SOCIAL CHANGE IN THE ROYAL NAVY 1924–1970

The Life and Times of Admiral Sir Frank Twiss

KCB, KCVO, DSC

For Rosemary
and the
Children

SOCIAL CHANGE IN THE ROYAL NAVY 1924–1970

The Life and Times of Admiral Sir Frank Twiss

KCB, KCVO, DSC

COMPILED AND EDITED BY
CHRIS HOWARD BAILEY

Royal Naval
MUSEUM
PUBLICATIONS

SUTTON PUBLISHING

First published in 1996 by
Sutton Publishing Limited · Phoenix Mill
Thrupp · Stroud · Gloucestershire · GL5 2BU
in association with
The Royal Naval Museum

British Library Cataloguing in Publication Data
A catalogue record for this book is available from the British Library

ISBN 0–7509–0610–3

Title-page illustrations: background: on board HM Drifter *Leeward*, 1934 (RNM Collection, neg. 79); inset: Second Sea Lord, 1968 (Courtesy Godfrey Argent; RNM Collection, neg. 98).

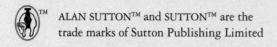 ALAN SUTTON™ and SUTTON™ are the
trade marks of Sutton Publishing Limited

Typeset in 12.5/14pt Garamond.
Typesetting and origination by
Sutton Publishing Limited.
Printed in Great Britain by
Hartnolls, Bodmin, Cornwall.

CONTENTS

CONTENTS

*Admiral Sir Frank Twiss signs the Vistor's Book at the Drumfork Club on the
Churchill Estate, Helensburgh, as CPO R.E. Sceel, Chairman of the Club, stands
next to him, 24 June 1969. (Crown Copyright, Imperial War Museum {IWM}
HU 69913)*

FOREWORD

This is a life story of a remarkable sailor, one of a rare breed of men whose mental resilience and physical stamina overcame the terrible experience of three and a half years in a Japanese POW camp, enabling him to resume his naval career and reach the highest ranks in the Navy. Besides the indomitable spirit and strength of character which that achievement required, Frank Twiss possessed a quiet but sublime sense of humour, a memorable turn of phrase and a personality that created keen devotion amongst subordinates, especially if they were in need of practical advice.

In 1941 came his first momentous appointment as Gunnery Officer of the 8-inch gun cruiser *Exeter* that sailed for the Far East to join a mixed force of Allied ships. When engaged by a superior Japanese force in the Battle of the Java Sea *Exeter* was disabled and subsequently sunk. Frank Twiss was awarded the Distinguished Service Cross after the war for his part in the action.

Throughout his prolonged ordeal in POW camps, Frank suffered from malnutrition, dysentery and beri-beri. Worse still was the savage, inhuman treatment from his gaolers. At one camp, if prisoners were asked to state complaints then he was prepared to represent them, even if it always resulted in being beaten up afterwards. There is no doubt he was greatly admired by all other prisoners, British, Australian, American, Dutch and others. 'I would sure like to shake that little guy's hand,' said one American survivor. 'He was a hero!'

After liberation and when asked the secret of his ability to survive, he explained that any POW who had the benefit of Dartmouth training had acquired '. . . an inner strength, confidence, morale, pride of service, call it what you will', which enabled him to show some degree of fortitude even when things looked hopeless. '*Esprit de corps* allied with religious strength is crucial.'

Frank's first step in resumption of a naval career was command of a sloop in the West Indies. Then followed a wide range of jobs ashore and afloat with promotion to flag rank in 1960. After being Naval Secretary to the First Lord and Second in Command of the Home Fleet, he was appointed Commander-in-Chief, Far East Fleet. Physically, Frank was not a big man but what he lacked in stature he more than made up with a natural ability to speak with conviction, authority and wit – and people listened!

His marriage to Prue had been the rock on which his life rested and together they shared a strong Christian faith which sustained them both. Sadly, Prue died in 1974 but four years later Frank had the good fortune to meet Rosemary, widow of a naval Captain, and they were married and enjoyed fifteen years of total happiness together.

During the last two years of his life at Bratton in Wiltshire, Dr Chris Howard Bailey from the Royal Naval Museum in Portsmouth conducted a series of recorded interviews with Frank Twiss to produce not only the story of his life but also his views on the changing scene in the social life of the Navy. As far as I know, this treatment of an autobiography was unique and Dr Howard Bailey is to be warmly congratulated for her initiative and for collating the taped interviews into a book. I am quite sure that Frank would have been pleased with the result.

Capt. John Wells
CBE, DSC, RN

ACKNOWLEDGEMENTS

S uch a project as this does not come into being without the help, co-operation and support of many people. Therefore I would like to thank all those who have assisted me during the course of this book's development. Most especially, of course, my gratitude and indebtedness go to Admiral Sir Frank Twiss for so graciously allowing me into his life and patiently taking me through its various stages. This is his book and I hope I have rendered it as he would have wished. I must also thank Lady Twiss for her hospitality and her help in seeing the project to fruition.

I would also like to thank Admiral Sir Anthony Morton for first suggesting that I should interview Admiral Twiss; the Trustees of the Royal Naval Museum for allowing me the time to complete the book; Campbell McMurray, the Museum's Director, for his support and commitment to oral history and to this project in particular; Colin White, Chief Curator, and the curatorial staff at the Museum, for their encouragement, support and patience with my preoccupation; especial thanks are due to Val Billing, who skilfully and painstakingly transcribed all the interviews and who, along with Janet Denby, assisted on the project whenever needed; to Assunta del Priore, Hilary Parker and Roger Homer for assistance with the photographs; Matthew Sheldon for help with the documents, letters and journals; and Nigel Tallis for help with the computer; Reg Davis-Poynter for his encouragement; to Michael Forder a special thanks for his comments and advice on the details of the manuscript; to Michael O'Callaghan for his suggestions on the book's design; to the editorial and production staff at Sutton Publishing; to Chris Arkell and Denise Smith at the Royal Naval Museum's Trading Company; to the *Daily Telegraph*, *Bristol Evening Post*, Paul Kemp and John Delaney at the Imperial War Museum, and Godfrey Argent. Most particularly I am indebted to Sue Goodger for her assistance with the exacting preparation of this manuscript and for urging me on when I most needed it.

To Captain John Wells I owe a special debt of gratitude for his expert guidance on seeing this manuscript through to publication. He has been, to all intents and purposes, my assistant editor and I am deeply grateful for all his support and advice.

I would also like to thank Cora, Jim and my family for their constant encouragement and support and for enduring my absences while I completed this project. Lastly, I must thank all of those who knew or served with Frank who, when they learned of the project, urged me to complete it in tribute to a man they respected and admired so much, a man who was so special.

Dr Chris Howard Bailey
Royal Naval Museum
June 1996

INTRODUCTION

27 July 1993

Dear Chris

I have now replayed all the tapes I have recorded and so I write to give you my views, as you requested. The series is meant to cover the social history of the Navy, but it frequently strays from this to record various yarns on personal incidents with no particular social bearing. I don't know if you want such stories, though I do think they lighten the whole subject. I suppose that editing of the tapes could produce an interesting oral history of one individual's experiences of the 20th century Navy, but the task of doing this seems daunting. If you proceed and want recordings to fill gaps or mistakes, I will certainly help.

Yours,

Frank

This was the last letter I received from Admiral Sir Frank Twiss. We had worked together for two years recording his life history and reflections on his time in the Navy. I met him later in the autumn of 1993 and then for one last time in December. We had planned to meet in January 1994 to discuss his overall comments on our series of interviews but, unfortunately, he died on 26 January 1994. What he would have said we'll never know, but this book is, I believe, testimony to the life and times of a rare man.

I first met Frank in the autumn of 1992 when I travelled to his home in Wiltshire to interview him for the Museum's Oral History Collection. He greeted me on my arrival and helped me carry my equipment into the drawing room of his farmhouse, apologising for his faulty security alarm which had undoubtedly alerted the whole neighbourhood to my coming. He then introduced me to his wife, Rosemary, and it was only then that I realised he had difficulty seeing. He could see light and dark he said, but only dimly.

Such resilience in the face of adversity was, I came to learn, characteristic of Frank. What began for me as a potential day's interviewing became an odyssey. One where Frank came to assess his life in the Navy and I came to learn not only about the man himself (and the reason for his poor eyesight) but the social history of the Royal Navy in the twentieth century as Frank saw and experienced it.

At our first interview, it became obvious that two hours were not going to be anywhere near long enough to record everything he had experienced and knew. I asked him, therefore, if he would agree to a long-term interviewing process. He readily consented, saying that he had long had an interest in documenting his thoughts on such matters, but (and he said this with his customary humility) he never felt that what he had to say would be of interest to anyone. I reassured him to the contrary and, with some mutual excitement, we began the process. I'm not sure at what point the idea of a book came along, but when I suggested it, Frank was agreeable in principle but adamant that he did not want a conventional biography, and neither did he want another, as he termed it, 'sea dog's salt tales'. He was happy, though, to talk about his life and experiences in the Service within the context of the changing conditions in the Navy of his time. If this would be of any interest to anyone, he said, he would be happy to give an oral history. Over the next two years, Frank and I met to chart and record his experiences and his reflections. In between our meetings, we wrote and talked to each other about what he had said and where our discussions should go next time we recorded our interviews. Of that dialogue, twenty-three hours of interview tapes are now part of the Royal Naval Museum's Oral History Collection, which is available to researchers.

What they reveal is that the relationship between history and memory is a dynamic one. The history of our lives is what we remember it to be. What remains central in our recollections is what we choose to remain central. In a conventionally written autobiography the author will record, usually, those central recollections and present a scenario of his or her past which he or she wishes to present. Frank has not had the luxury of such an experience here. I, as interviewer, have gently prodded him to address areas he might not have thought relevant or important, and to analyse issues which I have felt needed explication but he has not. This in some ways, therefore, lays him bare in ways other accounts of self might not have. Consequently, it presents a perception of the past which is far more, I contend, enlightening and, indeed, candid.

It becomes quite obvious through this testimony, for example, that Naval Officers as they move from one commission to another, are continually having to redefine themselves. They have to take on new identities, assume new roles and fulfil new expectations. Such adaptations take place within social and spatial contexts which influence that process of adaptation. How the officers are known, indeed, how they wish to be known, therefore, is as much a product of the tradition of the job as it is of its nature or even the individual's own self-determination. Frank was a very special individual but he could not escape his background or generation or even the traditions of the Navy, no more than he could the rapidly changing times in which he lived. What he was able to do was skilfully harness his own sense of self and what he thought ought to be achieved, with all the disparate elements that were to affect his actions. This, I believe, becomes quite clear as we read his account.

What follows, then, is a greatly edited and distilled version of Frank's tapes and letters, as well as the additional journals, short stories and photographs which he shared with me. Unfortunately, towards the end of our interview sessions, Frank became ill; yet it was, I learned, characteristic of his life as a whole that despite such increasing ill health he was determined to see this project he had started through to its final conclusion. I have been equally determined, therefore, to fulfil this commitment in Frank's memory, and for his family and friends. Towards the end of our interviewing time, however, Frank was getting weaker and the strain of talking to me was great. He may have made comments in the tapes that if he had had time to reflect on further, he might have liked to alter. We will never really know. I must, therefore, accept full responsibility for the editing of this material and any errors I might have made in completing the task. I have tried rigorously to be as faithful as I could to what I thought Frank would have said.

The rendering of the spoken word into a written transcript demands a great deal of concentration. People, for the most part, do not speak as they write. The spoken word is ragged but immediate and does not easily allow for the studied reflection and manipulation that the written word affords us. The intermingling, therefore, of Frank's written work with his oral testimony was challenging. The challenge was to maintain a consistency of style while ensuring faithfulness to the oral testimony. For the sake of fluency, therefore, I have had to alter some text, including a few words of transition and some verb tenses. Where necessary, I have included in brackets any explanatory comments. I have also included in brackets the names of any people he refers to by a short name or nickname, but the individual's full title has been cross-referenced in the Index. I have also kept annotation to a minimum, including it only where it is essential to meaning so as to keep the account primary. The main thrust has been to present as coherently as possible a very special man's account of his life and of the Navy in which he served.

Dr Chris Howard Bailey
Royal Naval Museum
June 1996

PROLOGUE

[The following extracts here and in the Epilogue are from private letters sent by Frank Twiss to Chris Howard Bailey between September 1992 and July 1993.]

Dear Chris

I have put down a kind of résumé of the social story of the Royal Navy which might be helpful in our future recordings. The social changes between the wars were less fundamental than those since 1945, in the same way that technology has changed so much and so fast since 1945.

The end of WW1 left this country in a fearful state. The dreadful losses of men and resources made the idea of another war too awful to contemplate and the concept of a League of Nations seemed the best hope for peace. While the early 1920s saw reparations, the dismantling of Germany, the sharing out of territories and various tidying-up operations with Russia, the Colonies and the Middle East, there was, domestically, in Britain, much hardship in the working classes; particularly, among those who had been doing the fighting and who were now discharged into a country badly worn, having few resources and apparently with little hope of being helped by Government. The streets of London and other cities were filled with groups of ex-Servicemen winding barrel organs, or groups playing musical instruments, selling matches and virtually begging, yet wearing their war medals or exhibiting their wounds in a mute cry for help. The war had decimated a whole generation of young men and most of these were the ablest and best of their time. Those who survived were often the second eleven men, and on these new leaders we had to rely to get matters straight.

As if this was not enough, Socialism and Communism had started to seduce the senses and Britain's sea power was being challenged by America and Japan. In the Services, the Army had taken the bulk of the casualties and had to discharge the greatest number of its manpower. In the Navy, the harshest blow fell upon the officers where the Geddes axe was wielded with little compassion and dreadful consequences for those cast into civilian life with no training or resources. Yet Britain had still an Empire as large, if not larger, than pre-war, and this Empire could only be held together by a large Navy. We had no less than two main Fleets, Atlantic and Mediterranean, a sizeable Reserve Fleet and four overseas stations (China, East Indies, South Africa and West Indies), each with a Commander-in-Chief; and other small commitments in the Persian Gulf, New Zealand and Fishery Protection at home. These had to be maintained with economy in vessels and trained sailors.

To reduce passage time and use overseas docking facilities, foreign commissions were long and lasted for two to two and a half years. Yet despite these long periods separated from their families with low pay and uncomfortable living conditions, there was no difficulty in getting men to join the Navy and ships were happy units and men proud to serve. The grouping of officers was unchanged with Wardroom, Warrant Officers and the Gunroom [Midshipman's mess] in cruisers and above, and on the lower-deck, Chief POs, POs and ratings. From top to bottom, both officers and men were glad to have a steady job and put up with separation as an inevitable price to pay. This led to a minimum of central welfare support and a certain amount of 'Regimental' support by officers and their wives. In ships away from home a kind of 'family' spirit prevailed which was not apparent at home.

So it was that there were no great social changes in the Navy in the 1920s, and all seemed well until the Invergordon Mutiny in 1931.[1] Although it has been a criticism that the relations between officers and men were not as good as they should have been in 1931, in my view this was not a cause of the mutiny, which did not disturb ships abroad and was confined to the Atlantic Fleet. The causes lay elsewhere; politically, in weak

[1] See Anthony Carew, *The Lower Deck of the Royal Navy, 1900–1939*, Manchester, University Press, 1981, and Alan Coles, *Invergordon Scapegoat: The Betrayal of Admiral Tomkinson*, Stroud, Alan Sutton Publishing, 1983.

ministers not Navy-wise, due to the Board of Admiralty being out of touch with the Fleet. Socially, the event led to the introduction of new welfare measures, particularly in the Naval Barracks support and in the replacement of the old Canteen Committee with a Welfare Committee in Ships and Establishments. Though these improvements were democratically better, so long as foreign service commissions remained long and the manning of ships remained geographically allied to Home Ports, they were not fundamental and the onset of war left the Navy socially not greatly changed since 1919.

Yours,

Frank

CHAPTER ONE

Dartmouth Cadet,
1924–1927

MY EARLY YEARS

I was born on 7 July 1910 in India. My father [Colonel E.K. Twiss DSO] was at that time a Captain in the Indian Army and he came back from serving over there at the beginning of 1914. When the war started, of course, he was immediately called up to his old British regiment, the Devons. He served in France for half the First World War and after the best part of two years in the front line, ended up with a DSO. After that he was recalled for a staff job and then sent out to India to assist in the training of the Indian Army fighting on the Western Front.

I had a sister [Nancy] who was nearly three years younger than me and as was common in those days when one's parents went abroad, the children were, as it were, farmed out with some relative at home. We were put in the charge of an elderly and very beloved aunt and lived in Whitchurch in Hampshire from quite early on in the war until its end. My mother [Margaret Edmondson Twiss] who had been living in Budleigh Salterton when the war started, served as a member of the Voluntary Aid Detachment down there. When my father went out to India to train the Indian Army, she decided that she must join him. So our aunt took charge of us and off my mother went, on what was no doubt a very hazardous voyage at that time. But she reached India and lived out there from roughly 1916 to 1918, and we lived in Whitchurch, my sister and myself.

My aunt, a Protestant, was one of the old school and the whole household had prayers every morning at nine o'clock. We lived a very pleasant but strictly disciplined life under this old aunt, were instructed by an excellent governess and were very happy. I don't remember particularly missing my mother or father at all. Myself and my sister remained in Whitchurch until after the Armistice and one doesn't remember much about the details of life, apart from one or two things. One was that I had an uncle in the Royal Flying Corps who was shot down and killed, and I remember the news of his death came through at prayers in the morning. My aunt was very solemn and a wreath was put round his photograph and hung on the wall and we all prayed especially for him and his family. Then, on Armistice Day at the end of the war, I remember being taken out into the square at Whitchurch to see the celebrations, and being very surprised that everyone appeared to be drunk, and that, as a small child, was something I hadn't met before.

When the war was over, my mother came back from India and took us away from the aunt and we went to live in London with my grandmother whom I had visited from time to time during the war. I remember very well the Potters Bar Zeppelin raid because she had what was an air-raid precaution at that time, a strong wire net over the top of the roof. This was meant to catch any bombs which fell upon us; observing they were quite small, it might have been effective. I don't know. By that time, 1918, I was eight years old and the question of my going to a boarding school arose.

In 1919, on the equivalent of Victory Day, I was sent off to a preparatory school called Oakley Hall, at Cirencester. I was extremely unhappy to start with, simply from homesickness; but like all small boys in those days you were sent to a boarding school and you just lumped it. After the second term you got into the system. So I spent from 1919 to 1924 at this preparatory school. I got on quite well, was a very keen cricketer, considered to be a very accomplished bowler of my time, and had a nice, well-ordered life which suited me splendidly. During the course of this time, my mother became divorced from my father and we were extremely hard up, and therefore there was absolutely no question of holidays or anything else. It was almost impossible for my mother to come down and see me at school because parents were only really invited to do so once a term. So she would come down at half-term and we'd all go and have a 'blow out' at some restaurant and that was about it, except, of course, we always went to chapel.

My mother had to look to my future, and having no money she naturally took a look around to see which was the most economical way of keeping me at school. She had a cousin, who was a Lieutenant in the Navy at the time, and he suggested sending me into the Navy. I remember going on board HMS

Queen Elizabeth whilst on a visit with my preparatory school and being immensely impressed by standing under the 15-inch guns of that lovely ship. I'm sure that, so to speak, directed me towards what appeared to be a very fascinating career. It certainly convinced my mother, because if you passed reasonably well into the Royal Naval College, Dartmouth, and the family was in what was called 'reduced circumstances', the Admiralty gave grants towards one's education. I was lucky enough to get one of these and to the best of my knowledge I was educated for forty pounds a year.

DARTMOUTH DAYS

We went to our first term at Dartmouth by train in special carriages which had been reserved for us. We went a day early so that we could be, as it were, positioned before the rest of the college came back, and as soon as we arrived we were put in charge of two Cadet Captains and a very fine old Chief Petty Officer. Our first view of the Navy was getting out of the train at Kingswear Station, going down to the Dart and embarking on a steamboat which took us across the river and put us ashore at another pier at the foot of the hill upon which the college stood. The hill was extremely steep, and I remember lugging my hand bag, a sort of doctor's bag containing my night clothes, up the many, many steps. When we arrived at the college we were all totally exhausted and were immediately, of course, fallen in, and mustered and sent off to our respective dormitories. I can clearly remember now being fallen in, in two ranks, in a new building called 'D' block, and given a few homely tips by a Term-Cadet Captain and the Cadet Captain who were in charge of us. Both were about two years older than ourselves.

We cadets wore a best uniform of cap, a blue serge double-breasted jacket and trousers, with white shirt, stiff collar, black tie and black shoes, much the same as I did later on as a Lieutenant, except that we had a little badge on the collar to show that we were only cadets. We wore this in the evenings and on Sundays but on weekdays we put on our jacket over white flannel trousers, with flannel shirt, black tie and boots. Then we had games rig for sports or when we went sailing. All our kit fitted into what was called a sea-chest, which was hinged in the middle to make, as it were, a box which opened up into two halves, and one half sat on the other. There were a couple of drawers underneath and a couple of shelves in the top and a compartment in which you could keep your valuables or private affairs, called a private till. It was built into the chest, and had a key you put on your lanyard. Otherwise everything was open to view.

Dartmouth in 1924 was still, to some extent, run by officers who had been in the Great War, probably in the Battle of Jutland, and there was a strong element of the *esprit de corps* of the Grand Fleet. Our Captain was a distinguished submariner called Captain Martin Nasmith VC. Life was regulated extremely strictly. There were eleven terms, and the junior term was the absolute bottom of the pile and the senior term were the big nobs. Each term of forty or fifty cadets moved through as a block, from term one to term eleven, and as we got more senior so we got a few more privileges. The term also moved from one gunroom to another. The equivalent of prefects, or Cadet Captains, as they were called, came from the top year.

Each gunroom was a large room with two or three good-sized oak tables, a certain number of forms (I don't remember any comfortable chairs) and a locker for each of us. We did any of our writing home and we did a lot of evening preparation in our gunroom – that was our spot. The other gunrooms lay in lines away from each other; that is to say, there was a long corridor with six gunrooms opening on to it at one end of the college and another long corridor with five gunrooms opening on to it on the other. The rule was that you weren't allowed to walk past the front of a gunroom of a senior term, so we did an awful lot of running, particularly when we first joined.

The teaching there was, generally speaking, of a very high order, and the entry to Dartmouth was higher than the entry to a public school. It was stiffer than the Common Entrance, and the

Examination Curriculum included not only what you might call the ordinary academic subjects, including science subjects and naval history, but also, of course, a good many practical subjects such as boat sailing, rowing, engineering, drill, and I suppose you might say good orderliness. We didn't walk about the place very much. We were fallen in as a group and marched about. The principle behind it was that we were part, so to speak, of a military set-up. They were getting us into the business of carrying ourselves properly, marching in step and respecting authority. It soon became quite natural. For instance, when we went in for meals, we mustered; we fell in as a term, and doubled into the dining-room. When we sat down, we laid into the food just like anybody else. That was the way it was done.

The routine was fairly comprehensive. We did a certain amount of instruction before breakfast. Then came what you would call academic hours, morning and afternoon. Games were a regular feature, and everybody had to take a certain amount of proper exercise, which was known as 'doing a log', and was well defined. If you played rugby football, that was a log; if you ran from the college to a place called Black Cottage somewhere in the country and back, that would be half a log, and if you ran on a bit further it was a full log. If you sailed a boat on the river for four hours, that was a log; and you had to write down what you had done every evening. If you missed your log, you probably were in some sort of difficulty. Either you were told to do something extra or, if you'd missed it before, you might even be caned.

There were strange things, of course. For instance, we were building the tennis courts all the time I was there, and therefore digging was a log. We dug brand new tennis courts and filled them with clinker, or whatever it was. If you went beagling, out with the college's beagles on a Saturday afternoon, that was your log. And so exercise, including swimming, playing squash and tennis, was all measured for its energetic performance and you had to do something every day except Sunday. That kept you fit but there was very little time really to yourself.

We weren't allowed to have any kind of sweets in the college. If we wanted to eat sweets or cakes, we went to the canteen and bought them. Now the trouble with that was that we only got a shilling a week, plus any pocket money our parents could afford to give us, which was banked and available to draw on when we needed it. Of course, at that age we were always very hungry and the canteen, which was run by a splendid ex-Chief Petty Officer, offered us all sorts of goodies like bread and butter and honey, or cakes and bananas and so on at a price. On a shilling a week it was really not possible to get very much from the canteen and, certainly in my case, I had practically nothing else because my family was too badly off to give me more than about, I suppose, ten shillings a term to cover postage and any extra food I might buy at the canteen. So I really remember working out very carefully how my shilling should be expended in order to get more to eat. It wasn't really that we were in any way starved at all, but boys of that age are always hungry and you could get a thing called 'a penny bread' and 'a penny butter', which was two slices, thick slices, of bread, and a little bit of butter. Well, tuppence into a bob [a shilling] went six times, so there was one day in a week that you didn't get bread and butter and you had to try and work out which day you'd do it.

Later on, when you became more senior, you were allowed to go further afield from the college and there were a number of farms all around Dartmouth, within walking distance, which would put on excellent teas on Sunday for cadets. One got to know certain farms and certain farmers got to accept the same boys for two or three terms, and you could get a most marvellous meal but probably had to pay some very large sum like sixpence or ninepence for it. That took quite a slice out of my ten shillings. It was tough, but most enjoyable. Walking back after a thumping great Devon tea, probably of apple pie and large slices of bread and jam, I remember, was absolute agony, because you had to be back in time for evening chapel.

So there it was, a very regulated and disciplined life, with a curriculum very well taught, I thought, and covering what was generally regarded as a broad education. We started at seven o'clock in the morning and finished about four. We did our games and had our supper, and then maybe we had a little time off. There were no particular entertainments. I mean there wasn't a cinema or anything like that. There was, however, the quarterdeck, which was a very large teak-floored space, with an arched colonnade round the sides and a gallery over that, from where you could look down. On the quarterdeck, cadets danced with each other as there weren't any women. We danced foxtrots or whatever, nothing very energetic by today's standards. There was a small civilian band that played music, and various bands organised by the cadets themselves which produced rather jazzier music. Dancing was very much part of the old naval tradition.

The daily routine always ended up with prayers at Evening Quarters on the quarterdeck, a typical finish to the day. We prayed; quarters were then dismissed, and we had to scamper from the quarterdeck to our dormitory, undress, clean our teeth and be in bed in something like ten or twelve minutes. It was always a tremendous rush, and we had to lay our clothes out in a very special way. We had to fold our shirt, with our socks pointing one way and our shoes pointing the other way, our lanyard had to be secured to the top of our bed, our cap had to be in the middle of the sea chest which was at the foot of our bed and everything had to be very tidy. While we were in bed, Rounds would take place. The Officer of the Day would walk through the dormitories to see that everything was correct, that our clothes looked properly laid out and everything was 'ship-shape'. When we got up in the morning, we had a cold 'plunge' in a very large, open bath such as you find in rugby football clubs, with salt water in it, then we dressed and went down to fall in.

Generally speaking, there was little time to think about very much except actually getting through the day, although I'm not suggesting for a moment that it was tedious or harsh or anything else. It was just busy. By the time we'd been eleven terms at Dartmouth, we had to pass an exam, the passing-out exam, in which everybody had to qualify or they went back again for another term. We emerged from Dartmouth at the age of seventeen, probably for the first time knowing something about higher mathematics, how to weld, how to carpenter, how to cast things; we knew something about internal combustion engines;

we knew a certain amount about boat sailing and boat handling and rowing; we were generally quite a useful man about the house – the sort of chap that would mend the fuses and things. So we emerged from Dartmouth probably more technically trained and fairly highly educated for our age, and went straight off to sea, to the ships of the Fleet.

CHAPTER TWO

Cadet and Midshipman in the Atlantic Fleet, 1927–1930

MY FIRST SHIP

I passed out from Dartmouth in the summer of 1927 and found myself appointed to what was then the Atlantic Fleet flagship, HMS *Revenge*. I find it hard to believe that anything today could equal the excitement, the pride, the anxiety or the sheer physical challenge of the first few months as a Cadet and Midshipman at sea in the Fleet in the late 1920s. For four years we had been brought up in an atmosphere steeped in tradition and custom, taught the rudiments of seamanship, navigation and engineering, filled with naval history and stories of courage and leadership, and drilled and chastised into a semblance of discipline and physical fitness within a college almost entirely cut off from the outer world and, in particular, girls. We had been constantly reminded of the motto over the main college entrance: 'It is on the Navy under the good providence of God that our wealth, prosperity and peace depend'. This and other similar sayings and prayers filled us with awe and humility. It was in this frame of mind that I set off to join HMS *Revenge*, a great battleship and the Flagship of Admiral Sir Hubert Brand, Commander-in-Chief, Atlantic Fleet.

At this time, my family was staying at a cottage in the Dorset village of Shillingstone, where my Great-Uncle Harry, an ex-Colonial administrator, was a much respected church warden, a sage and the Chief Scout of Dorset. My kit had been carefully packed in a green standard Dartmouth trunk and a new tin uniform case spotlessly painted a shiny black with flecks of red. In this kit was the 'Officer of the Watch' telescope from Dolland and Sons, presented to me by my godmother, Inman's Nautical Tables, a parallel ruler, and, of course, a dirk.

I arrived alongside the *Revenge* at South Railway Jetty by taxi from Portsmouth Station. The ship seemed enormously strong and powerful. The great 15-inch guns with their polished muzzles, the tall mast flying the Admiral's flag, the towering bridge structure, the row of 6-inch casement guns and above all, the thing that dwarfed everything: a massive funnel as large as a block of flats. Just imagine, I thought to myself, I am about to live in this monster ship and to be allowed to be part of the strictly disciplined life and mystique of one of Britain's most powerful vessels. I was at the same time frightened but exhilarated, proud but humbled, captivated by the aura of power and majesty and tradition.

I rushed up the brow, doffed my hat at the ship's side and announced myself to the Leading Seaman on deck who directed me aft to the quarterdeck to report to the Officer of the Watch. It was a Friday. Much activity reigned; it was a mixture of preparing to sail on Monday and getting away for the last weekend before the autumn cruise. Nobody paid much attention to half a dozen newly joined cadets and we were left to occupy ourselves, 'sling our hammocks', and keep out of the way. *Revenge* was due to sail on Monday afternoon. Accordingly, I was ordered to report to the Engineer Officer of the Watch at 0400 on Monday, to spend the morning watch observing the procedure for raising steam, a prospect which gave me some apprehension since I knew little about battleships' engine rooms nor was I accustomed to start the day at 4 a.m. However, I found my way to the engine room and reported to the Engineer Officer of the Watch, who clearly was too busy to give any attention to instructing me, and told me to go away and make a sketch of the closed steam system, whatever that was, and above all to keep out of everyone's way.

It was an impossible task. To begin with, the engine and boiler rooms were a mass of pipes, some hot, some cold. There were endless machines pumping or grunting or whizzing, and everything was on a series of levels or platforms joined by steel ladders. How different from the small sloop we had learned in at Dartmouth, where the reciprocating engines were push and pull and you could see them turning the propeller shaft, and the boilers were furnaces into which you shovelled coal at intervals or used a massive bar called a 'slice' to remove the clinker. However, with a little help from friendly stokers I was able to make some progress and began to get some clue as to what happened to the steam after it had rushed through the turbines. But it was a dreary, hot and oily task. I was very tired and soon looked for some diversion to help while away the hours.

I found it in a boiler room lift, a fine, solid box with folding metal doors, a brass control box with 'stop' and 'go' buttons, and two or three levels at which entry or exit could be made. It was quite interesting going up and down in this lift, checking your whereabouts at each stop and establishing a relationship with the long iron ladders which led down to the entrails of the machinery spaces.

What made it more interesting was that once or twice the lift did not accurately respond to the appropriate brass button. It was not long before I found out why. On opening the gates and stepping out at the top floor, so to speak, I was met by a very angry and abusive man dressed in dirty brown overalls, a filthy cap with an oily, once white, cover, no visible badge of rank, dirty boots and a torch. He pounced on me, shaking his torch and shouting various questions, notably, 'Who the hell are you?' 'What the hell do you think you are doing removing the lift from me just as I am about to enter?', as well as a variety of oaths. I politely explained that I was Cadet Twiss under instruction in engineering. This was too much for the fellow, who screamed, 'And who the hell do you think I am?'

About this time I formed the impression that this must be some stoker, and maybe he thought he could frighten me so I replied, again very politely, 'I'm afraid I don't know.' This caused a further explosion, which when translated said, 'I am the Senior Engineer.' Now I should explain that we never had such a person at Dartmouth, nor had I ever heard of such a post. Engineer Lieutenant yes, and Engineer Commander also, but Senior Engineer never. I was confirmed in my mind that this was a stoker of some sort trying to get one-up on me and I wasn't going to fall for that. So I said, quite politely, 'So sorry,' and walked off. Alas, that was not the end. After much interrogation, much concealed mirth in the Wardroom and no doubt due justice, I faced a rather painful rendezvous with the Sub-Lieutenant in the Gunroom bathroom. But that came later and was made all the more depressing by a sad encounter with the Commander the same afternoon.

A battleship, especially a Flagship, leaving Portsmouth was a major event. All harbour traffic was stopped, tugs lay at readiness, special flags were flown and the great ship, with her crew fallen in on deck, the cable officer standing in the bows, the blacksmith ready to knock off the slip on a huge anchor in case of need, the Admiral on the bridge and the Royal Marine Guard and Band in white helmets paraded on the quarterdeck, awaited the moment of departure. Stationed on the quarterdeck were an Officer and a Midshipman ready to see that all was in proper ceremonial order, each wearing frock coat or bumfreezer according to rank and equipped with a telescope.

I was greatly honoured and immensely excited to have been told to join the Midshipman on his duty and to understudy his role. Immediately prior to the wire hawsers being slipped or the tugs secured there is feverish activity on the quarterdeck. The Admiral on his way to the bridge is possibly conferring with some Staff Officer, last-minute messages arrive, people leave the ship, salutes are rendered according to status, the Commander prowls around satisfying himself that all is properly prepared, the gangway or brow is ready for the crane to hoist it away and the Captain is on the bridge reassured by the report that the ship is ready for sea.

It is, to a new cadet, most bewildering but there is little time to worry. 'Do this Snotty.' 'Get that.' 'What is the tug's name?' 'Have you seen so and so?' 'For heaven's sake tell Lieutenant X to dress the front rank of his division properly.' I rush here and there with my new telescope under my arm. Suddenly, the Commander sees me. He looks surprised and then in a stern voice addresses me: 'Snotty, what have you got under your arm?'

I am amazed at such a silly question, but I know better than to say so.

'My telescope, Sir,' I reply.

'Where did you get it?' booms the Commander, fixing me with an unnervingly fierce look.

'My godmother, Sir,' I reply.

'Ah!' explodes the Commander, 'Well, understand this, boy: it is not a uniform one. I never want to see you come on watch with it again. Go and get a proper one.'

Of course, I was devastated, crushed, humiliated, heartbroken. Was not my telescope clearly marked 'Officer of the Watch' and was it not a very fine telescope through which you could see beautifully? Indeed, it was, but it was also of rather large diameter, perhaps 3 inches instead of 1½, and that was not the uniform diameter. So off I went to the Gunroom, where I borrowed the Gunroom telescope. It had no lenses left in it and you could see nothing through it, but it was of uniform appearance. And though the Wardroom Officers kept borrowing my own telescope whenever they saw a pretty girl in a boat, the fact that I didn't know it was too big, added to my ignorance on the matter of the Senior Engineer, certainly knocked a hole in my enthusiasm, pride, and motivation for the Royal Navy. I wondered if perhaps I had really made a dreadful mistake in joining.

After six months as a cadet in *Revenge*, I was promoted Midshipman and transferred to HMS *Rodney* for her very first commission. The *Rodney* was a brand new battleship just added to the Navy and I did the rest of my Midshipman's time there. Our programme at that time, the late twenties, was quite a stable and pleasant one. I wonder how many have forgotten just how stable were the programmes of ships in the two main Fleets in the late 1920s. In the Atlantic Fleet the year was neatly divided into three so-called 'cruises'. There was the summer cruise, largely dominated by the Fleet Regatta in Scapa Flow or Invergordon, followed by visits to coastal resorts or possibly duty as guardship at Cowes. In September, after summer leave, the Fleet would set out for the winter cruise, somewhat dismally given over to practices and exercises, the King's Cup soccer final and, one year, the Fleet cross-country race. Then, by way of encouragement, in the New Year, came the spring cruise with its promise of better weather either in the Mediterranean or occasionally in the West Indies. It was this latter cruise that was the best, the fullest and in many ways the most testing.

The spring cruise started early in January with the Fleet assembling at Portland and proceeding thence to Gibraltar and the Western Mediterranean, exercising en route and possibly looking in at Vigo for a short break, with the feel of early spring in the air. Gibraltar would be the forum for many events and weekly practice programmes. In this period examinations for higher rate would vie with fleet boxing, fencing, running, hockey, football and tennis, to say nothing of a day or two with the Calpe Hunt, visits to Algeciras to sample the Reina Christina hotel, or to La Linea to see a bull fight or for less creditable enjoyment. There was also the Fleet concert to be put on, if not in the coal sheds or even the Gibraltar theatre, then in one of the battleships during a visit to Pollensa Bay in Majorca. But Gibraltar was the busiest period and the time when rivalry was most acute; Commanders of ships were most anxious about their paintwork or the behaviour of their liberty men, while girls, who had somehow arrived out from England, were most active in their search for young men and the excitement and fun of the chase.

This, though, was but a preliminary to the Combined Fleets assembly in March. Each Fleet was tuning up its muscles. The Home Fleet sailed out into the Atlantic for lengthy exercises, of immense boredom to the sailors and Junior Officers but of great interest and anxiety to Flag and Commanding Officers. It was their chance to make a good showing or a dismal performance in the handling of their ships or squadrons. Much depended on their knowledge and compliance with Atlantic Fleet Tactical Orders or the Fighting Instructions, and their luck in making an early and accurate enemy report, crossing the 'T' of a rival Battle Squadron or making a night torpedo attack in the dark and rainy Atlantic weather. This loosening-up period usually lasted about two weeks before we returned to Gibraltar to analyse the exercises and smarten up until the arrival of the remaining ships. Then early one morning over the eastern horizon would appear the Mediterranean Fleet, lovely in its symmetry, dominating in its formidable array of great grey battleships, steaming shorewards in line ahead and dwarfing the following columns of cruisers and destroyers. It was truly a sight never to be forgotten, a scene absolutely encapsulating British sea power.

The Mediterranean ships were always splendidly clean and glistening in their light grey colouring and in the sparkling paintwork of their hulls and upper-works. The Atlantic Fleet was always jealous of them. After all, the weather at home was a great handicap to polished brasswork and clean ships' sides, added to which the dark grey paint, which was the standard for Home Service, lacked the fresh summery look of the Mediterranean ships. Leading the new arrivals would be the *Queen Elizabeth*, flying the Flag of the Commander-in-Chief. Slowly, with salutes booming, bands playing, sailors mustered in ordered ranks and bugles sounding, the great ship would glide through a gap in the breakwaters and edge alongside the North Mole to join the Atlantic Fleet Flagship in what were the Admiral's berths. The Atlantic Fleet watched with critical eye, gauging how well the ships went alongside, how smartly they hoisted out their boats, spread their awnings or got out their booms. The dockyard mateys pushed forward the brows to make early disembarkation possible; Guards and Bands would be at the ready and just as soon as ships were secured in their berths, the ceremony of calls would start. Calls on the Governor, exchange of calls between Senior Officers, much bugling, presenting of arms and the music of military bands playing *Rule Britannia*, or, for the Governor, the National Anthem.

Gradually, the lesser mortals would surface. The Officer of the Guard, who had been despatched in the duty steamboat to meet the Mediterranean Flagship would be piped back on board. Messmen, postmen and orderlies would be seen setting off ashore; local officials, contractors, dockyard men and drafts from England would come on board until, eventually, peace reigned and the combined Fleets took stock and contemplated the days ahead. The pattern was well established: inter-Fleet sports of all kinds, meetings to discuss forthcoming combined exercises, dinners, drinks, socialising ashore, a visit to the races and maybe a battalion review of sailors on the race course and a march through the town. Old friends would meet, ideas would be exchanged, rivalries renewed, concert parties activated and for one and all the great brotherhood within the British Navy would boost the morale of even the most hardened sceptic. The Fleet was in, the girls and the naval patrols were out, and Gibraltar revelled in an orgy of fun and games.

LIFE ON BOARD IN THE 1930S

The way men were recruited for the Navy between the wars entailed the country being divided up into three zones, each zone being allocated a home port. This was Devonport for what was called the West Country; Portsmouth for the middle of the country; and Chatham which covered London and the East Coast. When they were signed on to join, men were allocated to one of those ports, and there they stayed throughout their service career. The idea, of course, was that (a) ships had people with the same kind of geographical background, and (b) that the ships went back there to give their leave between commissions or during service. That meant that the families could establish themselves within easy reach of the home port.

The result of this form of organisation was interesting. To begin with, it was naval policy to have barracks at each of these places; the Devonport division was called HMS *Drake*, for example, and naturally the Portsmouth division was called HMS *Victory*, and each port developed its own character. So when you were appointed to a ship in the West Country, you knew after some experience in the Navy that you had a crew on board whose general approach to life was somewhat different from people who had been recruited in Portsmouth and, perhaps, even more so than those from the East Coast and London. The West Countrymen tended to be enterprising, highly loyal and tremendously pro-ship people. The people from Portsmouth one always regarded as slightly more educated and possibly more able in running their ships in a general sort of way, while the people from the Chatham division were, broadly speaking, a fairly smart lot, one might even have called them a bit 'fly'. There was the sort of Cockney element that brought a kind of sharpness.

It was Admiralty policy at the time to keep a battleship's crew in the barracks at each of the home ports so that, in case of emergency, a battleship could be taken out from reserve and commissioned straight away. This, of course, provided a sort of shore service for the Navy which was made more so by the fact that each home port had its own training facilities. There would be a Gunnery School, a Torpedo School and so on, so that when men went for further training and for advancement they still were able to do it in their own home ports. So, as a system, it was quite a stable one. Also, it produced an enjoyable competitiveness between ships from the three ports serving in one of the main fleets. When the regatta came round there was intense competition between the West Countrymen, the Portsmouth men and the Chatham men, and winning the regatta became quite akin to winning the football league.

This system, of course, couldn't last when the Navy and thus the whole size of the Fleet was greatly reduced. It was altogether too expensive to keep three home ports, each with its own training arrangements, and so bit by bit the system dwindled away until it was necessary to man ships by getting the people with the right qualifications from whatever home port or recruiting area they could be found. This meant, particularly after the war, that men who were in a Devonport ship were regularly mixed with an equal number of men who really should have been in a Portsmouth ship. This, in turn, led to a good deal of disruption in the family life; every weekend, when the ship was refitting, with plenty of weekend leave, there would be a bus load of people going from Devonport to Portsmouth who would meet a bus load of people going from Portsmouth to Devonport. The whole thing became really rather ludicrous and, of course, eventually led to an entire reorganisation and the abolition of the home port system.

The number of officers and men in ships was dictated by the number required to fight ships in action. For example, a 15-inch turret required about a hundred men. This meant that when you weren't at war there were far more people living on board than were needed actually to keep the ship afloat, clean and working. It was, of course, accepted as gospel that men must be kept busy. People who weren't occupied became troublemakers; there was nothing else for them to do. So the routine in the Navy, particularly in big ships, was strictly designed to keep men working and keen. Looking back on it now, it was an astonishing performance. For example, a battleship in the Atlantic Fleet before the Second World War, might have nine hundred to a thousand men on board, of which only a proportion could regularly polish all the brass-work, clean all the paintwork, pick up the oil in the engine room or whatever it was, quite easily, in the first couple of hours. So what did they do for most of the day?

Well, they exercised in all sorts of ways. To begin with, the whole routine of the ship was that they were perpetually being mustered, counted, told what to do and sent off to do it. Seamen got up very early in the morning, and scrubbed all the decks; of course, they were wooden decks and they looked very nice after they were scrubbed. Everybody had a stiff broom and lots of water and sand and things, and they went up and down the decks. A Petty Officer stood in front of them saying 'scrub for'ard' – 'scrub aft' for the other way – and everyone was quite happy and the place was kept spick and span. Then, after breakfast, they cleaned all the brass-work; they cleaned the guns; they prayed and sang hymns; they took physical exercise in the form of PT or doubling round; they fell in again at least twice to be told what to do and then, when the dinner hour came, rum was produced with a good meal. Before they could fall asleep for too long, they were fallen-in again, mustered, told what to do and so it went on.

Usually, this routine was carried out every day of the week. Mondays tended to be the day that you did General Drill. Drills were done, anchors were taken, enormously heavy things, from one end of the ship to the other and dropped in the water, or boats would be put in the water and rowed madly to different spots and back again, or imaginary holes in the ship would be patched up. They got down to all sorts of evolutions as well as a few funnies, like the well-known signal to all ships, 'Commander is to report to the Flagship with a fried egg'. This required a certain amount of initiative because the man had to go in the boat and the egg had to be fried, and it was all good fun – and it occupied everybody. And so a whole morning could be spent moving bits of the ship hither and thither and getting them back again. This kept people busy so they had surprisingly little time to devote to themselves.

Part of that time, of course, was devoted to sport. Because of its competitive nature, sport was much appreciated by the sailors and a great deal of it took place. Mostly between ships, but within ships there would also be competitions, between groups of men known as divisions. A good feature was an inter-divisional football competition in which the officers would play with the men of their division. Then there would be inter-ship matches and, indeed, even the inter-home port matches. And after football, of course, rugger came a very close second – a lot of good international rugger players were produced from the Navy. Men kept fit on board and when you went into harbour, a lot of the ports at home and abroad had special facilities for sport. For instance, Invergordon was a complex of football grounds, canteens, changing rooms and so on. Furthermore, it had a wonderful loch for holding a regatta.

The regatta was perhaps the most important competitive sport of the lot. The ship that won the regatta became Cock of the Fleet and their boats' crews would go round the Fleet in the biggest boat with a thumping great model of a cock, shouting the odds to tell everyone else that they were the best in the Fleet. That kind of competition kept people happy, and took up time which people would otherwise spend twiddling their thumbs.

Sport in this way was a form of discipline, and, as a rule, a ship that was good at sport wouldn't be an undisciplined ship. To maintain discipline, of course, there were punishments. A man who didn't come back on board on time before his leave expired was immediately punished by having his leave stopped for a certain number of days and a proportion of his pay removed. It was a fixed scale and sailors understood it completely and could work out whether it was worth paying the price or not. To be absent over leave if the ship was due to sail could get you into much more serious trouble. And if you were a repeat offender, and these punishments didn't reform you, you could end up in the Detention Quarters.

To go from losing two days' pay and two days' leave to getting, shall we say, ninety days in the Detention Quarters, required misdemeanours of a progressively serious nature. You could break your leave, or you could return on board drunk, for which you lost a day's pay. You could return on board drunk and four hours late, in which case you lost four days' pay and four days' leave. You could get so drunk that you missed your ship when it sailed, in which case you got clobbered more severely. You could then indulge in all forms of peccadilles right up to striking an officer or drawing a knife and going for somebody, which would immediately get you, probably, some form of detention or even a Court Martial. Now the Navy didn't have a lot of Courts Martial, unlike the Army which had a whole professional legal body that looked after that side of the discipline. In the Navy it all rested with the Captain of the ship, who was allowed to deal with crime and give summary punishments on his own.

Young people were caned; boys and Midshipmen were caned. They were quietly taken to one corner and thrashed on their bottoms, which was regarded as quite normal. A Midshipman was in the hands of the Sub-Lieutenant of the Gunroom, who took you to the bathroom, produced his cane and thrashed you, and it wasn't regarded, in those days, as a particularly unusual thing to happen. I mean nowadays people are simply horrified at the thought of doing such a thing, but in those days it was almost part of the daily life. Seaman boys were officially caned in a similar manner by the Master at Arms.

For more serious crimes there was the Detention Quarters, about which there was a certain mystique. The idea was to greatly improve the man's smartness, morale and make him not want to do it again. And so the routine was very strict. Men weren't allowed to talk to each other, and by today's standards of prison regime, it would be regarded as intolerable. It certainly wasn't in those days, when some of the more hardened characters would calculate what was going to happen, saying to themselves, 'I'll get ninety days ashore instead of ninety days on board. Admittedly my life will be made pretty miserable in that time, but there it is.' That, of course, has changed completely today, as has the penal system. It's simply moved with the times.

CHAPTER THREE

Lieutenant and Gunnery Officer, 1930–1939

After my time in the *Rodney*, I qualified for Lieutenant by going ashore to do a number of courses. In those days we used to do six months at Greenwich and then went on to be trained in the various schools round the Portsmouth area, qualifying in navigation, gunnery, torpedo and so on. At the end, you emerged with a record and qualifications and were awarded certain advances in seniority or otherwise depending on how you had done in the various exams. I finished my time ashore in 1931 and was able to get some advanced seniority so that I only had to do a limited time at sea as a Sub-Lieutenant.

MY FIRST YEARS AS A LIEUTENANT

When I finished my courses, I was appointed to HMS *Emerald* in the East Indies Squadron. This was surprising as I had asked to be sent there and the usual form was to be sent somewhere quite different. As I had four weeks' leave due, I applied to go out early and spend a little time with my parents in Karachi where my step-father was the Commissioner in Sind. In due course, I took passage in a P&O liner, the SS *Ranchi*. The voyage was a three-week holiday of enormous fun and excitement, much enlivened by the presence on board of a most attractive and lively redhead. Together we danced, played deck games and swam, all the way to Bombay where sadly our ways parted. After staying a couple of nights with the Admiral commanding the Indian Navy, Admiral Walwyn, and his charming wife – friends of my mother – I started off again in a small British India steamer for Karachi.

I suppose my leave in Sind was one of the best times in my life. My Indian bearer was the son of my mother's and father's bearer before the Great War, named Molah Buksh, and he looked after me as if I were royalty. Life in Government House was grand, yet easy and enjoyable, and Karachi seemed to me to be full of fun and games. I stayed over Christmas and travelled with my parents up country where my step-father toured in a splendid caravan of tents with horses, camels, cars and bearers, holding

27

daily court and dealing with a multitude of petitions, litigation, crime and administration. He had a remarkable grasp of the local dialects and habits as well as sufficient firmness not to be taken in by the amazing Indian capacity to pull a fast one. As the country through which we passed boasted some of the finest duck shooting in the world, with bags to a single gun of over a hundred birds, and largely owned by wealthy landowners anxious to keep in with the Commissioner, we enjoyed some of the most superb shooting in the whole continent.

During this splendid holiday the Viceroy, Lord Willingdon, for whom my step-father had worked, came to Sukkur in North Sind to open what at the time was the largest barrage in India, if not the world. Stretching across the mighty Indus River, the barrage diverted the water into three huge canals each as wide or wider than the Suez Canal, and thence into various smaller canals which distributed the water over hundreds of square miles of parched land. For this event, we all stayed in barges which were part of the Commissioner's caravan and provided accommodation for the Commissioner, his staff and office and his servants and horses. It was a marvellous opening as only India could provide and I, as the only Naval Officer present, did my best to appear at ease in a blue frock coat, white duck trousers and sword. But all good things come to an end, and soon after I was on my way to join my ship.

I found *Emerald* at Trincomalee, at that time a lovely tropical bay, and the main anchorage for the East Indies Squadron. I never enjoyed a commission more than the ensuing eighteen months, which was odd because the Wardroom contained some peculiar characters. The secret lay in the Captain, a truly delightful and most competent man called Jack Clayton. It was thanks to his lead and the mothering of his wife, who had only one other wife from the ship to keep her company on the station. Our Commander was Irish and clearly showed this. The Navigator was a crudish but simple bachelor; one officer was known as MTF or 'Must Touch Flesh' and had a habit of falling asleep in the middle of dinner; another officer was gravely over-sexed and none too reliable with the public funds, and the Parson was earnest but dull. But the Ship's Company was a splendid West Country lot and were much encouraged by a lovely man, the 'Schoolie' Commander, who ran the concert party.

We completed a happy and successful commission in June 1933, and paid off after a month at Devonport where I met my [first] wife-to-be, Prudence Hutchinson, for the first time. It was a strange meeting, for she and her sister had been invited to tea on board by the Paymaster Sub-Lieutenant. They went with some misgiving, as they had heard of the MTF character and feared he might be one of the party. It was not he but I who made up the numbers. However, it was to be three years before we wed. On leaving the *Emerald*, I was appointed to HMS *Malaya*, starting there in September after foreign service leave spent fishing in Wales.

The *Malaya* was a lovely great battleship of the Queen Elizabeth class in the Atlantic Fleet. I reported to her Captain at 0900 the morning after joining, as was customary, and was asked if I had any ambitions to specialise. 'Yes,' I replied. 'My previous captain had agreed to recommend me for gunnery.'

'Most unsuitable,' said my new Captain and sent me on my way. I was duly assigned to be the Assistant Torpedo Officer under the charming but somewhat scatterbrained Lieutenant Commander Noakes. My principal job was marching up and down the quarterdeck as Officer of the Watch, being second Divisional Officer of the top division and Chairman of the ship's dance committee. This latter task let me in for endless work, many strange encounters and much friendship with more socially active sailors.

It was again a happy ship with some strange characters in the Wardroom. The Commander was a workaholic and could only be persuaded to go ashore if he could ride a horse, thereby leading the Wardroom to devote much effort to hiring horses at different ports of call. The Engineer Commander ate glass on Guest Night, which never failed to amaze. The Major of Marines had a habit of falling backwards to complete a somersault off the fender stool, until he broke his neck and had to give it up.

It was the time when the Earl of Cork and Orrery was the Commander-in-Chief, Ginger Boyle as he was called, and he was still trying to shake up the Fleet after Admiral Sir John Kelly had started the process following the Invergordon mutiny. The favoured way of doing this was to keep everyone unhappy by ordering strange exercises or drills at any time of the day or night. One such event was a night exercise intended to simulate an attack by MTBs upon the Fleet at anchor. The attackers were to consist of the assembled picket and larger motor boats of the Fleet. Unhappily, the date was 5 November, and keen to enliven the evening and make the practice truly realistic, Bendy Dawson decided to be on board the *Malaya*'s picket boat armed, though we did not know it, with a quantity of fireworks and tins of petrol. Nor did we know that Bendy had fixed with Noakes, the Torpedo Officer, to have a small charge of explosive hanging over the side of the *Malaya*'s quarterdeck which could be activated by wires going to Noakes' night action position at the searchlights.

The great night came and all ships lay darkened with watertight doors closed and appropriate look-outs and hands at action stations. On the quarterdeck, waiting for the attack and acting as Officer of the Watch, was Lieutenant Twiss, soon to be joined by the Captain who had just finished his dinner. Together we peered into the inky darkness; in order to see better ahead, the Captain went out onto the grating at the top of the starboard gangway ladder. Suddenly, one of the Fleet saw the attackers sneaking in and switched on her searchlights. Everyone followed suit. Beams swept the harbour. More boats were spotted and all seemed to be fine when suddenly the night was lit by huge flames, rockets, sparklers, whizzing stars and a regular cascade of flames and fireworks. The Admiral ordered fire-fighters to rescue the burning picket boat, and to us on board could be seen the bearded figure of Bendy apparently pouring petrol down the boat's funnel. It was an awesome sight.

Recovering from my fascination with the spectacle and feeling I should do something, I called out the duty fire party. Suddenly there was a violent explosion and the starboard ladder, at the top of which stood the Captain, rose into the air. I rushed over expecting to see him in the water; but by some magic he was not dislodged and clung to the stanchion as the gangway ladder fell back into place. At this moment the Major of Marines rushed up from below, visibly alarmed and shouting that a large hole had been blown in the ship's side over his bunk. The damage was not as great as seemed likely. The small charge which the Torpedo Officer had so skilfully hung over the ladder and which he had triggered off in response to Bendy's splendid attack so as to represent a torpedo hit, had done some above-water damage. This was as nothing to the furore and Courts of Enquiry which followed, or the rage of the Captain at being trapped in such a conspicuous and embarrassing position.

Despite such exhilarating episodes, I found life as a watchkeeper boring and was glad when I was transferred to take command of the ship's Drifter, HMS *Leeward*, a lovely job. My wish for some more challenging post showed in the fact that during my time in the *Malaya* I volunteered for expeditions to both the North and South Poles. I failed in the latter as experience in sail was required. I reached the short list for the former, which was to be led by the well-known explorer Gino Watkins. When I heard that I would have to travel to Greenland by trawler from Hull, I was not too sorry when a doctor was chosen and even less sorry when the expedition had to be abandoned after Gino was lost in a kayak accident in North Greenland.

However, things took a turn for the better when my Captain suddenly put my name forward to specialise in Signals and I was accepted, a situation that fitted my wish for change at a moment when the names for the Long Gunnery course had just come out and I was not among those chosen. The situation did not last long however. During my last month in the ship and while at Cowes as Guard Ship, the Commander (G) from Whale Island [the Gunnery School], a charming man of great repute in the Navy named Rory O'Connor, came on board to see me. 'Why,' he asked, 'have you put in for Signals? Are you no longer interested in Gunnery?'

'By no means,' I said, 'but you have not selected me for the next long course and I need to get going in some specialisation this year and stop being a watchkeeper.'

'Well,' he said, 'if you really want to be a (G) we have decided to increase the size of the next course by two and if you like, I think I can get you on it.' And instead of becoming a Signalman, in September 1934 I started a Gunnery career with all that flowed from it.

PROFESSIONAL GUNNERY OFFICER

I spent a very happy year at HMS *Excellent*, doing my course in company with a most delightful group of friends under the tutelage of a charming officer, Bob Elkins [Vice Admiral Sir Robert Elkins]. In 1935 I qualified as a Lieutenant (G) and won the Egerton Prize because the two cleverest people in my course were removed early to fill jobs in ships being brought forward for the Abyssinian campaign. As was customary, the top graduate went as 2nd (G) in HMS *Nelson*; so by the end of the year I found myself en route to relieve [Admiral of the Fleet Sir] Varyl Begg in the *Nelson*. The ship's Gunnery Officer was an old friend who had been the 2nd (G) in the *Rodney* when I was a Midshipman in that ship. With the large number of officers to be found on board *Nelson*, which wore the flag of the Commander-in-Chief Atlantic Fleet, Admiral Sir Roger Backhouse, I acquired a great number of friends. My arrival was not without incident. As I came up the ladder from the boat, I saw the Gunnery Officer being taken down another ladder to go to hospital. I was in at the deep end; I was now the new Gunnery Officer! When I reported to the Captain next morning, he was clearly not at all pleased with this arrangement. But as the ship was due to sail for exercises off Portland, he had little option but to accept the situation.

When I joined *Nelson* at the end of 1935, I found myself almost straight away involved in considerable efforts to improve the anti-aircraft defence of the Fleet, because the Commander-in-Chief, who was himself a Gunnery Officer, was determined to do so. Well, the weapons we had were precisely the same that had been fitted in *Rodney* when I was there as a Midshipman in 1927; there was no change in them at all. So we were already ten years adrift. The rearmament programme was just getting underway, and the very serious restrictions we had had to work under, for example, the amount of oil used, the speeds at which we steamed and the number of shells we fired and so on, were lifted. Up until 1935 we were hampered by the 'Ten Year Rule,' which said there would be no major war for ten years; so nobody wanted to spend money on bullets and guns if it was going to take ten years before you could use them. In the Home Fleet we were naturally influenced by what the Commander-in-Chief wanted us to do. I mean, I would see him personally, occasionally speak to him on the bridge and, as well as being a keen Gunnery Officer, I had had considerable experience in that class of ship. We had begun to think about the possibility of war, and were starting to build new battleships of the King George V class, and a new class of cruisers. New classes of destroyers had always been produced at fairly regular intervals.

In May 1936 I became engaged to Prudence Hutchinson, and in November of the same year we were married at Yarborough in Devon. Such was the frailty of the international situation that I was not allowed to go abroad. We spent our honeymoon, therefore, in London and Kent going to theatres, football matches and dining and dancing, between spells of listening to the radio news of King Edward VIII's abdication. From now on events began to occur with increasing effect upon our lives. I sailed off for the spring cruise of the Fleet and was joined by Prue in Gibraltar where we lived in one room, with a lovely view over the dockyard to Algeciras. Prue had to face the daunting experience, for a new bride, of sitting on the right of the Commander-in-Chief at a formal dinner in his Flagship. No sooner had Prue returned home than the Spanish Civil War started, Hitler became more troublesome, and Mussolini got going in Abyssinia.

When I got home, the coronation was approaching and I found myself in training to carry the King's Colour of the Atlantic Fleet in the ceremonies in London. When the great event neared, the Fleet anchored off Southend and the sailors, lining the route on either side of the Admiralty Arch, were taken by bus to London and billeted at Olympia. It was intended that they should leave about 0500, to be on parade by 0600. Unhappily, there was a bus strike, so the sailors had to start at 0300 and march to the Mall, proceeding round the Serpentine to keep out of the way and reduce the noise. Meanwhile the Guards, who had their own transport, lay abed for a further two hours. It was a lovely May morning and as the sailors swung along with occasional bursts of music by the bands, a couple jumped up from the grass in Hyde Park and ran off. A sailor called out in a clear voice, ' 'Ave yer?' to be answered from someone far down the line, 'Of course they 'ave.'

We arrived on the Mall and took up position, and in the ensuing hours platoons were marched away for a short break and an issue of Horlicks Malted Milk tablets and buns, as there had been no breakfast. Most of the buns found their way into the mouths of the many lions and other bronze animals which adorn the buildings around the Admiralty. The Guards were on the Navy's left, and between each carriage procession, of which there were many, a horse and cart came from Trafalgar Square to pick up the manure on the road. When the carters descended from their carts with a shovel to collect the offending droppings, the horses, encouraged most improperly and surreptitiously by the sailors, were fed Horlicks tablets as they moved down the line towards the Guards. Expecting further delicious tablets from the soldiery, the horses nuzzled up to these men who produced nothing. And so the horses spread upon their lovely scarlet tunics quantities of saliva and froth resulting from an orgy of Horlicks. This amused the crowds hugely and it caused the utmost horror to the Guards' Sergeant Majors.

Not long after the coronation came the Fleet Review in Spithead where not only were many of the ships of the Royal Navy assembled, but also representatives of several Foreign Powers. As I was appointed to be Gunnery Officer of the First Destroyer Flotilla shortly before the actual Review, I transferred by boat from *Nelson* to HMS *Grenville* so missing the one event that made the newspaper headlines. This was when Tommy Woodroffe, a retired naval officer and the BBC commentator on board *Nelson*, who was well known for his love of a glass or two, made his famous description of the night fireworks and illuminations by saying (between hiccups), 'The Fleet's lit up.'

A day or two after the Review, we sailed for the Mediterranean to relieve another destroyer flotilla on the Spanish Non-Intervention Patrol off Almeria. Unhappily, on our way to Gibraltar, the Captain of *Gypsy* fell down the bridge ladder and was killed, so that my first task in the flotilla was to conduct his funeral at Gibraltar. Thereafter, we went to patrol off Almeria, where one of our destroyers had recently had trouble with a floating mine.

Some four weeks later we were relieved and went to Malta, where my wife had preceded me. She had found a lovely, small but new flat at Tigné, whose landlord presented us with an agreement which, due to confusing 'Tenant' with 'Landlord,' bound him to pay us the rent (ten pounds monthly), a proposition to which we readily agreed, but did not enforce!

As a young married couple, we were supremely happy in our stay in Malta, although the international situation took the destroyers frequently away for weeks at a time, either on Non-Intervention Patrol or on Nyon Treaty Patrol. Each return to Malta was a moment of enormous pleasure, while each departure was a moment of agonising sadness. Little did I know that that precious spell of one year in the Mediterranean, with all its partings, all its anxieties and all the friendships, was to be the last of an era, and my last peacetime commission for eight years.

'The Non-Intervention Patrol', of course, was an attempt by British and to some extent, French ships, to prevent supplies getting into Spain to assist the Civil War there. It involved patrolling outside the three-mile limit and intercepting ships coming in, to try and find out what sort of cargoes they were carrying. We were also taking refugees from Valencia and Barcelona and places like that, up to Marseilles and away from the dangers in Spain. They were quite obvious dangers because I remember quite a number of people who had been tortured, burned with cigarettes and various things like that. Others had got into British Consulates or the Embassy and were smuggled out of Spain, via destroyers. Since we were neutral, we had to do the same for both sides, so we were neither pro-Franco or pro-Government and we visited the ports of both. Franco held position in the Balearic Islands, in Palma, and the Government was doing well in Valencia. And, for good measure, we used to

35

get the benefit of some of the bombing. It wasn't specifically aimed at us, but was unpleasantly close, particularly in Palma.

During that whole appeasement period, then, the feeling from people actually serving in the Navy was that war was imminent. The Commander-in-Chief in the Mediterranean was the man who eventually became the First Sea Lord in the war, Admiral Sir Dudley Pound, and his number two was Admiral Sir Andrew B. Cunningham, who became Commander-in-Chief of the Mediterranean Fleet for the greater part of the war. In addition, there were a number of extremely able and forceful Admirals all determined to prepare for war. We were being not only worked very hard on these patrols, but at every possible moment exercised in various forms of tactical operation which were thought likely to affect us when a war started. Admiral Cunningham had a healthy disregard for the Italian Navy and was absolutely determined to weigh in and bash them at the first opportunity.

An example of the tension and readiness of the Fleet at that time, perhaps, was apparent when peace was signed at Munich in 1938. By that time, the Mediterranean Fleet was at a high state of readiness and it was part of the plan to remove ourselves from Malta and go to Alexandria when war started. The Commander-in-Chief decided that as the situation looked so grave, that was what we would do and the whole Fleet left Malta and sailed for Alexandria. We did so in battle formation, with all the ships at the appropriate degree of readiness, and we steamed down towards Alexandria. I remember the night before we got in, we suddenly got an air-raid warning of aircraft approaching the Fleet and everybody went to action stations. The whole Fleet was gazing at this particular thing which had been sighted and we all thought it was some kind of enemy aircraft coming for reconnaissance or to attack. But it never got any nearer. Eventually, it turned out to be the planet Venus, at which all the guns were aiming! I suppose we learnt a sharp lesson from that, but it was interesting that the Fleet, so to speak, went to immediate action stations on a visual sighting. Radar had not yet arrived.

I came home just after the Berchtesgaden meeting, when Chamberlain came back and talked about 'peace in our time'. As a result, preparations of war tended to slow down. The Fleet went back to normal peacetime arrangements, but other preparations for war, such as the digging of air-raid shelters, the filling of sand bags and preparations for the evacuation of children, of course, continued.

STAFF COURSE AT GREENWICH

I arrived in England about November 1938. I was glad to get back because I had been sufficiently influenced by the international situation to think that I was going to start my married life overseas and get involved in a tremendous war and possibly never see my family again. It seemed a short run for a marriage which had only started in 1936. To my relief, I found that I was going to be the instructor to the new course of Lieutenants going through for Gunnery Officer. To me it was a very pleasant assignment and quite a leg-up, because you didn't get that kind of job unless you were thought to understand something about gunnery. My wife and I took a little house at Emsworth and embarked upon the business of having a family. She became pregnant and the date of birth was scheduled for September 1939. In fact, I didn't start the teaching job, because at the last minute I was sent to do the Staff Course at Greenwich. From Emsworth I used to go up to Staff College, spend the week there and get back on the weekends. It was a very interesting time to be doing the Staff Course.

I remember I knew how to knit. I can't think why. My mother taught me or something and when my baby was on the way, I said, 'I will knit a pram blanket for this child.' And I worked out that if I did the whole Staff Course, I would get so many weekends, and if I did sixteen rows, or whatever the number was, of knitting every weekend, I would finish it in time. Of course, when August came and it looked as if the war was coming, I could see I wasn't going to get a year at the Staff College and, therefore, I wouldn't have enough weekends to finish the blanket. So I spent my last week before I was sent off to Rosyth, knitting like mad, to finish the blessed thing, which I did.

The Staff Course was a year to get PSC [Passed Staff Course], which was the naval equivalent of the course at Camberley and the RAF course at Bracknell. It's difficult to say why I was selected, because I was, in fact, the most junior officer that had done a Staff Course up until then. At Greenwich, we were encouraged to read a great deal. We were given a course of lectures by people very well qualified in the particular subject that was being studied. There were schemes like, for example, studying submarine war in the Atlantic, and the control of contraband. We learnt about politics and government and how the country's affairs were run and we studied subjects such as Communism, Nazism and current affairs; generally it was an endeavour to educate us in a broad way to understand the affairs of the world and to train us in clear thinking and clear expression, so that we could write orders. We could write appreciations of the situation; we could write out the operation orders for some landing force that had been decided should go somewhere. Because, of course, for all those operations in the war, lengthy orders had to be produced, co-ordination had to be done and large staffs were involved. As new conditions came along, like combined operations, more and more demand came for people who could think and read and write, and express themselves and the subject they were dealing with succinctly and clearly. That was really what the aim of the Staff Course was.

We used to visit places of importance. They would usually put on some kind of lecture for us first, with discussion afterwards, and then we would be taken round the London docks or the London Fire Brigade or Scotland Yard. We went round places like the Port of London, which at that time, of course, was immensely important to the economy of the country, and saw all the warehouses and talked to the head people. We went to commercial centres like Birmingham and Manchester. We were taken over armament areas. We went to Wales to see the Welsh miners in the Rhondda Valley, and we even went down a coal mine. As a result, we learnt a lot about particular activities and places where they were being carried on in the country. Linked with these visits were lectures on government by senior members of the Civil Service, MPs and so on.

One of the outings we made was to the *Daily Telegraph* office when they were turning out the next day's paper. We were in the offices when the ticker tapes started to bring in the news that Hitler had marched into Czechoslovakia. That really was very much a turning point. Czechoslovakia was a tremendous arms production area, with a good little army and was very anti-Hitler and pro the rest of Europe; we lost a great bastion to the Nazis in that move. Hitler got away with it, and, as we all know, went on from there, ending up in Poland and starting the Second World War. But in the *Daily Telegraph* offices that night the place was absolutely humming with this red-hot news coming through and all the editions of the paper were being up-dated. It was a fascinating exhibition of how the media reacts to top headline news and gears itself up to pump the stuff out. This [staff training] was really all part and parcel of learning how the country is run, what media operations go on, the media generally, and in this particular case, one paper.

One talk that I particularly remember was given by the American Ambassador, Joseph Kennedy. Kennedy was not pro-British. He had made up his mind that Britain had had it, that the Nazis were going to conquer Europe and that they were the people of importance. He came down and spoke about America's position *vis-à-vis* England and his view of the way Hitler was behaving and the Nazi forces. I remember at the end of his lecture, he just said to us, 'Well gentlemen, that's all I have to say tonight. I can only say to you that I'm glad I'm not in your shoes.' That was a devastating remark for the Ambassador of the United States to make to a Staff College at that particular time. It simply meant, 'I've written you off. You're going to be bombed to death.'

The war hadn't started then, and in the period from January until August 1939, life took its usual course. Normally, in peacetime in August we had two months' holiday from Greenwich, in the course of which you toured parts of Europe, then you did some attachment to another Service and, in fact, I was all lined up to join the Army for their summer manoeuvres on Salisbury Plain. Instead of that, the Fleet mobilised and I never got my summer holiday. I went to Rosyth to commission a flotilla of destroyers which were in mothballs and join HMS *Malcolm*, the flotilla leader. Luckily the ships were very unsophisticated and few defects came to light which could not be remedied by ourselves. The guns all had to fire four full charges by way of a test, and most of the sailors regarded this with great trepidation. So much so that, as the Flotilla Gunnery Officer, I found it necessary to go to sea with each ship and personally oversee the firing of individual guns on the spot. Within a week our flotilla and others were at sea en route to Portland where the King was to review the Reserve Fleet. It was an impressive event. Row upon row of ancient destroyers, cruisers and sloops were anchored in Weymouth Bay looking and acting like any good warship and manned by as fine a body of ex-sailors as you can imagine.

I spent August getting the flotilla ready and taking it to the great review in Weymouth Bay, subsequent to which we were all dispersed to our war stations. When war came there was a War Book operated by the Admiralty and every ship had two envelopes. One was called envelope (A); the other was called envelope (B). Envelope (A), when you opened it, told you what your war station was, and the executive for opening the envelope was the signal, 'Open envelope (A)'. So it was a frightfully exciting signal to receive. And that was only done when war was pretty well inevitable. Envelope (B) prepared you for something else. So, while we were working at Portland, we were sent out into the Atlantic to escort a convoy of ships, and while we were on our way back from this job, the message came, 'Open envelope (A)', and to my delight it said, 'Your war station is at Portsmouth to escort the British Expeditionary Force across to France'. So I went straight from Staff College to the other extreme, so to speak. I was the Gunnery Officer of sixteen old destroyers, escorting the British Expeditionary Force to France. That was our task.

I went back to Portsmouth and turned up at our house in Emsworth and said to my wife, 'Believe it or not, I've been assigned to Portsmouth for a bit and so I shall be seeing you.' My son, Roddam, had been born by this time and I was able to see him after he had been christened, within the first few weeks of his life.

CHAPTER FOUR

Early War Years,
1939–1942

THE BEGINNING

The winter of 1939 was exceedingly cold. My ship, as I've said, HMS *Malcolm*, was the 16th Destroyer Flotilla leader under Captain Tom Halsey. She was a tough old girl with five guns and six torpedoes but no asdic or radar and hardly changed since the First World War. She had a canvas bridge and I swear the wind actually blew through her side into my cabin. For eight months we plied to and fro, mainly in the Channel and sometimes further afield in the Atlantic. We were on the point of being sent up Oslo Fjord when Norway was invaded; eventually she came to action at the evacuation of Dunkirk.

The very week before Dunkirk, however, I was sent to stand by HMS *Trinidad*, then being built at Devonport, and so I missed the epic of Dunkirk. Such a move for me, though, was convenient because my wife was a West Country girl and her parents lived just outside Ivybridge. So we packed up our house in Emsworth and I sent her to her parents as a safer place for her and our son during the war. I went down to Devonport to stand by this cruiser and throughout 1940 and the early part of 1941 I lived in my mother-in-law's house, and went every day to Plymouth to do my bit. I was employed on all sorts of extraordinary things like sitting on the tops of hills with machine-guns, trying to shoot at aeroplanes that were laying mines in Plymouth Sound. It was a time of considerable excitement and activity and in any spare time I trained the Home Guard unit for Ivybridge and Bideford. By this time the invasion scare was at its height. Britain was being bombed; Coventry had been badly hit; public anxiety was at a high level. My wife stayed in Ivybridge for the rest of the war and, of course, got deeply involved in various activities. She became an air-spotter and used to sit on the top of Dartmoor looking for enemy aeroplanes, and by night became a sort of air-raid warden; she finished up by running the collection of all the food that was thrown away by the Americans in Devon.

I was transferred to Devonport Gunnery School and there, in common with every other officer and man, became subject to immediate despatch anywhere. At least once a day we mustered on the parade ground, where parties for one need or the other were sent off to assignments such as laying mines in the Elbe, beach parties for evacuation of French ports, crews for the fifty US destroyers given by Roosevelt, and so on. My task was to requisition every naval gun available in the dockyard or the Armament depot, mount them upon ten-ton lorries provided by the Army, test fire the result and despatch this mobile weapon to Army centres for the defence of Britain against an invasion. We must have sent forty or fifty such armed lorries before I was suddenly ordered to take 120 brand-new conscripts to Bath and prepare to defend the city against a possible airborne assault.

Bath was a possible target because part of the Admiralty (which included the Ordnance Department) had been evacuated there at the beginning of war. The Deputy Controller of the Navy and his departments took over a girls' school and several hotels, and set up a sort of ancillary Admiralty – they had in mind the idea of evacuating more staff from Whitehall if the invasion came. Somebody came up with the idea that the city might be invaded by parachutists, so it must have some form of defence. Well, they couldn't get any soldiers because they were all wanted for anti-invasion purposes – at least, they were all trying to rearm and retrain – so they said the Navy must do it. It was Gilbertian. With a Boatswain as my second-in-command, four Gunnery Petty Officers and 120 men who only a week before had been civilians, I boarded a special train in Devonport Barracks and set out for Bath. We spent the journey getting the men into their equipment, seeing that each one had a rifle and a bayonet and knew which shoulder to put it on.

At Bath Station I was met by an Admiral who, taking me to one side, informed me that the morale in Bath was none too good and the Irish had been causing some anxiety. What he wanted was for my naval party to march through the city with fixed bayonets to encourage everyone. I caught my breath and thought of my 120 conscripts, but naturally, as expected, I replied, 'Aye, aye sir', and set off to find my senior Gunnery Instructor. He never turned a hair. Within minutes he had the

7. Receiving the Mayor of Scarborough on board HM Drifter Leeward, *1933.
(RNM Collection, neg. 76)*

8. Officers and Ship's Company aboard HM Drifter Leeward, *1933.
(RNM Collection, neg. 104)*

5. *HMS* Rodney, *1930.*
(RNM Collection, neg. 2210)

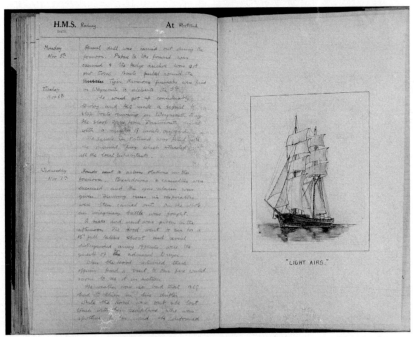

6. *Entry in Midshipman's Journal, HMS* Rodney, *5–9 November 1928.*
(RNM Collection, JD6, neg. 2247)

3. Parade Ground, Royal Naval College, Dartmouth, c. 1920.
(RNM Collection, 146/81)

4. The Quarterdeck, Royal Naval College, Dartmouth, c. 1925.
(RNM Collection, 987/81)

1. Frank Twiss (standing) with Nancy Twiss (sister, on pony), with friends Mary and Frances Moor and Bonnie the pony, c. 1925. (RNM Collection, neg. 81)

2. Cadet Frank Twiss, c. 1927.
(RNM Collection, neg. 100)

9. Wedding day, November 1936.
(RNM Collection, neg. 101)

10. Frank Twiss, 1938.
(RNM Collection, neg. 103)

11. How Christmas dinner used to be served [HMS Glasgow, 1936].
(RNM Collection, 47/80)

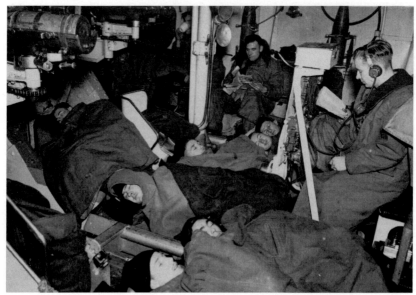

12. Six-inch gun turret, second degree readiness, c. 1942.
(RNM Collection,neg. 154)

14. HMS Exeter, *1942. (RNM Collection, 298/78)*

13. Burial at sea of pilot of Walrus *aircraft,* HMS Exeter, *Indian Ocean, 1941.*
(RNM Collection, 407/91)

15. *Frank Twiss shortly after he*
was liberated, c. 1945.
(RNM Collection, neg. 82)

16. *Liberated prisoners of war at*
Singapore, August 1945.
(RNM Collection, EF.19532)

17. *Scenes of the Japanese surrender of Singapore, 12 September 1945.*
(RNM Collection, 225/82)

men assembled behind trucks in the shunting yard. He placed a rifle with a fixed bayonet on each man's shoulder, told them to keep it there until told otherwise, fell them all in by fours and after making it clear that any man who failed to carry out his orders would never again be recognised by his mother, reported to me: 'Ready to move off, Sir.' Heaven knows how those men stuck it, but they marched in reasonable order slap through Bath and partly uphill to an infants' school where we were to be billeted.

I spent just on six weeks there, by which time I had trained my sailors to become very useful sentries, to fire their rifles and use their bayonets and, together with the Home Guard, who had been put under my command, to man a number of key positions and, hopefully, put up some resistance to an airborne landing. By now, well on in the summer of 1940, I was wanted back in Plymouth to take on the job of Gunnery Officer of HMS *Exeter*, which was in the process of being largely rebuilt and modernised after the River Plate action. Throughout the Battle of Britain period I was in Devonport either overseeing the work on board or organising new air defences in the dockyard, or sitting on hilltops trying to shoot at German minelaying aircraft as they came in to drop magnetic mines in Plymouth Sound and the Hamoaze.

Many and wonderful were those pathetic efforts, especially as some of my equipment was left over from the First World War. All the while I was gradually receiving men for *Exeter*, where the policy was to do as much training as possible before the ship commissioned so that we could man our anti-aircraft armament and support the air defence of Plymouth. I trained endless parties for other endeavours, including the local Home Guard. I went out night after night with my mobile machine-guns and I even lectured the Army on naval co-operation. All through the winter the dockyard worked on the ship and I worked on the available men.

The actual group of men that I started the war with were nearly all bus conductors or bus drivers or engine-drivers or what have you. Men who were splendid types of people, who left their families and off they went, and I couldn't have asked for a more loyal and splendid people and as they were going to ships that hadn't changed at all for nine, ten, twelve, fifteen years or whatever it was, they didn't have any great difficulty in taking them on. They all knew the rudiments of running destroyers, certainly from the time they'd been in the Navy. You'd have great difficulty in doing that today because technology moves too fast for people to keep up and there aren't those sort of Reserves left, of course; they just don't exist.

In 1939, of course, we had a Fleet that might have been called, so to speak, the 1928 Fleet. It was at least ten years out of date, generally speaking, with no radar and no radar fuses. We took a great knocking for it, not only in gunnery. Sonar and submarines were also problems. Of course, we had put an enormous amount of effort into sonar and were probably as well up in it as any navy in the world at that time. But the trouble with sonar is that layers of different density in sea water produce false echoes which make it difficult to achieve the kind of underwater measurement of range and bearing that is needed in order to destroy a submarine; even to this day, it produces the most difficult problems. So it might be said, I think, that the Navy was well prepared for undersea fighting but much less prepared for above-water fighting. Much less prepared, in the sense that our equipment was out-dated, and although much of the technology was available, we hadn't managed to get hold of it, introduce it to our ships, train people to use it and really modernise the Navy. It was too busy. We never had enough ships and they had to get on with what they had.

Between 1939 and 1941 there had been some progress. There was very little we were able to do with the longer-range anti-aircraft weapons, though; that is to say, the 4-inch guns for long-range air defence. They were operated by visual methods and our concern, as much as anything else, was about the fuses for them, because the fuse was a clockwork thing which we more or less had to wind up and set for a time to go off in the air and hope it was near the aeroplane. It was by no means affected by nearness to the target or anything like that, and though we knew that the Americans were well advanced in that particular form of fuse, we had not got it and much wanted it. So there was very little that could be done except exercise and practice against aircraft flying at us, picking them up visually, getting our armament effectively pointing in the right direction and opening fire, and getting the drill and the swing of a high rate of fire with a mechanical system for setting this clockwork fuse.

It was, of course, fairly crude by modern methods, because the effectiveness of the clockwork fuse depended not only on being able to measure the range and altitude of the aeroplane, but also on the accuracy of the clock keeping the time and the right time being set on it to go off near the target. It was affected by all sorts of things, by the shock of being fired into the air, by the temperature of the upper air, and altogether it was not at all easy to score a hit with the long-range anti-aircraft armament. We put up, though, quite exciting barrages of this fire, and, indeed, had various patterns of fire which started at long-range and ended up as quite close-range barrage.

None of it really was very effective, because what we wanted ideally was some kind of detection apparatus in the bullet that we had fired at the aeroplane, and that came very much later. What was being more urgently pursued at the time was close-range firing technology because of the worry of the dive-bomber and the close-range torpedo attack. The Stuka, the German dive-bomber which dived at an immensely steep angle to a very low height, and made a terrible noise, had really devastated and frightened everyone out of their lives in the German advance into Belgium and Holland. As soon as we got into the war, of course, it was used against our ships. It was a very frightening weapon and very accurate because it dived directly at you. It was, therefore, not at all easy to deal with, by gunnery, and it was thought that the only way to do it was to put up an immense amount of shell fire in front of it through which it had to fly and this might be able to destroy it. So, there was a great emphasis in the naval gunnery world, then, on close-range fire.

The question was: what means could we come up with to (a) produce the volume of fire and (b) aim it correctly? Well, they devised a system which depended on a sight which was like a spider's web. It was a visual sight and you looked at the aircraft through it, and if it was coming straight towards you, it flew in from twelve o'clock towards the middle; the middle was where the bullet was meant to hit the aeroplane. It was called eye-shooting, and required much the same skill as shooting at pheasants or anything else. And that was used for the close-range ship armament, which was mostly, at that time, the pom-pom. The pom-pom having been, in various forms, going for some years, had a small shell and fired at a very fast rate and we had produced by then multiple pom-poms; that's to say, instead of the single pom-pom which was very often fitted in destroyers, we had eight barrels on one mounting, all firing at the same time. It was commonly known as the 'Chicago Piano', I think, in the Navy, and it was hoped that it would produce a devastating amount of fire at anything being aimed at. It was supposed to go off if it hit an aeroplane or explode at a fixed range, but it was, in fact, a disappointment.

Other than that we only had ½-inch machine-guns, which were fired in the same way and which had solid bullets and were not really very effective. We had not, at that time, achieved or obtained any of the rather better and smarter guns which were then coming into use in places like Sweden. The Oerlikon gun was a revolutionary gun of its type, light and quick-firing, an excellent gun, but made in Sweden, and although we got round to making it in England, they really didn't get fitted in the Fleet for a very long time. I don't remember Oerlikon guns being available in any old ship before about 1940/41.

We had a close-range anti-aircraft school at Eastney, Portsmouth, where we trained personnel. It depended, though, to a large degree, on the personal skill and judgement of the gun-layer, like the chap on the grouse moor or the pheasant drive aiming a gun. There was very little apparatus to guide him when aiming his gun, apart from the cobweb, this clock-face of wire in front of him, as I've mentioned. We knew at that time, that improved methods of aiming were coming into force and were actually being used by the American Navy, which had devised a method using automatic optical sights which measured the speed at which the target was going across your line of fire, and how much to aim off to hit it. They measured it and cast off the barrel appropriately to help the gun-layer. But we didn't get those. We had none of them in the *Exeter* in 1941, when we commissioned. We entered the war and really had to fight a great deal of it with the weaponry of the thirties. We had to do that because there simply wasn't time to make the weaponry, put it in the ships and train the people while we were still at war. It could be done if a ship was in for refit or damaged or something; it might be possible to modernise its equipment but otherwise we had been forced to go into the war with what we had in the larder in 1939.

This, of course, affected personnel. Immediately, there was a shortage of people with sufficient electronic knowledge or ability to learn to deal with this new stage of equipment which was coming in, both the radar and what came to be called, the rate-aided system. When I use the term 'rate-aided', I mean it measured the relative speeds across the aim-off required for a shell to hit a moving target. As you can see, if we could have a machine that measured that an aeroplane was crossing the line of sight at a certain speed and set the sights to match that speed, we were well on the way to being able to get a hit.

The surface side of gunnery, that is to say, firing at other ships or bombarding, was, of course, affected to an equal degree by radar, but that kind of gunnery doesn't need the same swift measurement of aim-off as you have in aircraft firing. For example, if two battleships are firing against each other, you're talking of speeds of 20 or 30 knots, whereas, even at that time, we're speaking of 200 and 300 knots for aeroplanes. There's a considerable difference.

By the time I came to commission *Exeter* in 1941, we had a Ship's Company, of which I think the figures were something like 60 per cent Royal Navy regulars or regular Reservists and the remainder Hostilities Only ratings who'd never been to sea before, just conscripted, given some brief training and sent to serve. During the war, of course, that percentage grew more and more. The percentage of professional sailors went down as more and more ships came into use and more and more people were called-up by conscription. The interesting thing really was the amazing way in which those people who only joined up during the war became extremely competent sailors at all levels by the end of the war, although some of the things that went on would have been regarded as 'not quite cricket' by the old fogies.

Eventually, when the time came for commissioning, I had received and trained all the men needed to operate the anti-aircraft system and its radar, including the job of tying up with the Royal Artillery defences of Plymouth. All sorts of Ship's Orders had been produced, the stationing of each man arranged, the organisation of each state of readiness agreed; in short everything done as far as was possible before we actually went.

The day before commissioning the Captain died. If sailors are superstitious, here it was on a plate. But, in fact, so busy was everyone on Commissioning Day that there was no time to brood. The Ship's Company bravely marched down to its new ship, bands playing, onlookers looking, dockyard mateys lounging and me, the Gunnery Lieutenant, proud as punch at the way it was all going.

Within a couple of hours of joining, the ammunition lighters arrived and we worked away getting in the shells and cordite, fuses and small arms, torpedoes and the many small stores needed to fit the armament. It took up most of the daylight hours that day and the next to get everything on board and stowed. When this was done, the ship was in the fully loaded state to enter the basin for the last test, the tilt test. So, on the second night of the mission, we lay in the basin of the dockyard ready to make the final adjustments before sailing for trials.

It was on this night that the Germans made their first big raid on Plymouth. We lay floating in the dock with the last boxes of ammunition being struck down when the air-raid warning sounded. We had practised for this event and here was our chance to show our mettle. The gun crews rushed to man their weapons, and a special team for working with the shore gunners dashed up to the bridge. It was pitch dark and you could hear the drone of enemy aircraft. As we made for the charthouse, from where we were to control the *Exeter*'s gun support for the Army, to my horror one of our AA machine-guns opened fire; I was certain that no enemy plane was in range and our bullets must have gone straight into St Budeaux. But nothing could be done for the moment.

Guided by the Navigator and others we made contact with the Army, laid out our special diagrams, calculated how we should direct our weapons and gave the orders to load and aim the guns accordingly. We were ready with the shore defences to fill a certain portion of the sky, through which the Army calculated the bombers would fly, with a barrage of shells. 'Stand by,' came the Army order, 'Five, four, three, two, one – Shoot.'

Exeter fired her first shells of the commission in anger. There was a tremendous bang, enhanced by the fact that the ship was in a basin surrounded by buildings. All the lights in the charthouse went out and the door fell down. Desperately we fumbled to put the door back, for it held the special Darken Ship switch, and we struggled to restore order and light. When at last we succeeded, we had missed two salvos and the first bombs were falling. Even more strange, each one of us in the chartroom was completely white from head to foot. The shock of the gunfire had not only blown down the door it had also dislodged quantities of the white cork dust used to spray the overhead decking to prevent condensation. This dust, left over by dockyard men who had never cleaned up after work, had been lodged in the ventilation shafts overhead.

In a moment we burst out laughing. But then the business in hand reasserted itself and we resumed our liaison with the Army. For the rest of that raid and on the repeat raid the next night the *Exeter* blasted off many 4-inch shells into the sky barrage. With what effect we could not judge; but when the evening papers came out it seemed that everyone knew that our ship was on the job. I'm sure that every West Countryman had the greatest confidence that, if nobody else, the *Exeter* would drive off the Nazi planes.

It was a fierce attack though, and the dockyard and Plymouth were badly knocked about; when we sailed two days later the city was still on fire. Even so, the plain fact of the matter was that we weren't fully ready, the ship had not been properly tested, a great deal of the new equipment wasn't functioning properly and we had a Ship's Company on board in which most of the junior rates didn't know the bow from the stern. With difficulty we made our way up to Scapa Flow arriving in a blizzard.

In Scapa, we spent some weeks in working the ship up to a state of proper efficiency, at the end of which we were assigned to patrol the Denmark Straits where we expected to see the *Bismarck* try to break out. That was our first real operational assignment. After two weeks in the Denmark Straits, we were sent down to Glasgow and assigned to be ocean escort for probably the most important convoy which had sailed from England at that time. This was an armoured brigade going out to the Middle East, almost the last of our available armour, which Winston Churchill had decided must be sent to the Middle East.

We sailed from Glasgow escorting a mass of merchant ships, with a great many destroyers under Captain Philip Vian, together with a dummy battleship. This was HMS *Centurion* of First World War vintage, on which they had built a number of plywood turrets which looked just like HMS *Anson*, the brand-new battleship. As part of our escort, she was safely tucked away in the middle of the convoy and the idea was that we would fool the Germans. Well, there was not much question of fooling the Germans because we hadn't been out more than a few days before the *Bismarck* broke out and we found ourselves in the middle of the Atlantic with this enormously important convoy. All our destroyers were removed as the Atlantic Fleet sailed to search for the *Bismarck*. HMS *Hood* was sunk and we thought we would be mopped up by *Bismarck* should she come our way. Of course, we didn't know that she'd been slightly damaged in the action and I remember very well steaming through the night, pitch dark, and at action stations trying to locate the *Bismarck* with our radar. I'm sure that practically everyone on the bridge thought they saw the *Bismarck* once or twice during the night but, in fact, it wasn't her and later on we discovered that she'd passed 40 miles ahead of us.

We continued with that convoy round the Cape [of Good Hope] and discharged it to the Suez Canal from where we were assigned to do some anti-raider patrolling in the Indian Ocean. We made our way to Bombay, down to Colombo and then went to sea on one or two alarm reports which never turned out to be anything very much. We were based in Colombo until about November 1941 when we were sent to Calcutta and told to escort a convoy of troops for Rangoon, but on our way we were told to go and join the Fleet that was being formed at Singapore to defend Malaya against the Japanese. After delivering our convoy we arrived in Singapore at the very moment that the *Prince of Wales* and *Repulse* were being sunk on the other side of the Malay Peninsula.

CIRCUMSTANCES OF WAR

I recall many pleasant visits to Singapore, steaming down the Johore Straits with the sun glistening on the deep green of the mangroves, the murky vegetable-stained water, the occasional bright white bungalow and the dockyard buildings coming through the haze. But our arrival on that dreadful day, when the Japanese destroyed two of our finest capital ships, was very far from pleasant. In due time, the survivors of the *Prince of Wales* and *Repulse* began to arrive to be received on board the *Exeter*. We gave them a tot of rum and some clothes and looked after them, comforted them, kitted them up and sent them ashore to await dispersal. It was far into the night before we had done our part, and it was with heavy hearts that we took what rest we could.

Next morning, coming on deck for 'Colours', I remember looking out across the waters to Johore and along the empty jetties of the dockyard to see just one single First World War destroyer. We were a cruiser, the largest and almost the only ship between Singapore and the Japanese Fleet. I felt very small and immensely lonely and frightened. It would not be unfair to say that Singapore was not only unready to face a crisis of this dimension, it was not ready for war. To us, who had been through the perils of air raids in Britain and sailed in the face of submarine and surface attack, the atmosphere and attitude of Singapore seemed unbelievable. There were no arrangements for co-ordinating AA gunfire, a reluctance to meet requirements of ammunition or spares and a slowness of reaction to events which was really frightening.

In due course, the Shore Command stirred and we were despatched to Colombo, rounding up and taking along with us every merchant ship we could discover. The battle for Malaya had begun, and, though we did not know it, the first step of events had been taken which would lead to the greatest disaster of British arms.

It was an enormous relief to pass through the Sunda Straits, put Singapore and its disasters behind us and be once more where a cruiser should be, out on the ocean. But relief was short-lived. At Christmas we were on our way back through the Sunda Straits escorting a convoy of reinforcements to Singapore. We steamed up through the islands, where there was so little room to manoeuvre and none whatever to evade, and sure enough the Japanese aircraft found us and went for us.

I cannot now recall how many times we repeated this trip. Each time we were just allowed far enough into the Indian Ocean to rendezvous with a new convoy and back we turned, watching with envy the escorts who had brought the ships thus far, steam away back to Colombo. It seemed to us crazy to go on pouring ever more men, more equipment and more valuable but crated aircraft into Malaya, when the speed of our retreating forces was rapidly narrowing the possibility of deploying the reinforcements in time to stop the rout. We certainly had never believed Singapore would hold out if the Japanese were not defeated at the landings, and the more our forces withdrew and the more Singapore filled up, the less viable became the morale and the confidence of the locals.

It was no surprise when we were redeployed to Java, where a new base was being organised at Batavia, only a few hours inside the Sunda Straits. In mid-February Singapore fell and the scale of attack on ships trying to reach that port increased alarmingly. By this time the *Exeter* was a hardened warrior, experienced in facing Japanese bombing and accustomed to hours and hours at Action Stations in the steamy heat of the East Indies. We had achieved some degree of success, first in getting several convoys of reinforcements into Singapore and then in rounding up and dispersing a great quantity of Allied shipping caught in the South China and Java Seas by the war.

If we had any doubts about what we were in for, these doubts were dispelled when the news filtered through of 'strategic withdrawal'. We had heard this phrase too often in the first two years of the war, and the fighting men, who are not easily fooled, had given it their own expressive but rude description. It was, alas, just this. Our overall Commander-in-Chief, General Wavell, was going to Burma; new commanders were being appointed and Allied Forces were being redeployed. Strangely, I do not recall people being unduly depressed by all this. We all thought we could get away, out through the Sunda Straits into the Indian Ocean, and then, who knows, we might even get across to that city of lights and delights, Durban.

Tanjong Priok, the outer harbour of Batavia, was not a comfortable berth, though it was admirable for providing an all-round field of fire and a view to seaward. Batavia itself was virtually devoid of AA defence and had no effective radar. The place was in chaos. Ships were unloading supplies including a large amount of whiskey for the NAAFI. Soldiers and airmen were coming in from Singapore and Malacca, reinforcements were still arriving from India and all in all it was impossible to find out what was happening and who was in command.

The result was that the AA defence of the place fell almost entirely on *Exeter*. Japanese aircraft soon began attacking and our stay in harbour became no more restful or secure than at sea. It was not long before we were ordered to Surabaya, a long way east and into the Java Sea, far from the Sunda exit. Our task was to join an Allied Task Force of ships from the Netherlands, United States and Australia, under the Dutch Admiral Doorman. It took a full twenty-four hours to reach Surabaya and we reached the port just in time to attend a briefing before we sailed.

BATTLE OF THE JAVA SEA

We were a very mixed bag: two Dutch cruisers, *De Ruyter* and *Java*, the USS *Houston*, HMAS *Perth*, and *Exeter* with perhaps eight destroyers from the different nations. We had no common communications, had never seen each other before and had no idea of each other's capabilities or personalities. But there it was. The situation was desperate and we just had to do the best we could. We steamed east through the night, turning back in the early morning to sweep along the coast back to Surabaya. Nothing was seen or heard. We were nearly back in Surabaya where the destroyers expected to refuel when we received our first enemy report. A convoy of ships had been sighted a few hours steaming to the north. The Allied Force cracked on to full speed and turned to close the enemy convoy. There seemed likely to be a pause before we could make contact, so in the best naval tradition, the hands were sent to tea. I went down and donned a clean white uniform suit and clean underwear, just as Nelson's Officers did before action. We had barely returned to our action stations, fed and clothed, when things began to happen.

A Midshipman, sent up to the crow's nest to look for ships, reported something far ahead. From my Director Control Tower (which was an armoured box on a pedestal standing up above the bridge), I trained my binoculars on the horizon and there, sure enough, was a very small, thin stick, just showing over the line of sea and sky. Very soon others appeared, the sticks grew larger and I saw what looked like a dozen or so masts and yards. My heart leaped; we were into the convoy. But it was not so. The masts revealed that they belonged to two Japanese cruisers and twelve destroyers in two columns. For a time we were outside each other's maximum range, but this did not deter the Dutch cruiser *De Ruyter*, ahead of us, from opening fire, despite her smaller 6-inch guns. We followed shortly with our 8-inch guns and the battle had begun. The leading Japanese cruiser fired, and seeing the flash of her guns, I realised for the first time, that somewhere between us and her, shells were screaming through the air, menacingly directed at what felt like me personally. I had often wondered at Dartmouth whether in action I would be terrified and it was a relief to find that I was not. Momentarily, I was concerned to think that many thousands of miles away, my wife would be going about her business unaware of the spot her husband was in and I hoped that she was not going to have bad news after our action was over. It was a vague, if anxious, thought; but there was no time to philosophise further for the action was developing fast.

The cruiser we were firing at made a lot of smoke and turned away. We thought we might have hit her and turned our attention to her consort. Then came the call from the bridge: 'Engage the enemy cruiser on the starboard beam.' We slewed round to find three such ships apparently heavily engaged by the other Allied ships astern of us. The sea was a mass of shell splashes and it was impossible to make out who was firing at what. Up until then I had no idea there were other Japanese ships in sight and the appearance about 10 miles away of these large ships, quickly identified as modern 8-inch cruisers, was a nasty jolt. After a frustrating time, we began to sort out the splashes of our own and our allied ships' shells, and all the *Exeter* guns were soon pounding away. Suddenly, there was a gigantic thump and the ship seemed to jump. The feeling was exactly the same as when you puncture the lid of a sealed tin with the point of a tin opener. *Exeter* had been hit, but in the forward Director Tower it seemed rather remote and inconsequential. But not for long. In a matter of minutes lights began to go out, machinery stopped and power failed. The ship started to slow down, generators stopped, the 8-inch turrets came to a standstill and fell silent.

There was nothing I could do except relay information to the bridge. *Exeter* hauled out of the line and the next astern, unaware of our state, followed us. For a moment there was some confusion as the Admiral ahead of us was going straight on. After a time he turned back, collected the undamaged cruisers and returned to the fight while we slowly fell astern and eventually lost touch. By this time our damaged boilers had been isolated and power was again restored so that our guns could once more be fired.

The action could dimly be seen going on far away, and our orders were to return to Surabaya for repair. But the Japanese had not finished with us. Suddenly we became aware that a number of enemy destroyers were closing in, supported by one of the cruisers we had seen at the very start of the battle. We opened fire and since the range was now only a few miles our salvos were soon falling round the cruiser. She turned away and the Japanese destroyers, harassed by the gallant counter-attacks of our destroyers, fired at least two dozen torpedoes in our direction. We could see them racing towards us with a trail of air bubbles streaking out behind. *Exeter* turned away. One torpedo struck a Dutch destroyer which immediately blew into two parts and sank; none of the other torpedoes found a target. We had got away with it.

Under orders to return to Surabaya, we crept off the scene anxious in case other Japanese warships might come back for another bite. But our luck held and we safely reached harbour and berthed in the late evening. Our damage proved to be serious but not crippling. One Japanese shell had penetrated a boiler room, entirely wrecking it and killing the engineers in it. Another had hit the end of one of our pom-pom guns, splitting the barrel open like peeling a banana, but it had not exploded. Next day we found part of this shell on deck – it had British markings!

Next morning we set about clearing up, moving ammunition to even the supply between guns, repairing our AA armament, one part of which had been wrecked by the shell which entered the boiler room, and, of course, burying those killed in action. By superhuman efforts, the engine room staff patched up our steam piping and reported they could get the ship up to 25 knots. We were in business again. The question was, what business? Here was the *Exeter* in 1942 in just the same situation as the *Graf Spee* in 1939, wounded and in harbour with her enemy outside. In 1939 the *Exeter* and the other British ships were waiting outside for the *Graf Spee* to emerge; in 1942 the Japanese fleet was waiting outside Surabaya for the *Exeter*. Was there ever a greater naval irony?

The expression 'a proper turn-up for the books' certainly fitted the plight of the *Exeter* as she lay in Surabaya harbour on 28 February 1942. There was just time to confer with the local Dutch Admiral and speak by telephone with the British Liaison Officer, Admiral Palliser, who was in the capital, Bandoeng. It was quickly evident that there was not only a great paucity of intelligence but also a lack of air reconnaissance and a sense of near panic. Commodore Collins, Captain of HMAS *Perth*, had radioed the *Exeter* to break out and make for Colombo; yet nothing was then known of his whereabouts nor any of the other Allied ships. In the event, *Exeter*, *Encounter* and USS *Pope* were told to break out westwards through Sunda in the belief that exits from the Java Sea to the eastward were either mined or covered by Japanese ships.

To us it seemed crazy. Surely we should take our chance through either the Bali or maybe the Lombok Straits, risking mines or Japanese forces in a dash for Darwin. But our orders were to steam north towards Borneo and then westward to Sunda and the Indian Ocean; and our Captain was not willing to disobey. Despite the brave face put upon the situation, and, indeed, its obviously hopeless chance of success, the *Exeter* sailed with HMS *Encounter* and USS *Pope* on the evening of 28 February in an attempt to fight their way out of the Java Sea.

We did not know, nor did we hear until weeks later, that USS *Houston* and HMAS *Perth*, the only other surviving Allied ships, sailed at the same time from Batavia with the same objective. They were caught some few miles out, just inside the Sunda Straits and sunk by Japanese Naval forces. So, ignorant of news which might well have led us to turn a blind eye on our orders and head eastward for Darwin, we set out from Surabaya. Looking back, I am still amazed at the calmness, courage and determination to acquit themselves well which pervaded the ship. It could only be explained by the highest morale and it remains a tribute to a fine West Country ship's company.

We left Surabaya on a lovely, clear but dark, tropical night. We stood to all night and when daylight came, apart from one alarm about 0400 when we evaded a couple of merchant ships, we were, to all appearances, alone and undetected. But not for long. A small seaplane was seen on the horizon and we knew that our position was revealed. The ship held its breath; this was it. The weather was perfect; hardly a cloud in the sky, extreme visibility and no sign of those sudden black rain squalls which are common in the Java Sea. About 0900 we sighted the enemy: two large cruisers and one or two destroyers. We turned away only to find three other cruisers and some destroyers ahead.

It was only a matter of time. We weaved and turned, made smoke, reported the situation by wireless and fired everything we could whenever an enemy ship or aircraft came near enough. The battle continued for over two hours in this way with the *Exeter* by now bursting her remaining boilers to achieve 26 knots. Then we were hit smack in the vitals. A shell entered one of the remaining boiler rooms and cut the main steam pipe. Other hits followed and fires started. All the steam escaped, the generators stopped, the lights went out, power was lost and the guns fell silent unable to operate any more. I sat in my Director Tower above the bridge struggling with reports from here, there and everywhere. We tried every known 'stand-by' system but it was useless. The fires were bad, orders were given to flood the AA magazines. I looked around and for the first time realised that we had something like four cruisers and as many destroyers surrounding us.[1]

---

[1] For another account of Admiral Twiss' experiences at this time see Arthur J. Marder, Mark Jacobsen and John Horsfield, *Old Friends New Enemies: The Royal Navy and the Imperial Japanese Navy, The Pacific War, 1942–1945*, Oxford, Clarendon Press, 1990, pp. 72–3, 78–9.

CHAPTER FIVE

Prisoner of War, 1942–1945

A SURVIVOR

As *Exeter*'s Gunnery Officer, I was up in the Director Control Tower. I had with me a range-taker, two officers and two ratings and I was busy trying to find out what the state of play was and what was working and what was not working. I was not, therefore, aware that the order 'Abandon ship' had been given or that the Captain had decided that we must sink the ship and get out. One of the sailors, who was in the Tower with me, said, 'Sir, do you know they've given the order "Abandon ship"?'

I said, 'No, I didn't know that. Are you sure you've got it right?'

'Yes,' he said, 'and everybody seems to be leaving.'

'All right,' I said, 'abandon ship and you men get out.' It wasn't all that easy to get out from my position. We had to open a sort of trapdoor on top of us, climb out, disengage ourselves from all the telephone wires and climb down a ladder to the bridge. I made sure that all the men with me had moved out and then I climbed out myself, not at all sure whether we were doing the right thing, but I then found there was nobody left on the bridge at all.

I then remembered that as the Gunnery Officer it was my duty to throw all the confidential books on gunnery into the sea in a weighted bag with holes in it to make sure it sank. The outer covers of some of these books had lead in them. They were kept in a safe in the Gunnery Office, which was two decks down in the superstructure below. So I went down there. There was nobody with me at all by then, but I knew I must do it. I found, of course, when I got there, that the task was impossible because I hadn't got the key of the safe in which these things were lodged. I looked round and could see no way of doing it and as the ship appeared to be going to sink anyhow, I came to the conclusion I wouldn't bother any more. So I then made my way onto the upper-deck, arriving after quite a number of people had already started to jump overboard. I then found a whole lot of sailors trying to lower a boat; a bit of splinter went through the falls – the ropes with which you raise and lower it – and the boat crashed down. Generally, people were scurrying about, with most going aft onto the quarterdeck because that was the lowest deck and nearest to the sea and the shortest distance to jump into the water. By the time I got active, I thought I might be able to get a boat out into the water, one which was stowed quite high up and directly under the seaplane we carried. I tried to get up there but there was a very severe fire raging. In the end, I thought it's no good; I'd better go. So I went to the next deck down, which was quite close to the water for by that time the ship was sinking.

There I met the Chief Ordnance Artificer, a senior Petty Officer who had been in the Battle of the River Plate and was a very old and respected Chief. I said to him, his name was Johns,[1] 'Come on, Johns, I think we must leave the ship.'

He said to me, 'I can't do it, Sir. I've been in this ship too long; I can't leave her. I'm going to go for'ard and go down with her.'

I replied, 'I don't think that's at all a sensible thing to do; it won't do the ship any good if you go down with her; much better that you should come with me and we'll get into the sea.'

At that moment, the ship was struck by a shell and there was a tremendous rocking and bits and pieces, dust, debris and all the rest of it flew around, and I was absolutely peppered with what I thought were shots or bits of metal. I looked down and thought to myself, so that's what it feels like to be wounded. When I looked at my shirt, which was a white shirt, there was no blood on it at all, and there were no holes in it. Of course, what had happened was that when the shell hit the ship an immense amount of dust and material that lies on the top of cables on the decks of ships, had got shaken loose and peppered me. So I was still alive, and at that moment I said to Johns, 'Come on, blow up your life jacket and we'll step into the sea

---

[1] Chief Ordnance Artificer William E. Johns DSM, who later wrote an account of his experiences, *No Surrender* (George Harrop and Co. Ltd, 1969; rpt. W.J. Allen and Co., 1989).

together.' The sea was only about 12 inches away, below us, and so we stepped into the sea almost hand in hand, and swam away.

Eventually, from a distance of 50 or 60 yards, I suppose, we looked back and there was the ship listing over very badly. Then there was a tremendous explosion, and the ship was obviously hit by one or two torpedoes, with the result that it reared itself up in the sky, the bows went right up in the air and it then stopped, almost majestically. It was, so to speak, looking down on all of us, as much as to say, I don't think much of you people. Then it slid gently backwards and into the water. It was very impressive but immensely sad, of course, to see the ship sink. However much you're being knocked about, you don't want to leave it. It's been your life; it's been your home. You're deeply wrapped up in it. Your whole instinct is not to leave. So that when the moment comes – when it's clearly obvious you either leave it or get killed – it is a very moving moment.

Johns and I were separated shortly afterwards. A great deal of stuff had been thrown overboard, planks and bits of this and that. There were a number of life rafts, consisting mainly of floats and nets with corks on them, which were rolled up and tied so you could just throw them over the side. These had to be undone. Happily, as a sailor, I had always worn a knife round my middle, my 'Pusser's dirk,' so I was a popular fellow because I was able to cut the lashings and open them up. A great many of us were hanging on to them when we spread them out.

Eventually, a Japanese destroyer actually came and picked up quite a number of us. It was, perhaps, 300 or 400 yards away from me, so to swim that distance would have taken a considerable time and I just didn't try it. I just felt that I would stay where I was. I had a floating net to hold on to, and I still had a sort of stupid feeling, perhaps, that somehow I would be picked up by somebody who wasn't Japanese. Then, for the first time, I realised I was going to be made a prisoner. I hadn't thought of it at all. Sailors, except perhaps submariners, are not people who think about being picked up by the enemy.

I had got oil in my eyes and, as the sun was hot, bit by bit, it started to be extremely painful. Hanging on to anything isn't easy. I actually discovered a ping-pong table floating fairly close by and got hold of that, but it wasn't by any means easy because it kept tipping up. Such rafts and floating nets as were available were being used by a very large number of men, rather more men than there were billets on these floating nets. So one settled down, really, holding onto what you had and thought of things. I simply don't know how that night passed. I remember falling asleep and waking when my head fell into the water. I remember how hard it was to keep hold of the table and I remember that I became aware that I was making rather dreadful noises as I breathed. Beyond that I have no recollection, until sometime in the morning when I became aware that the night had passed, that I was still afloat and that to open my eyes and look was difficult and dreadfully painful.

At some period that morning I must have drifted close to a Carley float on which were a number of men, one at least of whom had been wounded. They called to me to come to their raft and somebody helped me over. But the raft was already full inside and I was too weak in any case to scramble on board. So I thankfully caught hold of one of the rope beckets on the side of the raft and settled down to wait again. It was a good deal more restful than the table tennis top.

Gradually, I got noticeably weaker and it was really very difficult to do anything but just hold on. On the whole, I was surprised that I had any strength left at all seeing that I had been afloat for some twenty hours; but I still was conscious and could move my limbs. What I could not do, except momentarily, was open my eyes; and this was horrible. There were people all round and although they were remarkably spread out, they were trying to keep together. The only thing we had been taught, really, about survival in those circumstances was to try and stick in one bunch, because if you were going to be picked up nothing would be more difficult than being spread all over the place. My eyes were extremely painful, and it was just a question of opening them to take a peep around, when I could bear it, to see if there was anything going on.

Then out of the blue, came a Japanese destroyer. It came right into the middle of our crowd of sailors and picked us up. When I say picked us up, we had to swim towards the ship and it was even more difficult to get on board. They threw ropes and nets over the side for us to climb up but we were very weak. So it was hard work getting on board and I was helped by a Japanese sailor who removed my signet ring in the course of getting me on board, which was not very difficult to do as it was a bit oily by then.

We were ushered forward onto the fo'c'sle of this ship and just lay down absolutely exhausted. Eventually, they brought us water and biscuits and really treated us quite reasonably. The Japanese weren't in any way brutal or beastly. They didn't ask us any questions; they were just amazed to have so many bodies lying about their ship. By that time I wasn't really seeing anything. I just opened my eyes quickly to see where I was going and feel my way. The effect of oil was very unpleasant, and remained unpleasant for several days afterwards. I can't remember how long we were on the destroyer, some few hours, before they transferred us. Funnily enough, the only thing I remember about the destroyer was its smell. A Japanese ship has a sickly smell of sweet biscuits; I don't know why. It was very strong. I mean, if I went on board a Japanese ship and smelt it again, I would recognise it at once. When they transferred us, I was more or less semi-blinded because it was so painful to look into bright sunlight. It wasn't until I got on board the hospital ship to which the destroyer took us some hours later, that I was able to get water and bathe my eyes. It took some days to get rid of the oil and my eyes were red and sore for quite a time.

MACASSAR CAMP

The ship sailed into Macassar Harbour and we were all transferred ashore. We then came under Japanese guards and were marched from the landing place to an old Dutch army camp which was about half-a-mile or so away. That was an experience on its own because, of course, I had no shoes by then and the ground was exceptionally hot, and marching was a matter of hopping from one place to the next to ease the burning soles of the feet. It was extremely painful, then, marching in a very bedraggled column, assisted by various shouts and blows from the Japanese, who by that time were getting somewhat rough in getting us into the order they wanted.

I was then put into a large building with a concrete floor; there were about fifty or sixty of us shut in there, where we spent two nights. That was the first time I discovered how uncomfortable it was trying to sleep on a plain concrete floor with nothing else to help you. In the course of the following days, we were gradually moved around and put into other buildings in the camp. We were hardly bothered at all to start with, until some officer arrived who started getting very stroppy, beating people up for any reason. They would give orders that nobody understood and when you didn't obey them, they'd hit you on the head with bamboo poles. It was a display really of 'We're the bosses now and you do just as you're told.'

Of course, by then everybody had heard how beastly the Japanese were. They had gained a reputation for brutality from the campaign in Malaya, and, although we weren't seriously molested, one or two sailors were rather nastily beaten up for doing something which annoyed the Japanese but of which the sailors were unaware. Generally speaking, though, it wasn't sufficient to make us do anything but watch out and keep as clear as we could of doing or saying anything that might lead us into trouble.

My first camp was quite big and had been an army barracks. It was filled with us and sailors from the other two ships who'd been with us, and with quite a lot of Dutch military and civilians. The Dutch were not too badly off because they had accumulated a certain amount of food and things and had some money. The local people, the Indonesians, would come to the wire in the dark and, if you had a bit of money, you could buy a banana or two. It wasn't much good to us because none of us had any money. There was a little bit of bad feeling between the Dutch and the British – we felt they ought to help us out a bit.

It was a time when morale and naval discipline might go for six. Yet to maintain our esteem, our cohesion, and, in due course, to be able to treat the Japanese authorities with a sense of proper leadership and position, it was tremendously important to keep up our own naval discipline and authority and so remain a unit. I think the day was largely saved by our Navigator, who somehow managed to get to our sailors and establish communication with them sufficiently to gain their respect and admiration; because he was seen to be actively reporting to our Captain and because it became clear that as officers we were getting no privileges at all, the anxious wobble in *Exeter*'s morale smoothed out. We were as one again.

I was there at Macassar for about five or six weeks, and generally speaking it was quite comfortable. We weren't bothered too much and we were living in quite sanitary blocks with our own people. Suddenly, I was told that I was to leave. The Japanese had decided that they would take certain people, who they'd captured, up to Japan for questioning. And they knew who they wanted. They'd obviously bought Navy Lists over the years, and they'd picked out the Captain, the Commander, the Engineer Officer, the Gunnery Officer, the Torpedo Officer, the Navigating Officer, the Cypher Officer and three Telegraphists, three Chief Petty Officers and Petty Officer Telegraphists. They did the same sort of thing in the other ships. They issued us all with civilian clothes which had been captured and we were then marched down to the docks and put on board a rather old cargo ship and we were stuffed into one of the holds, where we were not too badly off. We were given some sort of blanket and we set off from Macassar to go to Japan.

OFUNA PUNISHMENT CAMP

I think we left Macassar early in April. This ropey old ship was simply stuffed with rats and rather large cockroaches, enormous cockroaches. Otherwise it wasn't too bad: they fed us quite well; they didn't bother us at all; they just kept us locked up. Quite a number of Japanese soldiers and sailors were on board, and we didn't see anything very much of them except occasionally when they got very drunk and made rather a noise; but they didn't bother us because we were locked down below in the hold.

We set off for Japan and we all rather thought we'd probably be torpedoed on the way, in which case we speculated whether we'd be sunk with the ship or find ourselves swimming around once again and perhaps able to escape. Well, we weren't torpedoed and we made a very slow trip to Japan. We called in at Taiwan and at two other ports, I think, before we eventually arrived in Yokohama. I should think that must have been early May by then. It was quite a long trip, perhaps six weeks. When we arrived in Yokohama, we went alongside one of the jetties, where we were put ashore, wearing these strange civilian clothes of all sorts and kinds and descriptions. I mean we didn't have many clothes each, and we looked as though we were from a jumble sale.

We were marched from the docks to the railway station where we got into an electric train like an underground train. All the Japanese were moved out and we were shoved into a carriage and we set off for some unknown destination, which we arrived at after about three-quarters of an hour. We were then decanted again, fallen in, and marched up a hill, to a stockaded camp of wooded huts, like chicken huts, with a Japanese flag flying on a post and a lot of guards.

We were marched into the camp and this was where we were to be locked up. It consisted of, I can't remember, thirty or forty, perhaps more, cells in a sort of E-shaped block, and a small parade ground and associated lavatory accommodation, which was fairly elementary. We were fallen in and everything was taken off us except the clothes we stood up in. By that time, of course, we had beards. I had a splendid beard. I'd always wanted to grow a beard but my wife said if I did she'd divorce me, so this was my chance. In addition, I was one of those chaps who had a rather fine moustache I could twirl. The Japanese don't like beards; they're not able to grow them themselves and so it was quite clear that the guards didn't care for anybody who had a beard. We were then put into cells. I suppose each cell was about 6 foot by 4 foot, with a wooden door with a little window in it and a small barred hole at the back which was the window for ventilation and, to our amazement, we were locked in there, one of us in each cell.

We hadn't thought of being locked up like that, in solitary confinement. We'd thought we were going to go to some rather splendid Japanese castle for some reason and be incarcerated there, but not a bit of it. We were locked up in this wooden set of buildings like a glorified hen-house. Shortly afterwards, we were assembled again on the parade ground and a very perky Sub-Lieutenant in the Japanese Navy gave us an address; it was not very easy to understand because it all had to be translated. He shouted and gesticulated a good deal, but the gist of it all was that we were very lucky to be there. We were a pretty shameful lot of people because we had allowed ourselves to be taken prisoner, but the Japanese were a nice, kind people and just so long as we behaved ourselves it would be all right. If we stepped out of line at all, though, our heads would be cut off, and there was a demonstration then by this Japanese officer who drew his sword and slashed it around to show how heads could be cut off. We must remember, he said, that we were not prisoners. We were just in Japan. There was no question of us regarding ourselves as having any status as prisoners. We were men who'd been captured and put into this place, and by golly we'd better behave ourselves. So there it was. Then we were marched back to our cells.

A couple of days later, the place was enlivened when an enormous fire started raging in the undergrowth outside. They thought the whole place was going to go up, so we were all paraded again and the Japanese officer got frightfully excited because, of course, if it did catch fire there'd be absolute chaos for the prisoners who'd be trying to run away. So the Japanese Sub-Lieutenant rushed round screaming and waving his sword and getting very excited, but the camp didn't catch fire. We were then put back into solitary confinement. We were exercised on the parade ground three times a day. From time to time we were addressed by the Japanese Sub-Lieutenant telling us how good Japan was and how all the ships of the US Navy and the

British Navy had been sunk, and a whole lot of absolute rubbish about what they called 'War News'. There we stayed right through the summer.

Towards the middle of the summer, they brought in a whole lot of Americans and some Australians from ships which had been sunk in the original Java Sea battle. As with us, they brought the Gunnery Officer, the Torpedo Officer and the Captain and so on, and as there wasn't accommodation for all of them, they doubled up on some of the cells. I acquired an extremely nice young American Lieutenant Commander, who was the pilot of the aircraft on board USS *Houston*, and he and I shared a cell from July onwards. It was absolutely forbidden to talk at all. It didn't mean you didn't communicate because, of course, it's very difficult to stop people talking when they're in a small cell. We remained in that state waiting to be questioned.

From time to time, important-looking people came and I think one or two people actually were questioned, but it was fairly obvious that they weren't interested in the British any more because there really weren't any British ships operating in the Pacific. We'd all been sunk; and they were only interested in the Americans, particularly when they raided Japan. They got very excited about that, and we expected to be joined by one or two people who had been shot down or something, but we never were and so there we stayed.

Round about August somebody got dysentery; the Japanese were very worried. Unhappily, it seemed to spread and I caught it. I can't think how, but I did. By that time we had, perhaps, six or eight people with dysentery and the Japanese were worried, because, I think, their instructions were to keep us available for questioning, in reasonable health, but not too strong.

I was taken off to hospital with six or eight other people, in a lorry. We were taken to a Japanese port called Yokosuka, where there was a naval hospital and something like eight of us were put in a ward with, I think, four beds, which was awful. There was practically no medicine nor was there anything much to eat apart from a sort of rice gruel. Nevertheless, we all recovered and were sent back to the camp.

In Ofuna the guards were a very rough lot, particularly on Saturday nights. They used to get very drunk and line up all the prisoners and find some excuse to object to one or more of them and beat them up. It was an extremely alarming and unpleasant experience to be fallen in, in two ranks on a sort of half-square with the guards finding fault with somebody, or asking us some question. If we didn't answer it, they beat us over the head with their bamboo sticks as a form of Saturday entertainment. I suppose, perhaps, the most difficult thing was if one of your friends was being beaten up a couple of paces from you. It was extraordinarily difficult not to try and interfere, not to try and go to his rescue, but if you did, you'd be battered to the earth along with him, and it was clearly stupid to interfere. If you were the one who was being beaten up, well you were that Saturday's offering. Nobody died from it, but it was all part and parcel of a very strict regime, with the unknown quantity of fear and brutality lurking there all the time.

We were taken out of our cell three and four times a day for exercise, which was PT. That was all it was; we marched round the compound, then spread around and did all this Japanese semi-musical PT. Generally speaking, in the Navy, unusual and difficult jobs were nearly always given to the Gunnery Officer because he was the man who controlled the greatest number of sailors in the ship. I had therefore been told by my Captain [Captain Oliver Gordon RN] to conduct PT on board. So, it was me who used to conduct the PT in Japanese, and bit by bit, with a few blows and things, I learnt enough to count. But it was, in fact, quite a good performance. Every morning at dawn we were fallen in on the parade ground, turned towards the Imperial Palace and bowed three times, and the things that were muttered under people's breath on those occasions were simply staggering.

Life at this time was very low. I remember sitting in my cell and hearing the songs of birds outside. One song in particular was louder and clearer than the others and always made me think how lovely it must be to be a bird, free to sing, free to fly away, free to go back to its own home. From time to time even now I hear a bird song which instantly and painfully brings back the memories of how I felt in the Ofuna cell.

From time to time the guards would hold special days. Japanese Army Day was a great day in this camp. We were all mustered and instructed to put on a marching or military display for the benefit of the guards, after which they would show what useless people we were by doing Japanese drill. I drilled the British contingent and thereby achieved a position of some eminence, being the only Gunnery Officer ever known in the Navy who drilled a squad of which the front rank, right-hand man was his Captain and the rear rank, right-hand man was his Commander. Nobody's ever likely to have a chance to do that again.

Then, at regular intervals, we would be fallen in to get the 'War News', which consisted of a series of disasters to any form of Allied enterprise. The American Fleet was sunk several times over and it very soon was so obviously nonsense that one didn't worry about it any more. It was an anxious time because there we were, miles and miles away from any of our compatriots at home, not reported as prisoners, not considered as prisoners, entirely at the will of the Japanese, being ill fed and ill treated and with little knowledge of what was going to happen to us. One couldn't see any end to the war. We didn't know what was going on apart from all this false news and, therefore, to that extent it was both mentally and psychologically extremely difficult.

ZENTSUJI CAMP

Somewhere about September 1942, they decided that they would get rid of a number of prisoners from Ofuna, and replace them, presumably, with other people they had captured. Little by little, we were taken away. A group of ten or twelve would suddenly be fallen in and taken away and we, in fact, all ended up in one of the southern islands of Japan, on Shikoku Island, at a camp called Zentsuji. It was a great relief because we travelled down to Zentsuji by train and across in a ferry and were marched into the camp where there were several hundred Americans,

Australians, and Dutch. For the first time for six or nine months, certainly from March to about October, we were allowed to talk. It was tremendously exciting, actually, to be able to talk to other people.

There we were, then, down in Shikoku Island in this camp which was probably as good a camp as the Japanese were running in Japan at the time. Most of the camps had the same sort of thing. They had one or two sadistic people, a number of rather frightened people, and, in our case, a great many sentries who marched about and were supposed to guard us.

We were told that we had to sign a paper to say we wouldn't try and escape. Well, that wasn't allowed, that was one of the few things we knew about being a prisoner of war: that you didn't do that. Your duty was to escape. So we all refused to sign. The British were all then incarcerated in one building and told that they would have no mail. They would never be reported until we signed this thing. We didn't sign it and eventually they got bored and let us out and we joined the rest of the throng. A great many of the prisoners there had signed it. They all said, 'Oh, rubbish to this,' and signed.

We then started a period, a lengthy period, when it was made clear that unless we worked we wouldn't get anything much to eat at all. The question was: what was work? Work was all sorts of things that the Japanese invented. I worked for some little time with a sort of pick-axe, digging up hard tennis courts in the local naval or military club in order to plant vegetables. Then, because I got into some trouble, I was given the unpleasant job, with a friend, of emptying all the latrines with a bucket and a bamboo pole. So for quite a time I worked as a coolie at one end of a bamboo pole and it was all right because it was better to do that than sit about doing nothing. Bit by bit, over the period, things got really more and more stringent. The food got less and less palatable, and the work went on.

Unlike many camps of prisoners of war, we never ever had a radio set or anything like it and our sole means of information were the enlisted American men who used to be taken down to work in the docks about 10 or 12 miles away. They were able to steal Japanese newspapers and bring them back. We happened to have in the camp a Japanese interpreter who had been studying in Japan before the war and was caught up when the war started. So we were able to translate the Japanese newspapers and by setting one piece of news against another, we got a reasonable idea of what was going on. As MacArthur slowly advanced up the Pacific, the newspapers reported that the Americans had landed on Tarawa, or wherever it was, and they had all been decimated; two or three days later, in spite of all being decimated, they were still there.

I stayed at Zentsuji from the end of 1942 until the middle of the spring of 1945. By this time, in some extraordinary way, after about eighteen months of incarceration, our names had been reported back to England. I think it was during a visit by the Swiss, or somebody, to the camp that we managed to smuggle over to them a list of people who were in the camp; and so for the first time my family at home heard that, although I'd been missing for some time, I was still alive. We were then permitted to write twenty-five words a month on a postcard, which was better than nothing at all, and so we used to write home. Occasionally I'd get a letter of twenty-five words back from my family, which made a tremendous difference. My wife had become a widow by then and was on a widow's pension and was delighted, therefore, to go back on to full pay.

The period in that camp was, on the whole, marked by steady decline, but there were no great brutalities. Quite a number of people died of at least the indirect results of malnutrition, but the camp staff of officers didn't vary and they were not unreasonable people. It was just that there wasn't enough to eat and the work at times became hard. I was told, at one point, to run a chicken farm, which was an extraordinary business. We had to begin by building incubators with horse manure and straw and all sorts of things. Then we got baby chickens and we used to be given small amounts of grain for them. Needless to say, a good many of the baby chickens were smuggled away to be cooked. Eventually, one day, they actually got to the state of laying eggs, and the very first egg that came out we paraded round the camp and gave it to the Colonel, who didn't think it was at all funny and couldn't make out why the prisoners were so pleased at this egg being carted round.

The situation then changed very dramatically, because, in the first months of 1945, the B29s started to raid Japan and they used to fly directly over us and the Japanese began to get very frightened. We were put to making air-raid shelters in the form of trenches all round the place. We went and dug air-raid trenches and the B29s went on flying over and then the Japanese clearly made a decision that they were going to get all the prisoners, more or less, corralled in convenient places, in case Japan was invaded.

One day, we were all told that the place was going to be closed down and we were going to be moved off, which did happen. All the Americans went to one place, all the Australians went to another place, the British actually went to two places in Japan, and the camp was run down to just the enlisted men who worked in the docks. That was somewhere, I suppose, in April of 1945. By that time we were extraordinarily weak, owing to lack of food and hard work. Indeed, we were in a very weak state and it was extraordinarily difficult to do any work without exhausting ourselves. We set off for our new camp and it seemed awfully difficult to carry any kind of thing at all. Not that I was actually encumbered with much gear, as I had none when I arrived and accumulated practically none during my time there.

Anyhow, we had jolly little to cart around with us, although most of us still had a toothbrush and you could get a little toothpaste. In one of the tubes of toothpaste we hid an account of the battle during which *Exeter* was sunk and a record of the whole of our time in the camp. The tube was screwed up and kept by Captain Gordon in his gear. He always had that battle narrative, which he actually was able to hand to the Allies at the end of the war. It was always touch and go because whenever one moved everything was searched and most small things tended to be taken away, but the Japanese had a great respect, apparently, for teeth, and so toothpaste and toothbrushes always seemed to be passed.

THE CAMP AT MITSUSHIMA

We set out from the camp in Zentsuji in April or May of 1945, went down to the port and got into a ferry. Now I should say at this point that I was in a group that contained all the people from HMS *Exeter*, about eight of us, and a few other British people and, needless to say, as soon as it was known we were moving, rumours spread as to where we were going to go. One of the places mentioned was where the atomic bomb was eventually dropped, Hiroshima. We seriously thought we were on the way to Hiroshima. That didn't mean anything very much to us, except that it was a place on the Inland Sea. Because most prisoners of war are reasonably optimistic, we always thought it'd be better than the last place we were in.

So, we found ourselves crossing the Inland Sea, that is to say from the Island of Shikoku, in a ferry which was loaded with Japanese passengers as well as ourselves. We went across to the mainland where we got into a train and we set off. After we'd been in the train for some little time we came to Osaka, which is one of the great towns of Japan; when we reached Osaka there was a first-class B29 raid in progress and we were stopped in our train at a junction outside the town, while the place was absolutely blasted by the B29s. The difficulty was that this junction had also been visited by the American Air Force and was more or less in ashes. We made our way through hot, burning bits of timber into a smaller train and chugged off into the hills and went up some considerable way inland. We chugged away for many hours and got quite high up in wooded country and the train eventually stopped at a small station. We were ordered out and marched down a hill, a very steep hill, at the bottom of which was a river in a ravine with steep hills on either side and a camp quite close to this river.

We were marched into the camp. By this time, we were absolutely all-in, what with the effort of this journey and the poor state of our health, the bombardments, and arriving at a totally unknown place and moving into this camp, which had a great big stockade round it and a great gate. It was a place called

Mitsushima, which we eventually discovered was about 60 miles from Tokyo up in the hills. It was, in fact, an old Chinese coolie camp which had been taken over by the Japanese and was now a punishment camp. It was a place where tiresome prisoners were sent to in order to get them out of the way and I don't think it was a registered camp. I don't think anybody knew of its existence.

The buildings were large, wooden affairs with earth floors, a table down the middle and two shelves round the walls, one about 2 feet off the ground and the other about 12 feet off the ground, on which were palliasses and that was where we were to live. We were told we should be working and we would start work at six o'clock in the morning and we were all to be fallen in by that time. We then started a regime of extreme unpleasantness. To begin with, the place was dirty; it was between quite high hills, so the sun really didn't fall upon it until ten or eleven in the morning and disappeared about four o'clock in the afternoon. The only bright thing about it was that a very old friend of ours who had been in the camp at Zentsuji was there to meet us.

George Williams was a Britisher who had been captured in the Gilbert Islands. He had been taken by the Japanese, together with American officers there, up to Tokyo and, as he was a very able and amusing entertainer they tried to make him broadcast for Tokyo Rose. He was frightfully brave. He refused to have anything to do with Tokyo Rose and he was cast into a special camp. I think he was actually put up to be shot more than once, but he survived it and was eventually sent to Mitsushima, the punishment camp. He'd had his officer status removed and was therefore better off because he was working in the galley, which was very much better than being an officer and going out to work every day. So George Williams was there to greet us, and he put us in the picture as to what was going on around there, and it was a very remarkable reunion.

We found ourselves, then, in a worse state than we'd ever been before. We were miles from anywhere, the buildings and camp were unpleasant and we had this absolutely loathsome Sergeant who, it turned out, was well known as being one of the arch sort of brutes of the prison camp system. He was a gentleman by the name of Watanabe, Sergeant Watanabe. His word went everywhere. Although there was a Colonel in charge of the camp, he seemed to have no influence at all and was seldom, if ever, even seen. Watanabe, though, was always around carrying his stick and beating the daylights out of people whenever he felt like it, which was fairly frequently.

We started a routine of working ten days on end and one day off. The first job that I had was back on the old bamboo pole, because this particular site was where the Japanese were building a hydroelectric scheme, but, owing to what had gone on in the war, they had decided they weren't going to get it going in time and so they were therefore going to make the tunnels that they'd made for it into underground factories. Our job was to fill up the bottom half of this tube – which had been drilled through the mountains to bring the water – to make a floor for machines and things; that was done by two people carrying stones and rocks on a straw mat suspended between bamboo poles. The Japanese stood over us and made us shovel the stuff in and if they didn't think it was enough they would beat us on the head and we'd shovel some more in and off we'd totter with this stuff and tip it into the base of the tunnel. It was hard work and we really weren't fit enough to do it, but we did it anyway from six o'clock in the morning till six o'clock at night, when we set off back to the camp.

Generally speaking, life was pretty awful. We were beginning to go downhill fairly fast. There was no way out of it. This chap Watanabe saw to it that our life was made miserable and the prospects seemed extremely grave. We had, of course, very little idea how close the Allies were, although from the B29 raids which we'd been through on the way up, we knew that Japan was taking a tremendous pasting and it was fairly clear that the Allies couldn't be far away. Our news, however, was very scanty because we hadn't got with us our Japanese interpreter. One of our RAF compatriots, though, had managed to hoist in a certain amount of Japanese, and when we did manage to get hold of a paper, which we did from time to time because we went out of the camp on these working details, we were able to make out some things, but it was extraordinarily difficult to make out exactly what it said. We got some idea one way or another that things were going quite well for the Allies and to some extent that boosted our morale.

Somewhere about July 1945, the Japanese came along and said, 'You have got to practise evacuation.' We didn't know quite what we were going to be evacuated for. They said, 'You will practise. You will all fall in and you will go to these cellars [they had big cellars under the buildings there]. You will go into these cellars and when the bombing starts here, you will go down and you will be safe down there.' They practised it and we were marched down there and the doors were closed and it was rather like the Black Hole of Calcutta. We couldn't see the purpose of that at all, because it seemed very unlikely that we should get heavily bombed way up in the mountains in this unreported camp on the river with no target of any significance nearby. However, it began to dawn on us that there was something more behind this, and we had a nasty suspicion that it was a rehearsal for how we would be bumped off if landings were made on Japan. A theory, I think, which was well substantiated afterwards, when we found out a bit more of what was going on.

Anyhow, be that as it may, we worked there right up until the early part of August, and our condition was getting worse and worse. One or two people died, and we were deteriorating fast: the work was too hard; Watanabe was too beastly; and winter was coming on when it would undoubtedly be extremely cold there because the sun didn't get at it very often. The outlook was very, very bleak.

CHAPTER SIX

Captivity to
Liberation,
1942–1945

THE WAY WE LIVED

From the time we were captured by the Japanese we lived on rice and vegetables, the amounts of which varied quite considerably from one camp to another and from one area to another. When we were in Macassar first of all, food was supplemented to a certain extent by a quite easy supply of black-market tropical fruit like bananas, coconuts and those sorts of things, and so we could get something else to fill up with. When we got to Japan, and while we were in the ship going up, we had, I suppose, what was the standard Japanese ration – not necessarily in quantity, but in kind – of rice and bowls of a kind of vegetable soup. It was mostly just vegetables and rice. There was very little meat or anything else in it. We didn't see bread or any of those things; just rice, usually three times a day, accompanied by soup, occasionally accompanied by bits of fish or pickled vegetable.

When we were in Ofuna, we received this ration of rice and vegetables or pickles, but I don't remember ever having any kind of meat at all. Our food came three times a day in a rather small thing about the size of a tea cup. It was issued, and since we were in a cell with a little peephole and the guard could see into our cell, the door was opened and we were given this ration. We had two chopsticks and were told to get on with it. There was nothing wrong with it, except it wasn't very substantial and, as Europeans, one wasn't quite used to feeding like that. I didn't find it difficult, I suppose, because I had lived in the Far East a little, when my parents were in India and I spent a few years there. Perhaps I was more used to that sort of diet and temperature.

Food, of course, became an obsession, because we were hungry all the time. People used to sit about practically dreaming of splendid forms of eating, and if you ever got hold of a European magazine, and from time to time one would be found lying about somewhere, which had a picture of Spam in it, it drove you absolutely crazy, for this appeared to be the height of enjoyment: a tin of Spam.

When I arrived in the camp at Zentsuji, they were at that time issuing a very small roll of bread each day, which was very pleasant; otherwise, it was exactly the same ration of rice and vegetables but a little more generous than it had been at Ofuna. We used to have to send a man to the galley with a great big wooden bucket, which would be filled up with rice and that would be brought to our room and be served out. The great trouble, when everyone is hungry, is to make sure that nobody gets more than anybody else. When you have a bucket of rice, and perhaps sixteen men to share it, the one who's in charge of handing it out provides sixteen rations, and then there's always a bit left over, and that bit left over then has to be parcelled out too. Nothing could lead to more bad feeling in a POW camp than if some got an extra half-cup of seconds, and others didn't.

The food at Zentsuji wasn't different from anywhere else; it wasn't great; it wasn't designed to keep you particularly strong; and there was very little variation in it. We practically never got any sort of meat, though very occasionally we'd get a little ground-up meat in the soup. Mostly, it was nearly all vegetables cooked in some way or other, pickles and rice. We soon got used to that sort of thing. There was no question of Red Cross supplies at that stage. I don't remember quite when it was that the idea of getting a Red Cross parcel first came along, but it must have been at least a year after we'd been captured before we even heard of such a thing.

As for clothes, well, when we arrived at Zentsuji I'd had, you remember, a civilian coat and my uniform trousers and shirt. By this time, and I'm now talking about October 1944 and me being captured in March 1942, I'm sure they were getting in a very bad state. We were then issued with this Victorian army uniform of a tunic with brass buttons and khaki trousers in a very hairy sort of material and that was our uniform. That was what we wore throughout the time I was at Zentsuji camp. However, quite a number of prisoners who'd come up from places like Malaya and Java had been able to bring with them a certain amount of luggage, so the variety of dress in the prison camp was very odd. It would be almost possible to find a man walking in a top hat, except there was no purpose in doing so. Quite a lot of men had bits of uniform, bits of shirts, odd pairs of trousers, shorts and so on.

We slept on the wooden shelves with a straw palliasse and a blanket. In the winter it was very cold and I think we must have got hold of a second blanket, because I know we used to try and get hold of Japanese newspapers to put between the blankets in the winter because it was so very cold and blankets interlined with a bit of *Mianichi* were so much warmer. We also had a hard pillow. It was about 12 inches long and 6 inches in diameter, stuffed with straw or something, I suppose.

Of course, the other thing we all had in our bedding was bed bugs. The place was riddled with them. They lived in the woodwork and we used to complain constantly about them, but there never seemed to be any way of getting rid of them. The Japanese did give us bed bug traps, which were pieces of wood with holes drilled into them which we put at the foot of our mattress; bed bugs got into the holes and the idea was that you picked it up in the morning, banged it so that the bed bugs fell out, and then you killed them. It had absolutely no effect, of course, on the total population of bed bugs!

The Japanese were very strange about some things. Usually rooms had sixteen or thirty-two people. The big rooms had thirty-two in two halves and the smaller rooms had sixteen, and most of the time I was in the smaller rooms. As we were generally segregated by rank, I lived in a sixteen-bed room and by the time I'd been in the camp for a little bit, I had acquired some useful things. I'd acquired a button and a very small stump of pencil. We had no money, we weren't paid anything, so we couldn't buy anything and one would acquire strange little valuables. I mean if somebody had a pair of scissors or something, that was a great thing.

When we used to go to bed, I always used to make a tremendous song and dance of emptying my pockets and putting my valuables, consisting of this pencil and so on, on a shelf, which was just above where I laid my head, and on which I was supposed to fold my clothes and put them. The Japanese used to get wildly excited about this and asked why I did it, and I explained to them that every gentleman in England, when he goes to bed, takes the things out of his pockets and puts them on the dressing table – his money and his pencil, or whatever it was that he had in his pockets. He puts them on the table so that next morning he can pick them up and put them into his pocket again, and that was a very old English custom and I didn't feel like giving it up. Well, they said it was contrary to Japanese rules. You couldn't do that because you might have them stolen, to which I replied, 'Oh, but they are all British in my room of sixteen; nobody would steal anything, no question of them stealing anything.' This put them in an awkward position because, if that was what I felt about it and my things disappeared, then it could only be the Japanese who were stealing them. And so this question of me putting my valuables on the shelf became a sort of joke among all of us and a cause of strange infuriation to the Japanese. They didn't actually like to take the things away and it was very difficult to stop me and they used to come and watch me do it. The guard used to come and watch. I'm sure he'd had special orders to watch me do it – as if it was going to blow the place up. So that gave us quite a lot of quiet amusement and gave me something to do each evening.

When we first arrived in Zentsuji, we were rather depressed. There was no entertainment at all. To that extent there wasn't anything to boost one's morale but the British group that came down from Ofuna, and those who came up from Malaya, did contain some quite able people, and before very long the British organised a regular display of theatrical or pantomime-type performances.

The very first one was a pantomime. I was the princess who lost her shoe, or whatever it was in Cinderella, and we dressed up in all sorts of clothing which we borrowed from anybody who had an odd bit and, as I said, quite a number, particularly the soldiers who came up from Malaya, brought a surprising amount of clothes with them. Those who'd been fished out of the sea, of course, had none. So we started, really, quite a strong theatrical group; people put a great deal of thought into it and it got better and better. So the British theatre was quite reasonably high class.

Theatrics were also taken up by the Dutch, who were extremely clever at it, and the Australians joined us as well. The

Americans didn't go so much on theatre but they were very much better at a thing like barber shop singing. We ran a choir and became quite good, though we had no music at all, no note of music, no way of making a note, no instrument for playing it. We just did it all by singing. In Zentsuji, we eventually put on a performance every week, one nation or another, the Americans, the Dutch and the British, one after the other. Among other things, we put on most of the Ralph Lynn and Tom Walls shows because people would get together and go over the play, as they remembered it, and we would reconstitute it, reconstruct it rather, and replay it within the limits of our staging.

Now the stage was quite an odd one. We had for our use what had been at one time a sort of Japanese canteen. We were in an old barracks and at one end of the canteen there was a counter which went across the room and cut one end off from the other, behind which, I suppose, at some time, they'd served refreshments or something. The counter stood about 4 feet or so high with an entrance at one end and behind it was a space.

All the acting was done behind this counter and so really what happened was the audience only saw the top half of people; they didn't see the lower half at all. All the acting, if you can imagine it, was carried on, as it were, in a shop, with the audience on one side of the counter and the players on the other. This gave scope for an immense amount of fun and games as to what could be done in the way of scenery changes and tricks of one sort or another, out of view of the audience, but in full view of the people who were acting. I remember in the Tom Walls play, one scene involves a double bed. I can't remember exactly how it went now, but a character gets into a double bed with a pretty girl, and, of course, we didn't have a double bed. However, if you fixed up two pillows so that they showed above the counter, you could move just as if you were in a bed with your head resting on the pillow, while the rest of you was standing on the floor. From the audience, it looked like a double bed. All those sort of tricks gave a great deal of amusement.

We ran those shows pretty well, eventually. Every now and again we'd get into trouble with the Japanese because, of course, every show had to be censored. We therefore had to supply the script, which was extremely difficult because we had practically no paper or pencils or anything like that. We eventually hit upon the idea of copying out two or three of Shakespeare's plays because we'd got hold of a book of them from somewhere, some prisoner had brought it up with him. We used to put in a Shakespeare play and every week we had a performance and did something quite different, not related to it at all. But the Japanese never hoisted that in. They didn't understand the reading; they didn't understand English, let alone Shakespeare's English, and we'd obeyed the rules. We'd put in something to show what we were supposed to be doing and that satisfied the rules. They didn't seem to mind that. They were quite enthralled with it.

Occasionally, one would get into trouble. One or two shows we put on outside, sort of Vaudeville shows, and I remember I was taking part in one and I was singing a song about golf which had been written in the camp, and I had a stick, and, as part of the illustration of the song, I took a swing, as it were, with the golf club, and very unfortunately hit a stone which hit the Japanese interpreter in the face. He went absolutely wild and shrieked with anger and proceeded to chase me and I was quick enough to fade away from the stage and run off. He pursued me round the camp, but never actually managed to quite get his hands on me, much to the delight of the audience, who thought this was a great performance. He was a Japanese interpreter with no great athletic prowess and he got over this all right, but for a moment we thought that I was in deep trouble and I'd be bound to be thrown into jail. You could never quite tell with the Japanese, you see; it wasn't funny to him at all, it was an insult.

We did run quite a lot of education at Zentsuji. Although we were supposed to work for our living, there was not enough work for everyone to do and so we ran a sort of academy and I actually learnt Spanish. I spoke quite good Spanish when I came out, which I learnt from an American who was Mexican by birth. And lectures: we gave lectures, quite a number of us had specific lectures that we gave round the camp. By this means we kept ourselves mentally, so to speak, more or less in tune. The

Japanese took no part in this. They were very suspicious and watched us very carefully and they sometimes came and listened to a lecture just in case we said something we shouldn't, or something that insulted the Emperor.

When there was anything that had to be dealt with that required real punishment, such as, for example, people breaking out of the camp or somebody attempting to do so, then we might be put in a cell. It wasn't particularly difficult for people to get out of the camp; it was just that it was an offence. In some cases, if a guard or a sentry reckoned he'd been rudely approached by a prisoner of any sort, the prisoner might be brought up, and be thrown into one of a series of cells, which were known as the brig. You might be thrown in there and given nothing but a little water to live on, on a stone floor, and very uncomfortable, for two or three days. That was their sort of punishment.

In our second camp, we didn't get assaulted by the guards that I remember. There might have been the odd occasion of bad temper but it wasn't part and parcel of their discipline. Whereas at Ofuna, of course, it had been, and in a number of other Japanese camps it was a regular feature to be pushed around. I was badly beaten up at the last camp by this awful fellow Watanabe, who nearly killed me one night because he got so mad with me. I was sent for by Watanabe and told that I was to rear fifty baby chicks, because he understood I was a great expert at looking after chickens. At Zentsuji, as I've said, I had had this particular experience with chickens, and I told him, 'Well, as a matter of fact, I don't have great experience. We don't keep chickens in His Majesty's Ships,' and that infuriated him. He said you'll do it and go away and you're to build all the necessary things and there'll be horse manure and straw and you'll bloody well get on with it.

Then I got these fifty chicks and a certain amount of stuff to feed them with, but nothing like enough. The place that I built for them wasn't very cleverly built, because I didn't know very much about it, and I'm afraid to say, the rats got them. One by one the chickens went and eventually there weren't any baby chickens left at all and no eggs. The whole thing was a dismal failure. It was a dismal failure because the equipment was totally unsatisfactory. I wasn't an expert and I didn't really want to do it.

Watanabe got absolutely mad about this and had me up and accused me of sabotaging all sorts of things. He shouted and screamed and hit me and knocked me down and picked me up and knocked me down again. All my fellow prisoners in the camp thought I was being murdered; so did I. He eventually got bored with it, and I slowly crawled back to my hut. That was typical of him. He would get absolutely mad; he'd have a strange look come into his face and it was no good; you just knew you couldn't escape him. There was nothing you could do. He used everything. His fists. He used this bamboo stick, a truncheon they used to carry around, and he'd knock you flat on the ground and make you get up again. Then he'd knock you down the other way and he'd shout and scream and ask questions and say, 'Why don't you answer me?' There was nothing to do, but to just stand there and take it on the chin, so to speak, and just look at him. He knew what you were thinking of him, but he was that way.

There was really only one other Japanese man with whom I had any communication. We had as an interpreter in Zentsuji, an extremely nice Japanese man whose father had been in the diplomatic service and I think had been an ambassador in Paris or somewhere. He himself had been educated partly in England and had been to Cambridge and was known popularly in the camp as 'Cambridge Joe'. He was married to Admiral Yamamoto's daughter, who was an extraordinarily pretty girl and really the only woman we ever saw. When he came into work, occasionally she would come with him, cloppity clop in her little wooden slippers. He disliked the whole business of the treatment of Japanese prisoners of war. He thought the whole thing was brutal and beastly and he didn't want to have anything to do with it, but he couldn't escape. He was considered not fit for military service. His name was Asobuki and he was connected in some way with the Royal Family, so I suppose to a degree he had some protection. He couldn't do anything but follow the routine of the camp. He was never in any way beastly. He did his very best to represent points of view, but he was steering a difficult course, between getting into trouble with his own people where he might find himself suddenly demoted to private and sent away, and retaining a position as interpreter in the camp. He spoke perfect English, very educated English, and, therefore, from time to time, one could occasionally say something to him, which is quite normal between two civilised people. He is a man I have seen since the war.

I made a great many friends in the camp at Zentsuji. There was no opportunity for friendship at the camp at Ofuna because we were shut up in cells, except for the man who shared my cell with me, who I got to know very well and have corresponded with ever since. I became very friendly at Zentsuji, though, with quite a number of people, including one or two Americans. One American was a Lieutenant in the US Navy, and I got on particularly well with him. We were both learning Spanish together, from the American Army officer, and he managed to get my name back home, for the Americans were able to write letters because they had signed a paper to say they wouldn't escape home. The British weren't able to do that until the war had been going for about two years. He managed somehow to send a message in his twenty-five words which gave his father and mother sufficient clue to indicate that I was alive. We became very friendly.

From time to time, there was talk about escaping. It was a very difficult situation. There was no difficulty in getting out of the camp; quite a lot of the work we did took us out of the camp and we were very poorly guarded. It was quite clear the Japanese would have got more work out of us by doing the work themselves and letting us be the guards, rather than the other way round. We broke practically all their tools and generally did everything we could to be useless, but it wasn't difficult to get out of the camp. In fact, it could be quite difficult to get into the camp, once you got out, because they couldn't believe that you were who you said you were.

We kept our spirits up by these forms of entertainment, and by a certain amount of education and lecturing; also by working parties, which occupied our time to a certain extent; and by a very limited amount of reading. There was no library or books. One or two prisoners had arrived with a book, but about the best thing one could do was to get hold of a book every two years or so. It was really a question of keeping each other's morale going.

I think if you talk about how being in the Navy helped us survive, then undoubtedly it was the way we'd been brought up; the way we'd been trained. I had been trained ever since I had joined the Navy, in a highly disciplined way. I had been trained in what was quite a rugged form of life, that is to say Dartmouth. A Midshipman's life in the Fleet was a strangely rugged life: half-sailor, half-officer, rather at the mercy of both. To that extent one was imbued with a certain amount of tenacity, and with a considerable amount of *esprit de corps* in the Navy and your ship. You were very much concerned with not letting the side down. That is to say, not doing anything which would bring disrepute on the Navy or your ship or on your Captain, or your Senior Officer, not necessarily a Captain but whoever is your senior Naval or Military Officer. I was with my Captain. We had been brought up in a disciplined force to take orders from our seniors, so as we had our Captain with us we saluted him every morning as a matter of routine. It used to annoy the Japanese because we didn't salute the Colonel. He used to get very cross about it from time to time. He found it very difficult to make everybody salute him.

We did a lot of things to annoy the Japanese. It was great fun; it was a way of keeping up our morale. If we could really aggravate the Japanese in some way, make them have to work harder or look stupid or whatever, we did it. That did us good; it might get us into trouble but it was worth doing. We used to play the most awful tricks on the sentries. We had a lot of sentries round the camp, for example, not only at the entrance but at strategic points; they had a beat. They marched up and down or stood at certain corners; they were clad in Japanese military uniform, which was a sort of padded khaki coat and trousers with large jackboots and a certain amount of equipment with bullets stuck in it, and a steel helmet and a rifle almost as big as themselves with a huge bayonet on the end. They were quite well-accoutred, so to speak. Just standing up in all that gear was quite tiring and as it used to get very hot in the summer, it was a damned hot uniform to be on guard in and they used, undoubtedly, to find it very difficult. A

Japanese sentry had to be treated with the utmost respect. Every time a prisoner passed one, he had to stop, turn towards him and bow and the Japanese sentry was supposed to respond to it by bowing back, that was because he represented the Emperor. It wasn't very difficult to organise streams of people to go past Japanese sentries who had to bow to you. You bowed to them and then they had to stop and bow back to you. If you did that for four hours on end, the poor chaps were absolutely whacked at the end of their watches. I mean they hadn't done much in the way of doing sentry duties, but they'd spent an awful lot of time answering salutes. It was very difficult for them because they couldn't complain. We were complying with the regulations precisely. They didn't have the wit, and it was difficult indeed, to have sentries in useful positions and not have people who walked by or near them. So this was a splendid performance and annoyed the Japanese immensely.

LIBERATION AT LAST

And so the days went by. Suddenly one day, we got hold of a newspaper and after a tremendous amount of work by this amateur linguist of ours, we learned enough to know that a great bomb had been dropped on Hiroshima. This bomb, as far as we could interpret it, had disposed of Hiroshima in the twinkling of an eye and was known to us as the 'twinkle bomb'. We had no idea what a 'twinkle bomb' was but it was clearly something new in the ordnance field and the Japanese were exceptionally worried about it and became very jumpy. Watanabe became almost hysterical and we really didn't know what was going on.

Not very long after this, the guards came along and said, 'You will not go out to work today.' Now that was a very unusual statement. What's more, Watanabe wasn't there to help us understand this and we all said, 'What's going on? Fancy just staying in camp and doing no work. What's it all about?' We really couldn't make head nor tail of it, except that Watanabe wasn't to be seen. Watanabe disappeared and, we thought, well that's very funny and we became very anxious to get hold of more newspapers to find out what was going on. It was extremely difficult. Days and days would go by without getting a scrap of paper at all and when we did get a bit of paper, we couldn't make very much of it. It was quite clear that things had suddenly changed. We weren't being made to go and work. We weren't being hustled about. Such guards as there were, were known to be the better guards and weren't interfering with us, and we were in a state of limbo.

As the time went on, we were more and more anxious to try and find out. One day we managed to get hold of a newspaper and there was a picture of General MacArthur with the Japanese. This was a simply staggering thing to find. What was going on? How did General MacArthur get in among the Japanese military? We said the war must be over. There was a great deal of debate: some of us said that if the war was over, we'd go and tell the Colonel to shove off and we'd take charge of this camp and that's that. Others said, 'Now wait a minute; we may have got it wrong. Perhaps the war isn't over at all. Perhaps this was an old picture or something and if we do that we shall give away the fact that we are getting bits of news through, picking up newspapers, and we shall lose our last shreds of information.'

We decided to mark time for a bit and then we got another piece of paper with photographs in and it was quite clear by then, considering we weren't working and some of the guards had disappeared, in particular Watanabe, that the war must be over. So the two Senior Officers, the Australian and the British, asked to see the Colonel, and the Colonel, who was never much to be seen, turned up, and they said to him, 'Is the war over?' He replied, 'Well, I don't know yet.' Or words to that effect.

The Senior Officers then said, 'Come on, is the war over? We understand that the war is over; in which case, we're going to take over from you.'

The Colonel obviously was very worried about it and said, 'Well, I think the war is over. I have not been told officially, but General MacArthur has landed in Tokyo.' That was good enough for us and we told the Colonel where he could get off and took charge of the camp.

The camp didn't have many supplies, much food or anything else. It was tucked away in the corner. The villagers weren't really aware of what was going on and the question was, what could we do to get in touch with MacArthur? We had at that time a chap with typhoid who was very ill and we were very anxious to get a doctor, so a team was sent to sally forth into the village to see if they could find a telephone system. The long and short of it was, they did. They found a telephone set and managed to get through to Tokyo and got in touch with an American. They said, 'Look, we're in this place with a lot of prisoners, and we're in a very bad way and we've got a chap with typhoid and what are you going to do about us?'

And the American said, 'Well, we don't know about you at all. We don't know that camp but we'll bring some aeroplanes up and drop supplies on you.'

The next day, sure enough, a lot of US Navy planes turned up and dropped a whole lot of kit bags full of food and stuff on the camp – we having been told to mark it with letters on the roof. It was immensely exciting, of course, because these aeroplanes came over and threw out kit bags with parachutes and the very first one didn't open and came absolutely straight down and we were jolly lucky it didn't kill anyone. It went clean through the roof of one of the buildings and it was full of chocolate bars and burst into an absolute mass of chocolate, all over the walls of this building and the prisoners, of course, went mad, scraping the chocolate off the walls.

We got our supplies, and eventually MacArthur's people got in touch with us and arrangements were made to take us out. I think by this time it was 1 September. On 2 September we had instructions from Tokyo that a train would arrive. The Japanese had been told to escort us to the train and put us on it and we would set off for somewhere to join the American forces. We set off to the railway station, greatly excited; sure enough there was a train. We got into it, with a few Japanese guards to keep out the rougher elements of the civilian population, who I might say were absolutely as bemused as we were, and hadn't the slightest idea of what was going on, and we chugged off down the railway line. After we'd been going for about five or six hours, we came to the coast and we were trickling along the railway line with the sea on one side and the land on the other when the train halted and a whole lot of US Marines appeared and said, 'Come on you guys, we're taking you off. Who are all these Japanese people with you? Are they nice or shall we bump them off?'

We said, 'Well, actually, these are the better ones; don't bump 'em off yet.'

We were taken off in landing craft to an enormous US hospital ship which was lying off-shore. We went on board this ship where we were de-loused and issued with US Marines' uniforms with all the bits and pieces, and then we were supposed to be put into destroyers to be taken up to Tokyo Bay, which was about twenty-four hours travelling. I had beri-beri by that time, rather badly. My feet were swollen and my face was swollen, and, generally, I wasn't in very good shape, and although I had all this kit, I couldn't get my boots on. Because of this inability to walk, I was taken off going up to Tokyo Bay and put in a ward in the hospital ship. I was subjected to a lot of examinations by doctors, who gave me an immense number of different sorts of pills and raw liver and so on to try and get the upper hand of the beri-beri and get me into rather better physical shape. It was, of course, the time when you wanted to eat a horse, but the medical people wanted you to do it fairly slowly and not increase your intake of food too fast. So I spent, I suppose, nearly ten days on board this very well-equipped and very large US hospital ship until it sailed and went up to Tokyo Bay and joined the Allied naval forces up there.

From there I was transferred to a British hospital ship which was, of course, quite different from the American hospital ship. It had practically no supplies. It had come out from Sydney some two months before and was due to go right back and replenish, but had never got there because of the sudden ending of the war. So we were in a ward but didn't have any drugs of great value. It had a very enterprising Surgeon Captain, however, who said to us (I think there were about four or five British survivors who were not fit to travel at that time), 'Now look men, I haven't very much to give you. We'll feed you as good a diet as we can provide for your condition and you can have a glass of port three times a day, because we have got some port.' So our medicine really was three glasses of port a day, which I can assure you was as good as anything we were likely to get and did us a power of good.

THE LONG VOYAGE HOME

I stayed in this hospital ship for about another week; some of the swelling went down and I was eventually able to put on a pair of boots and was pronounced fit to be evacuated and was taken off by aeroplane and flown down to Okinawa. At that time there had been a terrible typhoon – a typhoon which, as we all know now, would have entirely ruined the proposed landings on Japan – and Okinawa was in a dreadful state. Everything was flattened. There'd been an enormous amount of rain and the camp into which I was put had about 6 inches of mud in it. It was only by getting up on to your bed that you got out of the swamp. So it was a most difficult place to conduct your life. You lay on your bed and when you got out you took your boots and socks in one hand and waded through the mud until you could get out and clean them and then went down a road or over a series of planks to get your food and went back again.

The devastation caused by that typhoon was very considerable. However, we weren't there very long before we were put back onto an aeroplane and flown down to the Philippines. We landed on, I think it was called Clark Field by then, right up in the north end of the Philippines, and were put in a train to go down to the main camps. These were down in the main capital of the Philippines, at Manila, where there were huge camps of prisoners of war being assembled, military of all kinds and sorts, and entertainments for the troops, including Gracie Fields.

Eventually from there we were to be evacuated home. I was to go by sea from Manila to America and across America and so back to England. As I was a Lieutenant-Commander, I had a little more status than some, and so was selected to be a sort of boss of a huge party of prisoners of war who were going to be put in an American troopship and sent across the Pacific. For this purpose I was given all their medical documents, which by that time were colossal, because every doctor that saw us wrote a report on us and stuffed it in the file, and I couldn't carry them. So I consigned the load to some sort of transport hoping it would reach me at the other end; needless to say, I lost the whole lot.

I arrived at this troop ship, then, in Manila Harbour, where we went on board with bands playing and girls singing, and a tremendous send-off, just like you see in the movies; there were thousands of people in the ship. It was absolutely packed. It wasn't only packed with prisoners of war – there were about a thousand or two – but a whole lot of GIs and other people who were trying to get home. And off we sailed.

On board, the day's routine was quite simple. There was a perpetual queue for something to eat because by the time breakfast was over, lunch had started for the next lot. The front was eating breakfast while the back end of the queue was eating lunch or vice versa. So there was always a queue for eating. We all had rows and rows of bunks, one above the other and really tremendously crowded. We also had very little to do. I made great friends with the Master at Arms, and he said to me, 'Come on, don't have anything to do with this lot; come down to our mess and we'll look after you there.' I was most wonderfully looked after by the United States Navy Master at Arms of this ship, so I had a much better passage.

On the way across the Pacific, plans changed slightly. We were to call into Hawaii on the way. So we arrived at Hawaii and I was, at that time, joined up with my Captain; he and I were together in the ship by now and he said, 'Now come on, we must write a full report of the action and here's the tube, the toothpaste tube with it in, and we will write it out and we will write the names of as many people as we can remember and any other information, so that I can hand it in when we get to the other end.' So I spent my days working with Captain Gordon, who was provided with somewhere to write and with paper, doing all the reports we could, of the loss of the ship and the account of the actual battle and so on.

By the time I arrived at Hawaii, we had more or less finished our work. Captain Gordon was delighted with it and there was in Hawaii a Naval Captain liaison officer who he knew quite well and so this liaison officer asked us if we'd like to go ashore, be driven round the Island of Hawaii and have lunch with him. So we said, 'Thanks very much.' We went ashore and this extremely nice Captain took us to his house in Hawaii and gave us a slap-up lunch which included a dry martini. I hadn't tasted a touch of alcohol for the best part of three-and-a-half to four years and I drank my martini and that's about the last thing I remember of Hawaii – I was in no time absolutely drunk as a lord. I managed to struggle around the island in a car, but couldn't take anything in because I was so frightfully drunk. Eventually, I was placed back on board. I did learn a sharp lesson though – that I wasn't fit to drink, especially American martinis.

We then went on to the Canadian base at Esquimalt, Vancouver Island, where we were put ashore into a Canadian camp. We were, of course, medically examined again. All the medics kept on examining us for possible diseases, and we were interviewed by a psychiatrist. The man who interviewed me obviously took a rather dim view of my condition – I took a look at what he'd written on his piece of paper and I saw he'd written me down as socially hopeless. He explained at great length that after all that time and what I'd been through, my life would be very difficult. My sex life, he said, would be extraordinarily poor. I went back to the barracks I was living in, and another friend of mine who'd been similarly examined, said, 'Well, he said something about me being socially no good, because he explained what my sex life would be and so on.'

I said, 'Well, rotten show; let's show them that they're totally wrong. Let's go to the Wrens' dance. We'll show them who's socially hopeless.'

So we went to the Wrens' dance. I was still dressed in jungle green and had these rather large jungle boots on, so I wasn't exactly dressed for dancing. Dancing, of course, had changed quite a lot while I was a prisoner of war. It wasn't quite the elegant foxtrot and quickstep. It was much more 'heebie jeebie' or whatever the modern dancing was called, where you fling

yourself about. This was in 1945, so what was it then? Glenn
Miller? Yes. I didn't know anything about Glenn Miller then;
I've learnt a lot about him since, because he's so good. It was
essentially a thing where you didn't necessarily clasp the girl
round the waist and go one, two, three, hop, but rather, you
flung yourself about in a very excitable fashion. Well, after I
tried to do this for a minute or two I realised that I really wasn't
strong enough. I simply couldn't keep it up; too much for me. So
I said to this rather charming Wren with whom I was trying to
perform this dance, 'It's no good. I'm afraid they're right, and
I'm socially hopeless and I'm afraid I must leave you.' I went
back to my barracks and went to bed, because I wasn't strong
enough to take part in this big social outing.

From Esquimalt we were taken across to Vancouver and put in
a train which went across Canada. Pretty well everywhere we
stopped, the Red Cross or someone came on board and gave us
more things to eat or drink and we really were fêted all the way
across Canada. We arrived at the other end in very poor health
from over-eating, really, and went into another camp, just short of
Halifax, where we were sorted out. Eventually, I was taken to the
Ile de France, one of the great big liners to cross the Atlantic. I
came across the Atlantic with thousands and thousands of other
prisoners of war and soldiers and sailors making their way back
and a whole lot of Wrens and other girls and, of course, we hadn't
seen a woman for a very long time, so it was really rather exciting.
It was a period when sweater girls were rather popular, and,
whatever the medics said about being socially hopeless I found the
girls very exciting, and the trip across the Atlantic was very
pleasant. It was like the one across the Pacific in the sense that one
was nearly always in a queue of some sort, waiting. I got some of
my energy back, but there were no dances on board. There really
wasn't room. The *Ile de France* was absolutely packed with people.
They used to take enormous numbers across. It was rather nice to
get back to your own countryfolk. I mean your own countrymen
and women and every lady was, of course, very nice to us.

My family was in Southampton to meet me. My mother and my
wife and my small boy of six were all there. I came down the

gangway and there was an awful lot of 'hoo-ha' going on. The Mayor of Southampton came to meet us and there was a band playing and, although we were all frightfully anxious to get ashore and go home, quite a lot of people had to be processed through other camps, for some reason or other. As my parents lived in the New Forest, though, I managed to slip away with my wife and small boy of mine, who, not having seen me for six years, looked into my face, which was very swollen and fat still with beri-beri, and said very solemnly, 'We've got a pig at home.'

CHAPTER SEVEN

Commander – Post-war Years, 1945–1951

I suppose everybody coming back from the war to their home country looked around to see what was different and there was no question that Britain was different; not only in the sense that it had elected a Socialist Government, rather contrary to what had been expected with Winston Churchill still in power, but also because the upset in the war had been so complete. Men had left the country and not come back for two or three years. Nations had been mixed up in an extraordinary way. The Americans, in particular, more than anybody else, were the strongest, and to that extent, the most influential power. They were actually living in our country, and could almost have been said to have occupied a lot of it. And I, coming back from three-and-a-half years of being a prisoner of war, was entirely out of that sort of situation.

When I got home, I fully expected to be told, well it's nice to see you, now go away and find another job, because an absence from England during some four years of intense activity in warfare leaves you so much behind-hand. It wasn't quite like that, though, because we had won. No doubt if we'd lost it would have been very much like that. So I was back home in my country, very badly knocked about, witnessing great shortages, sad losses, separations of people and an absolute Piccadilly Circus of men, moving to and fro, trying to get back into a peacetime routine. There were people who had been abroad for several years, people who had been to remote parts of the world, people who'd got more or less marooned in other parts of the world, people who were leaving the Services, people who were joining for the first time, and really it was a schemozzle of enormous proportions.

Looking back on it, I find it extraordinary that we managed to get through it, get back to our own families, and get some form of civilised life going as, we thought, it had been before the war started. Everything, though, had changed; not only were many, many things which had been available now no longer available, but many, many people had progressed in one direction or another in their professional and family lives. Also, somewhat ironically, even after all that period of fighting and disturbance, and coming out in a winning position, we really were in no position to start making good decisions straight away.

I, of course, did not go to sea immediately I got back. I did some eight or nine months ashore, where I found that the professional changes, the technical changes, great though they were, were not so far removed from what I had known about at the beginning of the war, and to that extent I was able to join in again more readily. But I was not at sea and the men who were at sea, the ships that were at sea, were in a strange place, situated between the pre-war discipline and routine kind of Navy that we once knew, and the post-war, somewhat 'do-it-yourself' Navy now in existence. In so many ways it had to be a 'do-it-yourself' Navy, because there was no other way of getting things done. We were too short of supplies, too short of all kinds of necessities, and the problems in front of us, of unwinding a Navy which had been very tightly and efficiently wound up for the war, were really formidable.

In 1945 I came back from being a prisoner of war and I had six weeks' leave. Then I was appointed to HMS *Excellent*, the Gunnery School, and put in charge of the close-range, anti-aircraft training section out at Eastney. I wasn't there very long before I was promoted to Commander, which was interesting for me because, of course, I had been overtaken by most, if not all, my contemporaries and was worried that I should have so fallen behind-hand, that technologically I wouldn't be able to pick up my job again. Happily, it didn't turn out like that as I had been well up-to-date at the time I was sunk in 1942, because the *Exeter* had been a completely modernised ship. I had already come in touch, therefore, with matters concerning radar and the experience of battle, anti-aircraft fire and all the kinds of weaponry concerned with a fighting cruiser. Teaching other people at Eastney, therefore, I put into practice quite a lot of what I had previously learnt, and then I got what every Commander hopes to get, command of his own ship.

FIRST COMMAND

It must have been the ambition of every young officer before the war to command one of HM Ships; yet, although much of the time spent as a junior officer was occupied in watchkeeping in both battleships and destroyers, few achieved command until well on as a Lieutenant Commander. My first experience of command, though not what was termed 'an independent command', was as a junior Lieutenant in charge of the drifter HMS *Leeward*, a splendid First World War converted herring drifter, attached to HMS *Malaya*. However, it was not until after the Second World War that I was given the chance of command by being appointed to a frigate, HMS *Porlock Bay*, one of three frigates, which with two cruisers made up the West Indies Squadron. Very naturally, I was thrilled by this chance, although somewhat apprehensive because my period in Japanese captivity had left me somewhat astern of my contemporaries in experience. So a chance to show that I was not entirely a write-off did hang very much upon a good performance in this, my first command.

A series of refresher courses was quickly arranged, from navigation, which I found had changed a lot from the Inman's Tables and Trigonometry format of Dartmouth days, to victualling, anti-submarine exercises, gunnery and, finally, the tactical course. It was during the latter course at Greenwich that I was able to pick the brains of many who had spent some years in command and could be expected to provide a few useful tips to a green beginner. On the whole, the advice was fairly simple: read the book and inwardly digest Captain Troup's *On the Bridge*:[1] always put a parallel ruler along the lines the Navigator draws on the chart, just to see that he gets that part right; write your own Captain's Order Book and make it short and simple; and above all keep your eyes on the rum, victuals and the Confidential Books. Armed with this advice and topped-up with the confidence of training at Portland, I set sail from the latter spot in a frigate for Bermuda. The weather was dreadful and it blew a gale for the entire passage to the Azores, by which time my terrible sea-sickness began to abate and I was able to take a little food.

[1] Troup, Captain J.A.G., RN, *On the Bridge*, London, Rich and Coward, 1932.

Arriving off Five Hundred Fathom Hole at Bermuda, it was arranged that I should transfer by whaler to the *Porlock Bay*, which was exercising with a submarine. In due course, feeling rather like Hornblower, I was pulled across to my new command and boarded her by jumping ladder. The Captain, a senior Lieutenant, was on the bridge taking charge of the morning's exercises and he received me civilly enough, but not perhaps with enthusiasm at the idea of giving up his lovely command to a new and inexperienced gunnery chap. I watched the proceedings from the bridge, trying to observe how skilful or otherwise were the operators, aware that the Ship's Company probably shared their Captain's reservations about the new boss.

I suppose we had carried out half a dozen runs on the submarine and dinner was not far off, when the Captain said to me, 'Would you like to take the ship for the next run?' I naturally jumped at this offer, keen to show that I had learned something at Portland when under training. My attack over, I gave, from the appearance of the marker which the submarine was towing, a fairly accurate performance. I was standing, therefore, at the voice pipe feeling mildly elated when a Leading Seaman came clattering up the bridge ladder calling out, apparently in some panic, 'Captain, Sir! Captain, Sir! I have let go a depth-charge.' Mine was certainly not the only heart that stood still on that bridge.

How could it have happened? Was the safety pin in? Would it explode at any second? What in any case might happen to a depth-charge dropped in such terribly deep water? We waited tensely but, by the grace of God, nothing happened. The explanation was all too simple. The afternoon exercise included firing a whole pattern of depth-charges and these were being prepared for the event. Hearing the fire buzzer sound off on the quarterdeck, the Leading Hand panicked, thought it must be the moment for the full pattern, for which he and his mates were not ready, and dashed to the stern to remove the retaining rails, thereby letting one charge roll down the chute into the sea. It was certainly an ugly moment. Over lunch the Captain and I pondered over who would have faced the Court Martial, he or I.

One or both. What, too, if the submarine got to hear of it? We decided that, above all, the incident must be kept secret, the Leading Seaman in no way punished and that on our return to harbour the Captain and I should invite the submarine Captain aboard to take a very strong drink or two.

In due course, badly shaken by the whole affair, I took over command and sailed next day to replenish with oil from a tanker lying in the tiny anchorage of St George's. It was to be my first 'alongside'. I took the ship slowly and carefully through the narrow channel and was happy to find the harbour calm and the oiler lying waiting for us. We glided along, bows pointing in what I estimated to be the right spot, speed just enough for steerage way, the men on the fo'c's'le at the ready with heaving lines and apparently all set for a good alongside.

Alas, pride comes before a fall. Just as I reached the oiler I realised for the first time that there was a marked flare to her fo'c's'le and her bow overhung considerably. From the way I was going, my awning stanchions were going to foul her fo'c's'le and we were clearly in for trouble, but too late to check the way. With a nasty rending noise the stanchions bent and broke and then, in one of those moments of utter silence which usually follow disaster, I heard a sailor's voice from somewhere aft, 'Away stanchions'. I never forgot that cry. It said everything the Ship's Company thought of their new Captain: cack-handed, no ship handler, spoiling our nice ship, not what we expected of you Sir, not what we look for at all.

I returned in some shame to the dockyard for repair and lay in the basin cleaning up and painting, awaiting Christmas Day, which was only about a week away. By Christmas Day I had recovered somewhat from the trauma of my first days in command, and was looking forward to the usual festivities of the season. On Christmas morning my cabin hand, a fine old three-badge seaman, failed to call me so I started the day late and somewhat testy. Hardly had I emerged on deck when the First Lieutenant came up and said, 'Sir, have you seen the Flagship's side?' I looked across the harbour where, to my consternation, I saw my own ship's pendant numbers painted in black figures on the cruiser's spotless side.

It wasn't long before the Flagship signalled, 'Commanding Officer to report on board wearing sword and medals.' I was clearly for the high jump. Indeed, this was an understatement. I was received on board HMS *Sheffield* and was taken to the Flag Captain, who was standing glowering at the after-end of the quarterdeck and here I was treated to a tremendous round of abuse, anger and recrimination. What kind of undisciplined ship did I command? What kind of respect had my ship's company for authority and the Flag? The incident was a disgrace and immediate steps were to be taken to remove all the black paint and repaint the Flagship's side a beautiful grey.

Very shaken, I returned to my ship to confer with my First Lieutenant and tell him what he had to do. He reported that the Ship's Company were extremely angry at the affair and denied vehemently that it was in any way the doing of HMS *Porlock Bay*. They were horrified, too, that their Captain should have had to face such indignity and, above all, on Christmas Day. In fact, it began to look as if any working party sent to put the Flagship's side to right would be a pretty bloody-minded lot. We were debating this situation when the Coxswain came along to report that he had irrefutable evidence that it was our opposite number, the frigate lying astern of us, which was the culprit. Not long after that, the Commanding Officer came over and offered to put the record straight. It all blew over in the end, but perhaps that did blow me some good. My Ship's Company never forgave their opposite numbers for painting our pendant numbers on the Flagship's side, nor for the indignity heaped upon their Captain. To some extent, perhaps, my poor ship handling had been forgiven. But this was not quite the end of Christmas.

My three-badge cabin hand again failed to appear on Boxing Day and I made enquiries of the Coxswain as to his whereabouts. It seemed he was gravely under the weather and so he looked, when eventually he came to my cabin. By that time I had discovered that someone had pilfered my small wine cupboard in which had resided what was probably the only bottle then extant of Drambuie. I was extremely cross and, after giving the man a piece of my mind for leaving me in the lurch for two days, I said to him, 'Cruickshank, can you tell me where my bottle of Drambuie is?'

'Yes, Sir', he replied, 'I took it'. At least this was a straight reply.

'And did you share it with your Messmates?' I enquired.

'No Sir, I drank it all myself.' No wonder he looked under the weather. It was another case of discipline or discretion. I chose the latter and never had a more loyal or more honest cabin hand.

By the end of the year, I had been in command for a little over two weeks. In that time I had certainly had more than my fair share of trials. What, I thought, lay ahead as we started the New Year, and as the Squadron sailed from Bermuda for Jamaica and all points West, I thought back to my friends' advice from the Tactical School. So far I had not run into any of the pitfalls they had highlighted but, alas, these came. Before the end of the year we had: lost the secret code wheels we used for the cypher machine which were kept with the Confidential Books; run all the ship's ledger accounts for three months using the wrong dollar exchange rate; been battered by a hurricane in Bermuda while the Commander-in-Chief was actually on board; and then been ordered home early because of the dollar crisis. Finally, the day after reaching Devonport with the paying-off pennant flying, we had all the butter stolen from the store room. It was small wonder that my next appointment was Gas Commander at Portsmouth.

GAS COMMANDER AT PORTSMOUTH

My first command time, then, was a very exciting and broadening experience. After that, I went to the Admiralty to find out what they thought they were going to do with me. They immediately said, 'Just the chap we want. We're going to put you in Intelligence.' Now, I always had a deadly loathing of being involved in Intelligence. I always believed that you got sucked into it and before you knew what was happening, you were encased in a network from which you were very lucky to escape, and, if you did escape, you probably never got promoted. So I said that I would rather not have anything to do with Intelligence, whereupon, the appointing system being such that it was, leaves were shuffled, tempting explanations floated in front of me of how jolly Intelligence was, and sinister innuendoes given that, of course, there was no other job as good as this. I mean, if I didn't take an Intelligence job I would get something very dreary. When I asked what that was, they said, 'Well, we've got a particular job in mind for you in Portsmouth.'

My mind ranged over all the best Commander's jobs in the Portsmouth area, and I couldn't actually locate one that seemed to be coming free. But I didn't have to wait long. I got a letter from their Lordships, saying that I'd been selected to be the Gas Commander at Portsmouth. Nothing could have sounded more awful. I was to take over the anti-gas training schools and reorganise them, I was to have an office in HMS *Excellent*, and I was to be known as the Gas Commander. My heart sank: this clearly appeared to be the kiss of death. I'd been Commander of a frigate; I was still moving upwards; and here was I, replacing a man who I think had something like six or eight years' seniority as a commander, and I was not really very interested in gas.

Off I went, determined if there was anything to be made of being a Gas Commander, then I would make it. I had an office at Whale Island, and I had one Petty Officer Wren to help me reorganise the anti-gas training of the Navy, which oddly enough had previously been in the hands of the torpedo men. It consisted of three gas schools, one at Chatham, one at Portsmouth and one at Devonport, and there everybody went through elementary training for putting on and taking off their gas masks. Very rapidly, though, we were expected to include training on the new gases, the nerve gases, and after that the bugs, all forms of bug warfare, and before I knew what was happening, nuclear defence; that is to say, defence against radiation from atomic bombs. I was ambitious to get my teeth into something, for I did not want this to be what gas training had been, a dreary thing in which you all rushed out and put on your gas masks and went into gas chambers and had cheerless and frightening lectures on all the awful things that could happen if you sniffed this gas. There was nobody, though, to tell me what to do; there was nobody to set an example. I had inherited two or three Lieutenant Commanders of some seniority, three little brick schools with gas chambers and all the rest of it, and I was told to get on with it.

It was a strange way to start and the only people who really had anything going at that time were the Army. So I committed to doing the Army gas course and spent many bitter days moving about Salisbury Plain in the winter, rushing through gas clouds and attending very dull lectures. Bit by bit, though, I built up some knowledge of the subject and then I went to Porton, where they kept all sorts of rabbits [for experiments], and people rushed about in gas masks and put on capes and did all the stuff that goes with gas training. In the end I entirely reorganised all gas training.

Of course, it was a subject which everybody in the Navy dreaded like mad. It was deadly dull and they all wanted to do other things. They wanted to be much more naval than going in and out of gas chambers and crawling about making their way through gas clouds in all the anti-gas clothing which they put upon you. I found myself, therefore, single-handed as it were, setting up all this training without an enormous amount of support; I mean in the sense that everybody hoped it would go away. I say I, because, of course, I was actually heading up this organisation which was simply a further development after the war. New weapons of mass destruction had come upon us. We had much more virulent gases available to us for killing each other. We were getting involved with extremely difficult and dangerous bacteriological offensive agents, and the whole business of radiological defence, the atom, the proton, the rest of it, involved quite a lot of both actual training and trials to invent an entirely new form of defence.

I started to look at the whole problem of these three: nuclear radiation, bacteriological agents, and our old friends, the gas clouds, which had now been very much up-dated. I had to run weekly courses in all these and try and get the thing started right throughout the Navy. It was a fairly formidable attempt altogether and I knew very little, of course, about bacteria and practically nothing about nuclear radiation. Although under the umbrella of HMS *Excellent*, which provided lecture rooms, gas chambers and all the rest of it, it was really being run from the Admiralty as a whole new science.

The first thing I was aware of was that the really important thing at the time was to get to grips with nuclear radiation. Of course, the place where nuclear radiation was really understood was America. As a result of the Bikini Atoll explosions, radiological defence in America had been set up, particularly in San Francisco at Treasure Island. A whole school had been installed there where lectures both in the science of radiological gases and radiation of one sort or another were taught in a very big way. So I persuaded my boss in the Admiralty that I ought to be taught something about this. I couldn't head up this affair if I didn't have up-to-date teaching.

Before very long I was sent to America. Three Englishmen were sent: myself – a Commander, a young scientist and a Naval Engineer Officer. We were packed off to do a six-week course of instruction in radiological defence from which I emerged qualified as a US Naval Radiological Defence Officer. Indeed, the three of us did rather well in this exam. I was amazed, because I had never done a degree in physics or anything. The training had involved a lot of theory; we used to do an exam every Monday morning concerned with the theory of different forms of radiation and what sort of things would come off what sort of bombs under what sort of circumstances. It also involved a certain amount of practical work in the dockyard in San Francisco, where they had taken one or two of the hulks from Bikini Atoll which were still hot. You know, we could go with Geiger counters and actually measure the radiation, treating it with the respect which was necessary. Of course, you couldn't do too much practical work without getting yourself ill.

I came out of it with a full qualification, and when I came back to England to my amazement I was invited to lecture to the US forces in Britain. There were a great many at different RAF stations and so on, and I actually gave five or six lectures to American military forces on the very subject which I'd gone to America to find out something about myself. It seemed a funny way to do it. But the attitude then was that we weren't going to go about the whole training scheme if, when you'd done it all, it wasn't any good. The essential part, therefore, was a knowledge of what we were dabbling with, what these nuclear radiations were, what harm they could do. At that time there was an immense amount of worry and myth arising from Hiroshima and Nagasaki, and it was felt that everybody, all the Armed Forces, simply had to know enough about looking after themselves, how to avoid the worst hazards, how to adopt what you might call a properly disciplined approach if they were ever likely to be in any kind of nuclear environment.

It was a great leg-up for me, because I suddenly found myself one of the few chaps in the Navy who really had learnt a bit about this. I was able to go ahead introducing courses for very junior ratings or expensive courses in the sense of the higher standard, right up to Captains and Admirals. Everybody in the Royal Navy was expected to have some knowledge of this subject and I was the chap who was told to get on with putting it over, to talk on the use of the atomic bomb, if we were going to be involved in any further hostilities. The Korean War was on our doorstep at that time and there was a considerable threat of nuclear war at the time. The powers involved, greater and lesser, needed to have some kind of instructions to avoid the very worse damage which could be done to their troops because of ignorance of the use of the atomic bomb.

All operations at that time, particularly land operations but sea operations as well, involved considerations of nuclear attack. All ships were being fitted with washing-down sprays. If we had to steam through an atomic cloud, all this nuclear fall-out would drop upon our ship, and there would be a serious danger that everybody would be polished off by radiation. The whole business of trying to wash down a ship after it had been through such a cloud was an enormous task and required a great deal of training, and holding your nerve. The art of nuclear defence, the art of integrating nuclear defence into tactics, therefore, had to be learnt. This new art of defending yourself, not just against mustard gas or whatever, but against nuclear fall-out, had become a huge business and involved large and cumbersome defence movements and training. But we had to press on if we were going to be able to go out and fight someone who might have an atomic bomb. Whether, in fact, it would have worked out or not we, happily, never found out.

We were, of course, just moving into the 'Cold War' period. The Soviet Navy was building up like mad, the American Navy had a huge stockpile of nuclear weapons; we had moved right out of the simple gunpowder bit, into twentieth-century weapons of mass destruction. It was just something that had to be incorporated into the training of military forces without, of course, ever having much experience as people could not be exposed to it for the sake of training. No one was ever deliberately exposedf to nuclear fall-out. Of course, they did tests on animals at the various bomb sites. It was the beginning of a dreadful form of war, though, to which the only answer was not to use it at all. We had to know, however, what we were talking about. The whole of that training, then, got incorporated into what, before the war, had been called Gas Warfare, dating back to the First World War – starting with mustard gas and all those sort of things, to, of course, Hiroshima, and later the trials on Bikini Atoll.

The fall-out from atomic bombs, what you might call the gas from atomic bombs, was infinitely more difficult to deal with than that which had been deployed during the First World War. It was an entirely new science to most if not all of the military people. Their tactical and defence training, therefore, involved a very large, very costly and a somewhat uncertain new defence need. Here was one thing which you couldn't muck about with; we couldn't pour it out of buckets and see what it did. This was something we had to study the theory of, and link up with such experience as we had from trials and Nagasaki. We then had to produce a training manual on how people should behave in the presence of nuclear fall-out. It was a kind of simulation; the first move towards simulation really. A lot of it was from theory; a lot of it was from picking up dust from desert islands in the Pacific. Everybody was trying to move forward to harness some kind of rational behaviour, in case we really did find ourselves throwing atomic bombs at each other. What would really have happened was anybody's conjecture. The one thing you couldn't do, was to say you couldn't do anything about it. There were a number of things which could ameliorate it, but whether having ameliorated it anybody would have survived to go on fighting, we've never really discovered.

To develop the training we brought in a lot of scientists, purely on physics. In other words, unless you understood something about the theory of it, the physics and the partitioning of the atom and all the radioactive by-products that you could get involved in, you really weren't going to get anywhere very much. It's not too difficult to understand tear gas. Somebody tells you this is a nasty thing and squirts some of it at you, you find out how it works, then you decide how to deal with it next time. If, however, the thing that you're playing with is lethal anyhow, it's difficult to make people understand what they're up against and to give them some kind of practical training which isn't actually thoroughly dangerous. All you could do was to simulate clouds, putting little bits of radioactive material on the ground and approaching it with instruments which measured its strength.

Then, of course, there was another whole new kind of gas – the nerve gases. These new gases were extremely potent, and quite easy to use once you'd made them. However, you could defend yourself in that you could detect them and put on clothing, or equipment. There was a defence against them. That is to say, you could go through a gas cloud with suitable equipment and clothing in a way that you couldn't go through a nuclear cloud. So they were, you might say, the second eleven of horrors, but even so Servicemen had to know enough about them, to be able to behave sensibly. Biological war was another concern, as if we hadn't got enough trouble! Anthrax, and horrible things like that, could contaminate the ground; people would go through it and then all die of the disease.

So we had three horrible things here. We had nerve gases, biological warfare – I mean bugs and things that could behave in the same way as gases – and, of course, nuclear radiation. A whole new range of horrors which we'd never known anything about before the war but with which we now had to grapple. I got involved in all this, and I became quite well known in the Navy because I spent a lot of time lecturing people of all grades. This included Senior Officers' war courses, Commanding Officers' training courses, Junior Officers' training courses, matters to do with Staff Courses – I used to lecture to the Staff Courses. Anybody I could get my hands on, so to speak, I would go and lecture.

Most of them knew nothing about the subject at all when I first walked into the lecture room to deliver my opening lecture. The art of getting it across, of course, was to make it interesting or amusing. With a certain amount of skill and effort, we did manage to make the lectures both accurate, or reasonably accurate, and not altogether too dull – falling asleep in the afternoon listening to a lecture on nerve gas is only too easy. We simply had to find ways of making the subject sufficiently interesting to listen to, and I think we were lucky in being able to do that. We used a certain amount of films; particularly, of course, line pictures, not so much photographs as diagrams and a lot of information. The people who were concerned with this were not science degree people, they weren't frightfully clever physicists, they were just like anybody else. And when you're trying to get the rudiments of a subject like this across, to get people to behave sensibly, in an action condition, you've simply got to get a sufficient number of the principles into their heads so that they know what's going on. It therefore became quite an essential part of people's training; a part that everybody would gladly get rid of.

AN EXECUTIVE OFFICER ASHORE AND THE UNWINDING OF A WARTIME NAVY

In the middle of all this, while I was struggling to go on with the training, I was hoping to goodness that I could get out of it soon and do something a little bit more to do with what I felt was my naval career, and a little less to do with the horrors of physics. You see, after I had done this shore job of teaching gas, biological and radiological warfare and so on, I found myself becoming something of a professional in this one particular branch. I had done my bit there and now I had to get away from it. I went out into the field, first of all in an executive post in 1949, as the Second-in-Command of the Gunnery School HMS *Excellent*.

The British Navy at that time was having problems with personnel and conditions of service. It was having problems in the change-over to a different type, a different class of young officer, and to some extent, to a different type and class of lower-deck rating. There was not really the same professionalism and cohesion in the lower-deck class as there had been before, and to some extent there was a rather looser standard for the young officer class: this was a difficult position, and perhaps could have become a dangerous one. Fortunately, it was at a period when we weren't involved in any large-scale military affairs.

We were moving into a much more difficult era of defence, though. Unable to practise little bits of it openly, because it was too dangerous, much of it had to be done as theory. [This was at a time, of course, of the run-down of the Navy, the disarmament, and the reduction of the ships. Although there was some rebuilding going on, essentially it was the run-down of the British Navy and the move in 1949 to the NATO approach to defence.] There was so much going on. To begin with, an enormous amount of equipment and ships were just being thrown away. All the war-time stuff couldn't be assimilated, couldn't be used, couldn't be paid for, and in any case advances of one sort or another in technology were coming so fast, spurred on, of course, by what eventually became the Cold War. So it was an extremely mobile period in which we were moving from a well-established, and somewhat immediately out-of-date technique, to all the new technology, all the new horrors of the Cold War, all the business of setting up NATO, the Korean War, and we were still trying to run the British Empire with insufficient ships, and with insufficient money to spend on armaments. It affected the British Navy faster than other

Services because it was already pretty skimped by this time anyway.

We also had the breakdown of the personnel. We had the Hostilities Only people leaving, the RNVR people leaving. Thousands of men who had been called up just for the war had to be demobilised. A great many ships had to be thrown away; they couldn't be maintained. The new ships that were coming along had to move forward very considerably to include the very things that we had been talking about, these modern things which you must be able to defend against, and, of course, a whole lot of other technology. Submarines were getting much more efficient. They had to be able to stay under water longer. They were getting nuclear power – the whole effect of nuclear power was enormous.

Therefore, the period between say 1945 and 1955 was an enormous one of shaking off old ideas and methods, trying to introduce new ones, and trying to introduce along with them the changes in personnel and social life which went with a total change after the war. The fighting man after the war had a whole different concept of the social relationships between officers and men. He also had learnt different ideas about separations from his family and what comforts to expect. [In April 1946 the Navy was debating in the House of Commons as to how they could get a more democratic system of recruiting the officers they needed at that point.] The closeness between classes, of the officer class and the rating class, had got very much greater, because of the way people had been living together for the last four or five years. There was neither the room nor the time to make the same differentiations between a Wardroom Officer and a rating in 1950 as there had been in 1940.

The Socialist Government had been wanting for some time to make the officer class and the rating class more or less a common entry. There had been a lot of opposition to the Officer Entry at Dartmouth taking place at thirteen. It was regarded as cheating to take them as young as that and try and fix them in what they learnt at that age, at thirteen. It was the Labour Government after the war that eventually did away with that entry at

Dartmouth. [The Education Act of 1944, which advocated educational opportunity for all, did a lot to herald change in the Royal Navy.] It was a very big change. The Thirteen Entry was just thrown out of the window and they started a dreadful thing called the Sixteen Entry, which was not a success. There was a very bad period of naval officer entry while this Sixteen Entry was going on. [The Labour Government in 1947 increased the entry age to sixteen and a quarter, and provided free board, lodging and tuition.] Then we got to the Eighteen Entry, which was also based on the general education standard, that is to say, you had to have two A-levels in order to get in to Dartmouth at the age of eighteen. This was five years later than the Thirteen Entry. And that in itself, I mean the mere fact that it had been changed by five years, meant that the Navy had been democratised in one swoop really, from what had been pretty nearly a one-class Officer Entry to one which certainly in theory was open to everybody. It threw the Officer Entry and all its class distinctions, I think, into complete disorder.

The transformation from thirteen, which was the end of one sort of school, to eighteen, which was more like the university entry, was a very great change and didn't allow for the same sort of, well I suppose, running-in, which the old entry had when they went to Dartmouth and did a period of not quite full secondary education before finding themselves at sea as Midshipmen. This new order was an entirely new social pattern for the Navy. People who wanted to put their children in the Navy, wanted them to go in for the naval entrance competition in a mix which was far less middle class than the old one, and which was far more orientated towards the lower class, or lower middle class. That is to say, they weren't people from professional families but from the general mix of people. This was something which the Naval Service had long wanted to do but had never been able to reach before because the clientele was, as it were, a one-type clientele; it was nearly all middle class. A much more general type came along with the removal of one particular age group, the thirteen to seventeen group, and the substitution of a more general age group, which was the sixteen year old, later the eighteen year old. That cast the net into a completely different sphere of young men to what had been before, when they had come from mainly the middle-class, public-school entry, which was based, to a large extent, on family connections and accepted standards: the 'old boy network' as it's called. In many cases there was a certain amount of leg-up towards passing these exams which would not be so readily available if it was a more open one-class system.

There were a whole variety of changes which could be achieved in our Navy, but only with the guidance of other navies, notably the American and Canadian. They had managed to fit-out living spaces for ratings to much higher standards than had ever been envisaged before. They produced bunks; they produced good lockers; they produced comfortable hangings in the mess-decks. They made the place more like home. We had to learn from them, and as soon as we did, the standard started to go up, and as the standard of living started to go up, the standard of amenities for living began to be raised in demand.

It was not considered good enough simply to have forms of feeding which were, so to speak, where the stuff was dolloped out from a ladle and you sat down in your mess-deck and ate it. They wanted choice; they wanted menus; they wanted modern galleys where you could actually see the food being cooked properly and dished out by modern cafeteria methods. The cafeteria method was well adapted to life in ships, but it was not adopted for a long time because it meant making important changes in the way the food was cooked, how it was kept hot, how it was served, and generally the conditions in which it was eaten. In other words, it was more civilised.

When all this began to become possible, conditions improved: things were provided in a better way; things were organised in a better way; more thought was given to it. So there you had the Navy, undoubtedly making improvements in the way that it was fitted with gear, in the way that it organised cooking, issuing, sleeping, sitting and entertainment. The whole way of life of the mess-deck was changed. The Navy's whole composition, from the point of view of the type of man who was coming into it, was changing very fast, and that in turn was beginning to be affected by education. The type of man coming in was ceasing to be simply cannon fodder. The Navy way of life was beginning again to be a life for a career man, and a career man who could see that if he behaved in a certain professional and reasonable way he would be better off. He would get a job which was better; he would get promotion; he would become more respectable.

These kind of changes only trickle through, though; but as they do and the sailor himself sees that these are better standards to work to, so the standard goes up. When men see a good standard being operated well, and they like the look of it, that standard also develops – one feeds upon the other. As soon as they got centralised messing, much better galleys, food served on a cafeteria basis, piping hot, dining-rooms to eat in as opposed to eating at a wooden table in the same place as they slept, as soon as all this began to happen then you were starting to raise the whole standard. Better sleeping arrangements, however, were much more difficult and slower to change. It was far more awkward to make notable changes in how and where you slept in a small ship, because anything that was worth doing required quite drastic structural changes, and, therefore, though it was nagged at, it didn't alter quite so readily.

As you started to raise the whole living standard, so you started to raise the whole behaviour standard. Then, of course, you ran into other problems, notably to do with engagement, and re-engagement; how long should you be parted from your wife and family; how important would it be that you should have rather more freedom for breaking your engagement at one period rather than another; in other words, a general loosening up on the whole framework of the way of life in the Navy.

Now all this was churning away in that period round about 1950. By the time of the Korean War, we were at last beginning to pull out of the old wartime ships and we were beginning to see improvemnets actually taking place in structure, in amenities, in bars, in all sorts of sleeping and living accommodation, and with it new types of routine. The whole business of life in a ship began to be much more civilised than had been the way before. For example, why should you scrub a piece of wood in order to make it shine every morning, when it contributed little or nothing to the improvement of the ship? Either the wood could be something which didn't need scrubbing all the time or the routine of doing it could be so worked into your daily life that it wasn't simply one of those horrible chores you had to do every day. Similarly, there were certain things which, nice as they would be to do, the ship would not suffer noticeably if you didn't do them. In other words, unnecessary work. 'Work study' became the great cry, and the way time was spent became important. You were getting away from such fixed things as routines.

In this way, the regulation of life in the Navy became much less rigid. There was a call for more deregulation, leaving things to be done by people without them being driven to do it. Hence there was a greater responsibility, and hence a less rigid form of discipline in a ship's routine. More time was given to examining the exact routine of running a ship, a small or large warship, with a view to providing a routine which recognised those things which had to be done and those things which were not essential.

If you were going to trust people to do things off their own bat, that is to say, you said that between ten and eleven o'clock, you must get on and clean all the Carley Floats or something, and left some responsible man to see that that was done, that was better than falling in fifty people and saying, 'I want thirty of you to clean the Carley Floats now before eleven.' There was no initiative in that. There was no particular interest in it. If, however, you were responsible for making the Carley Floats look very nice and it was done without falling in men, and then falling them all out again, and issuing them with soap or whatever it was, the whole thing was far less formidable. There was far less calling on people to do some routine thing which they didn't want to do.

It dawned on the Admiralty that there were areas which, if looked at further, could make ordinary life in ordinary ships, without too many alterations, very much easier – if they could face up to making changes. All these things took a slowish time to formulate, but bit by bit, they were worked out. What was breaking down was much of the wartime routine, and we were moving towards a lifestyle which was more fun. Additionally, people had more opportunities to get promoted and rather more reasonable regard as to how they could achieve higher posts in their career with the use of education, and the right approach to life. That was a gradually dawning process, between roughly 1945 and 1948/9.

There were still a lot of people in the Navy, though, who'd got awfully fed up with all the change and said, 'Look we've done our bit; we're all in favour of you; we don't wish you any evil intention, but don't you think you could let some of us out because we are really awfully bored with cleaning out the bilges every day. We've done our bit; we've applied to retire and in some marvellous administrative way we never seem to get there.' They then became disgruntled, of course, and that sort of disgruntlement spread, and you got a certain number of bad eggs – people who were staying on in the Navy and doing the minimum they could, but didn't want to be there at all. What they were contributing to the pot was half what a contented man was providing and we were really casting people into prison because they wouldn't stay on until the time they were due to leave the Navy came up. They couldn't ever see there was any special reason which made one cause a stronger one than another. People were held against their will and they just went sour.

These conditions and circumstances had, of course, affected me and my family. I was posted away not too terribly long after I'd returned as a prisoner of war. Naturally, we felt rotten about it, but we didn't, as it were, exactly experience the feeling until we found we were doing it, if you see what I mean. We made our plans. My wife was going to have another baby. I had one child already. I'd been away for four years. I had been promised that, because I'd been away for so long, I would be allowed a passage out to Bermuda. Passages were then not part and parcel of naval movement at all, but they were part and parcel of civilian movement. A passage meant actually going in a ship. They didn't have aeroplanes that flew people out then; we went out in a merchant ship and once every month or so there would be a draft of people who worked in the dockyards and civilian employment of that sort, going out to Bermuda with their families and everything else and the people out there would be relieved and come back, and sailors only got the benefit of that if there was a space left.

In many cases, the hardship suffered by the sailors was considerably more than that of the people who perhaps had been serving three years ashore in Portsmouth Dockyard and were being transferred to Bermuda for their next appointment. They still had their families with them and they weren't losing any family time apart, but sailors who were appointed out to Bermuda, in some cases to work in the dockyards or the tugs, if there wasn't a passage for them, they were put to the bottom of the list. They just weren't given the priority, and out they went and their wives and children followed them when there was a passage. So what happened? The family stayed at home, the husbands worked away in Bermuda, and maybe they'd be lucky and three months later they'd pick up a passage, or maybe they'd wait six months or maybe, like me, they'd get a passage when the husbands were within six months of coming back. It was not a clever way of doing it but like everything else it gradually got sorted out, although by the time it was sorted out they'd practically done away with all foreign service, so you know they cured it by more than one means.

We were officers, of course. We were supposed to look after ourselves and we knew there was nothing very much they could give you. They didn't have married quarters or anything. We had rented a house for ourselves. To that extent we were well suited. The only trouble that was my wife, who'd served for five or six years in Devon working for naval welfare, might have been thought to have earned a rest, and given a passage out to Bermuda, which is a very nice place, where I had rented a house for her; but it all went through the window. It was hard. It was a hard life and we were very bitter about it. But it was inescapable. By the time you'd got that type of thing sorted out, your time was up and you had to do something else. But the whole prospect of taking my wife and my son and setting up a little shop there, so to speak, would have been such fun, because there were other people round about my own age, who would have been doing the same. They'd have been living in a very nice climate, although I wouldn't have been there all the time, because they did two or three cruises, the ships from there.

I suppose the general effect of that period, 1945 to 1951, then, was that here was a Navy, which in the case of people like me, I had known for some little time and knew some of the tricks of the trade. But, for the junior rates, though, practically all post-war entry, it was difficult to assimilate into a Navy whose routine was a pre-war one, despite its having absorbed a great many entirely new things, from Coca-Cola to movies, to much more personal welfare, for example.

It was, in fact, a Navy waking up from an old system and trying very hard to put into effect some of the ideas it had absorbed or seen at work in other navies during the war. It was difficult, though, for the British Navy to get started on modernising because we were very short of people. We were discharging people as fast as we could. We were desperately short of money, and we hadn't really started to get the measure of the size of the task needed to turn over from a fairly tight pre-war system of running a Navy, to the much more relaxed up-to-date system, revealed by other countries' forces and navies that hadn't been under the same intense pressures of economy and, you might say, class pressures that the British Navy had. But bit by bit, these were becoming apparent, bit by bit they were being formulated, and bit by bit they were starting to throw up changes, which themselves threw up still more changes.

CHAPTER EIGHT

Captain – Ashore and Afloat, 1951–1960

DEPUTY SECRETARY TO THE
CHIEFS OF STAFF SECRETARIAT

One of the joys of the naval career is the variety it provides. If you are fortunate to be making your way up the ladder, the variety in your career comes in great measure from the sequence of your appointments and the broadening experience you thereby acquire. Looking back I can see how the Long Gunnery course, my first 'G' job at sea, the Staff Course, war experience, my first command and even Gas Commander, each brought some new and unexpected awareness of an augmentation in professional skill.

One job I particularly remember, in the immediate post-war years and before reaching Flag rank, was that of Deputy Secretary to the Chiefs of Staff. I was sent to this post on promotion to Captain and remember being horrified at what I imagined to be a kind of Paymaster's job. I knew little of the Chiefs of Staff except as a supreme body in the military field, and I had no idea whatsoever of how they or the defence organisations in Whitehall operated. Least of all had I ever thought of myself being associated with them, even in the most distant capacity. But there I was, full of zeal after being Commander of Whale Island, and literally thrown in at the deep end.

It was not a job you could readily take over from a predecessor. There were too many classified papers, too many variations with no particular subject or field in which you could feel you were the expert. My appointment simply read, 'To the Cabinet Office for duty as Dep. Sec. to the Chiefs of Staff'. I didn't even know where the Ministry of Defence was located. It was hard to guess, therefore, how I would get on with a Brigadier, three Lieutenant Colonels (all hand-picked high flyers in the Army) and two office girls who knew more about the inner workings of Whitehall than any prime minister.

It is quite simple, said the soldiers: you just write minutes, draft and send the signals to Commanders-in-Chief and so on, and get to know who is what in the Foreign Office, and the Colonial Office and the Service Ministries. Remember, too, they added, these great men seldom know exactly what they have agreed after a meeting and look to the Secretary to spell it out in the minutes. It all sounded straightforward, except that I had never kept any minutes for any meeting and now apparently I was expected to do this and process the decisions for three or four Cabinet committees in a Labour Government with a war going on in Korea.

I set off on my first day for Great George Street where, I learned, the Ministry of Defence, then running on a total budget of only £19m a year, was situated. I walked up the imposing steps, through the great oak doors, showed my pass and decided to go on walking up the stairs until I reached the second floor where my office was to be found. As I reached the first floor landing, I noticed the office in front of me was marked 'Mr Nosie, Assistant Secretary'. When I reached the second floor the door was marked 'Sir Harold Parker' [Permanent Secretary to the Ministry of Defence]. Strange coincidence I thought, and continued on my way to my new office. Here I was immediately taken in hand by a remarkable character – Vera, a lady of enormous ability and experience, full of fun and without question the linchpin of the Chiefs of Staff organisation. She was assisted by another extremely able and charming lady called Dora who, in fact, looked after me since Vera's job as boss girl included keeping the Secretary to the COS, Brigadier Robbie Ewbank, on the rails.

Vera then introduced me to Lt Cols Vivian Street, Fitzgeorge-Balfour and Bill Heald, as remarkable a team of talent as you could wish. They called themselves Section B. Somewhere in the background was a Major Johnson, who comprised Section C. I don't know if I was Section A, but I imagine that I was. Now a Captain in the Army is a junior officer, which I soon found out as when I rang the War Office I was automatically put through to someone who cut little ice in the set-up. So I adopted the title of 'The Sea Captain' and in this way managed, when ringing Ministries, to speak to someone of my own equivalent rank, an essential procedure in Whitehall.

It did not take long in such a team to learn the ropes. I soon found myself taking minutes or sitting in meetings with all the most eminent people in the Government and the Services. During my first months in the Cabinet Office the Labour Party was in power. 'Manny' [Emmanuel] Shinwell was the Minister of Defence. It was he who presided over the Defence Committee on which I was an Assistant Secretary to Sir George Mallaby [Cabinet Office Under Secretary]. On occasions I was present at other Cabinet Committee meetings where Clement Attlee, then Prime Minister, occasionally presided. It was always a joy to have him as the Chairman for he had a wonderful ability to sum up a discussion and with a concise and firm manner deliver his decisions. This could not be said of many Chairmen of Committees.

I recall one extraordinary meeting which the First Lord of the Admiralty [Right Honourable J.P.L. Thomas MP] arranged at short notice. It was to discuss with the South African Minister of Defence the future of the naval base at Simonstown. I was summoned to Admiralty House to attend the meeting at 7 p.m., not a very happy time since it was a Friday evening. Presenting myself at the door to Admiralty House I was met by the Admiralty Porter who acted as Butler-cum-Messenger at the First Lord's House. This man, a fairly well-known character in the Admiralty, let me in and informed me that the First Lord was in bed; but not to worry as he had given instructions that the meeting was to be in his bedroom and sandwiches and drinks were to be available. I looked at him in some astonishment and he obviously detected my unease as he remarked, 'I don't know what to do with the Labour lot, they have no idea how to behave and I've given up trying to teach them.' Whereupon he took me up to the First Lord's bedroom where I found him sitting up in bed in pyjamas reading his brief.

I don't know what the South African representatives thought when they were ushered in. Their Minister of Defence was a tough Boer, but not accustomed to Cabinet Ministers' bedrooms; their Chief of General Staff was even less at home there. However, they settled down on small chairs round the bed and held the meeting while I made notes for my record and dealt with the sandwiches and drink.

The Chiefs of Staff in 1951 were Admiral Sir Rhoderick

McGrigor, General Sir William Slim and Air Marshal Sir John Slessor, again a remarkable team, and they were backed by Vice-Chiefs Admiral Sir George Creasy, General Brownlow and Air Marshal Sir Hugh Saunders. In Washington, representing the Chiefs of Staff, was Air Chief Marshal Sir William Elliott, an extraordinary man of great ability and totally unlike a military figure. His principal staff assistants were Captain Alastair Ewing and a Lt Col Humphrey Prideaux, another extremely able officer, who later retired to become Chairman of NAAFI.

In the first months with the Chiefs of Staff, we in the Secretariat worked extremely long hours, as the Korean War was reaching a critical stage. The period when General MacArthur proposed using an atom bomb on the Chinese and his subsequent dismissal by President Truman, gave occasion for several tense and crucial meetings between Cabinet and Chiefs of Staff. But even when the Korean War was over, life was not very much easier. Large numbers of Servicemen had to be returned to civilian life and new military plans had to be drawn up quickly. It was a period when NATO was being set up, with Greece and Turkey still not members, and when the command structure particularly in the Mediterranean was still in need of firming up. The Chiefs of Staff were additionally worried by the British position in the Middle East where a huge military base, under General Sir Brian Robertson, was threatened by Egyptian nationalism and King Farouk was rapidly losing power. The return of Winston Churchill to Government brought with it much extra work too.

I recall so well that the election was concluded on a Thursday night. Next day Churchill assumed the office of Prime Minister and Defence Minister and immediately started in on the military establishment. Minutes began to arrive, the first being that all Labour Ministers were to be out of their offices by Friday evening. Then came his famous prayers, 'Pray inform me how many of the rifles I ordered to be stocked in 1945 are still serviceable' was one in the first twelve hours. Another was, 'I wish to see the Chiefs of Staff at 1100 on Saturday morning'.

The Map Room where the Chiefs met was duly prepared, Churchill's special swivel chair, which by chance had fetched up in my office, was brought back and on Saturday morning the great man quizzed the Chiefs of Staff and delivered an hour's talk on world strategy. It was a brilliant, if at times erratic, survey of the world as he saw it in 1951. Poor 'Manny' Shinwell left his office on the Friday after collecting his small staff together for a farewell drink. He loved the Services and I am sure stood up for them manfully in Cabinet. There were tears in his eyes as he left to go and succour his roses, for he was a keen gardener.

Things moved fast after that. Field Marshal Sir Harold Alexander was made Minister of Defence and Major-General Ian Jacob brought in as his Chief Staff Officer. General Robertson was called back to discuss the Middle East and King Farouk gave way to General Neguib. Field Marshal Sir Bernard Montgomery, who was now Deputy Supreme Allied Commander, Europe, to President Eisenhower, called in from time to time to tell the Chiefs of Staff how to run their business and occasionally President Eisenhower would come over to see Churchill. On these occasions Churchill would fix a dinner and collect his old wartime warriors – General Hastings (Pug) Ismay, Ike [Eisenhower], Alexander, Montgomery and Ian Jacob would form the quorum. And, late into the night, Alamein, Sicily, Salerno, D-Day, Arnhem, and the Battle of the Bulge would be refought, with salt cellars, mustard pots, ashtrays and anything portable used to mark the position of this force or that. How I longed to be a fly on the wall on these occasions.

Then, in 1952, a great plan was evolved to expand NATO to include Greece, Turkey and Egypt, these latter being grouped in what was to be referred to as the Middle East Defence Organisation. The idea was discussed with Eisenhower and the NATO Standing Group Chiefs in Paris, from where a delegation of the Standing Group was to sally forth and sell the plan. I went with the British Military Representative, General Sir William Slim, to the meeting in Paris, which was also attended by General Omar Bradley, US Chairman of the Joint Chiefs of Staff, and General Juin, the French Chief of Staff. The meeting was a tricky one and I had my work cut out keeping a record. Luckily I did keep this, because when the meeting finally broke up it was found that the Standing Group Secretariat who had flown in from Washington had forgotten to provide the 'verbatim' reporters for this occasion. So, perhaps for the only time, the Standing Group had to rely on the British style of minutes, far from verbatim, but perfectly adequate in our eyes since it contained a summary and the really important part, the conclusions.

Next day the Generals set off for Athens in General Omar Bradley's private aircraft (complete with doctor and hostess). Leaving Orly was a splendid affair – Guards of Honour and music for Slim, Juin and Bradley, all the top brass on hand, and tucked inside the aircraft with the hostess such lower Staff Officers as were being taken along. I was the only Briton. Arriving at Athens, we were met by the Greek Army Chief of Staff and welcomed by a Guard of Honour which was inspected by three NATO Chiefs of Staff, each receiving his own salute and music. During our stay in Athens the Greeks were won over to the plan and arrangements were made for their Chief of Staff to join the circus and fly to Ankara. Before leaving, King Paul and Queen Frederika of Greece gave the delegation a splendid banquet and for the first time in my life I dined off gold plate.

Once more everyone boarded Omar Bradley's plane, though by now the ceremony required to pay due farewell to Generals Bradley, Slim, Juin and a Greek General had become something of a marathon. En route to Turkey news came that President Neguib had backed out of the talks and that Egypt wanted no part in NATO. However, nothing daunted, we pressed on and were duly welcomed by a large and incredibly tough-looking bunch of Turkish soldiery, a Guard of Honour some hundred strong and a large band, each member of which was armed with an automatic weapon.

The occasion was not without its humour. Omar Bradley was wearing a raincoat and looked very unmilitary, Juin likewise had on some kind of Burberry, and the Greek General was rather small and looked hen-pecked. But Slim was looking every inch a fighting man. The Turkish Chief of Staff made a beeline for him, almost ignoring the others, and took him to inspect the Guard. It transpired that Slim had for a short time during the First

World War been a prisoner of the Turks and told them how glad he was to visit them this time as a free man.

The cavalcade motored back to Ankara, which was about 20 miles from the airfield. Every yard of the way, lurking behind boulders or standing by trees, were armed soldiers. Security was certainly made obvious. Discussions in Ankara lasted two or three days. I stayed with our Naval Attaché, a furious golf fanatic, and learned from his wife how attachés in Ankara found out what was afoot. It all came from the 'cooks' league'. Our Naval Attaché's cook was related to the Russian Embassy cook, as well as to one or two in other diplomatic houses. Through the grapevine, a steady stream of small gossip and information was obtainable and Naval Intelligence was provided with at least something to chew on.

Once back in England again the busy life of the Chiefs of Staff Committee continued. Greece and Turkey were integrated into Supreme Allied Command, Europe's command and further proposals were in the air for sub-commands at Gibraltar, Oslo and the Channel. But the most contentious proposal was the one for the Mediterranean, where Britain's historic role in that sea required some special recognition, particularly over the nationality of the new NATO Commander-in-Chief. Britain, and not least Admiral Mountbatten [Commander-in-Chief, Mediterranean], were pressing hard for the leading role.

Along with NATO matters, other problems were calling for attention. The Monte Bello Islands British atom bomb tests were in the pipeline and Professor Penney [Director of Atomic Weapons Research] was a frequent visitor to Great George Street. Egypt also was proving difficult and General Robertson, a one-time front runner for CIGS, was regularly being called home. Then Malaya began to get out of hand and General Sir Gerald Templer was soon in close discussion with the Chiefs on his possible appointment as Director of Operations. Templer was a fascinating man to observe in action. Wiry, somewhat ascetic and ill-looking, an absolute bundle of nervous energy but knowing precisely what he wanted, he would sit at the table, chain-smoking and almost trembling like a puppy wanting to be taken for a walk.

Without doubt, 1950 to 1953 were high-pressure years in the military as well as the political field. The relaxing of wartime rationing, the return of Churchill, the effects of Marshall Aid and the setting up of NATO alone were enough to fill the day. But there was also the American monopoly of the atom bomb, from which flowed the whole strategy of deterrence. And nobody was more active in propagating that than Air Chief Marshal Slessor, who saw in it a leading role for the RAF and was already active in plans for the V bomber force. So while the RAF saw a new light, the Army was busy looking for a new role in Europe while engaged with demanding calls in Egypt and Malaya, and the Navy was busy as usual trying to preach Command of the Sea and looking for wide opportunities in the Mediterranean, Atlantic and Channel areas of NATO. Small wonder that Planning and Intelligence papers flowed, that Foreign Office telegrams became a flood and the small Ministry of Defence groaned under the load of meetings, minutes and papers. Global Strategy was what Churchill wanted and much time and thought was given to updating the Chiefs of Staff's views on the 'Glob Strat' paper.

I went on one more great outing, this time to America. The matter in hand was the Mediterranean Command in NATO and the two representatives of the British Chiefs of Staff were Admiral Sir Rhoderick McGrigor and Air Chief Marshal Sir John Slessor. These two, with the British representative on the Standing Group, Air Chief Marshal Sir William Elliott, met with the US and French Chiefs of Staff and hammered out a command structure which, very happily for us, accepted a British Admiral as the NATO Commander-in-Chief in Malta.

When we came to fly home from an airfield close to Washington there was an amusing incident. The plane was ready for take-off, Slessor and McGrigor were waiting to board, but there was no sign of Elliott, other than a message saying he was on his way to see us off. Minutes passed but still no sign of the great man. The US Officers became restless and put out calls to locate Elliott, but in vain. Then, just as we were giving up, the

18. Whale Island, February 1944. (RNM Collection, 225/89(20))

19. Commander, c. 1947.
(RNM Collection, neg. 99)

20. Treasure Island, San Francisco,
1949. (RNM Collection, neg. 84)

21. HMS Coquette, *5 July 1954. (RNM Collection, neg. 2187)*

22. HRH Princess Margaret being welcomed aboard HMS Coquette.
(Crown Copyright; RNM Collection, neg. 2182)

23. *Aerial view of* HMS Gamecock, *Nuneaton, 1956.*
(Crown Copyright; RNM Collection, neg. 2237)

24. *Captain Twiss looks on as Vice Admiral Sir Caspar John inspects the gliding*
facilities at HMS Gamecock, *13 September 1956.*
(Crown Copyright; RNM Collection, neg. 2239)

25. Twiss pipped at the post in a sports final, HMS Gamecock, *June 1956. (Crown Copyright; RNM Collection, neg. 2240)*

26. Admiring gamecocks presented to HMS Gamecock *by the Mayor of Leicester, 1956. (Crown Copyright; RNM Collection, neg. 2242)*

*27. Captain and Mrs Twiss stir the Christmas pudding, HMS Gamecock,
11 November 1957. (Crown Copyright; RNM Collection, neg. 2241)*

*28. Leaving HMS Gamecock, December 1957.
(Crown Copyright; RNM Collection, neg. 2246)*

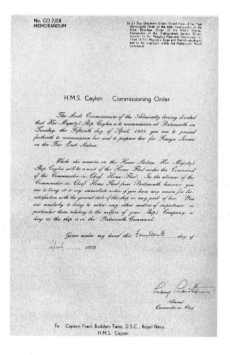

29. *Commissioning Order, HMS* Ceylon, *14 April 1958.* *(RNM Collection, neg. 2245)*

30. *Addressing Ship's Company, HMS* Ceylon, *15 April 1958.* *(Crown Copyright; RNM Collection, neg. 2259)*

31. In tropical working rig, Singapore, c. 1958–59. (Crown Copyright; RNM Collection, neg. 2194)

32. HMS Ceylon *leaving harbour after refit, Portsmouth, 14 July 1958. (Crown Copyright; RNM Collection, neg. no. 2258)*

33. Lady Macmillan arrives on board for a Service of Dedication. July 1958. (Crown Copyright; RNM Collection, neg. 2263)

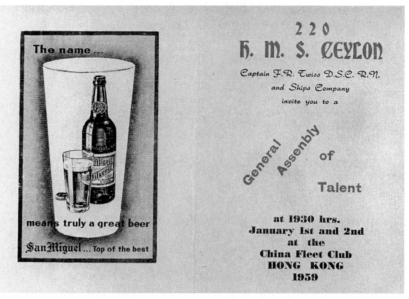

34. Ceylon's Concert Party invitation to China Fleet Club, 1 and 2 January 1959. (Crown Copyright; RNM Collection, neg. 2256)

Air Marshal appeared looking quite extraordinary in the bright hot sunshine at the airbase. He climbed out of his car wearing a black striped suit (similar to the trousers of a morning coat), black tie and a small black 'Derby' hat. As everyone else was in white summer uniform, this rig, quite unsuited to a military man in any case, took everyone aback. Looking pale, lanky and just like an undertaker's mate, the Air Marshal advanced to bid farewell. He was very angry. It seemed that due to his strange appearance, the US guards on the Air Base entry gate had absolutely refused to let him in or to believe he was what he claimed to be. It was only after his identity had been checked with the Pentagon that he was allowed to proceed.

We returned to England satisfied with the outcome of the meetings. NATO was well organised, Mountbatten was named Commander-in-Chief, Penney was on time with his bomb; nuclear deterrence was accepted; Templer had a grip on Malaya; the RAF were taking on the UK deterrent; Egypt was rumbling and Montgomery as Deputy SACEUR was mumbling. At that point King George VI died. Although everybody knew the King was far from well, the announcement of his death came as a surprise. In due course, the King lay in State in Westminster Hall where for several days an unceasing line of people walked past his coffin to pay their last respects. I was able to get a ticket for admission through the House of Lords and can remember even now the solemnity, the dignity and the extraordinary atmosphere created by a country and a people so quiet, so orderly. Little did I think then that in later years, as Black Rod, I should become closely involved in the ceremonial of Westminster Hall and be called upon to oversee the ceremony of Lying-in-State in an era when IRA bombing was prevalent.

It would be dreary to list the very many eminent people with whom I made acquaintance in those years in Great George Street. Certainly for the rest of my career there was hardly a Minister, Senior Diplomat, Civil Servant or military man of high rank in the NATO and Commonwealth Services whom I did not either know about or know personally. This was certainly, as it were, a credit card worth having in my wallet.

CAPTAIN –
FISHERY PROTECTION SQUADRON

While I was still working in the Ministry of Defence and my time was up there, the Naval Secretary, who arranges the appointments of Captains, said he'd like to send me to the West Indies in command of a Frigate Squadron. As I had done time in a frigate in the West Indies directly after the war I didn't want to go there again, since it meant being separated from my wife for a further period of eighteen months. So I asked if I could have a reconsideration and he came up with the Fishery Protection Squadron.

This was an unusual job because it had very little to do with the Navy as such, but of course a great deal to do with the fishing industry and with the regulation of the fishing industry, internationally and through the Ministry of Agriculture and Fisheries. So I set out in April 1953 to take command of a little ship called HMS *Coquette*, which was one of the wartime ocean minesweepers – a very small, compact ship, and a wonderful seaboat, with minesweeping equipment. It actually had two separate mess-decks, one below the water line and one above the water line; and when minesweeping, the crew used the upper one, but when just steaming hither and thither, they occupied the lower one, which was rather more comfortable.

My job was to keep an eye on our fishing fleets and keep in close touch with the Fisheries Department. I answered to the Vice-Chief of Naval Staff on the naval side, and altogether it was an entirely new business and very interesting. I was due to go down and take command of the ship just before the Naval Review for the Coronation of Her Majesty Queen Elizabeth at Spithead. When I arrived there, there was no ship, as she had had a collision in Norway with a tanker and knocked a great piece off her bow. So I found myself becoming Captain Fishery Protection without a ship, because it was in dock having a new bow put on. One knew at that time that relations with the European nations over fishing were always very tempestuous, but I, of course, didn't foresee the ferocity of the Cod War and at the time I took over we could still fish fairly readily in Icelandic waters and the fishing industry was doing quite well.

I kept in close touch with the fishing industry because I had my office in Hull, where one half of the whole ocean fishery catch was landed. The other half was landed at Fleetwood. But by having my office in Hull, I was in direct touch with the fishing firms and the fishing skippers and one thing and another. My ship having been damaged like that, the only thing I could do was to climb into one of the other ships in my squadron and go off and find out the form, which I did. The squadron was very small and select. There were five ships, and two motor fishing vessels. They were what were called ocean minesweepers. That is to say, they had big, heavy reels of sweep wire for cutting mines that were moored by chains, and some of the more modern equipment for dealing with acoustic and pressure mines. They had rather delightful names, like *Truelove* and *Mariner*.

After the best part of three months as a visitor, so to speak, in one of the other ships in my Squadron, my own ship *Coquette* became available and I thought I would set a good example by spending Christmas in the Barents Sea, in the fishing area off north Norway and north Russia. So off we went to monitor the fishing up there, and provide what was undoubtedly a very useful backing for our fishermen, in those wild and extremely cold waters. It was perpetual darkness, of course, when I got there, and I steamed out to where the fishing was going on. All those fishing vessels chatter away to each other on the radio and you could hear the word going down the line: 'That fellow, Captain Fishery Protection is around; look out chaps.'

Instead of being received with open arms, there was a general view that the best thing to do was to avoid me. This was a typical, so to speak, way of welcoming a newcomer, and I found that what they said rudely about me over the radio, bore no relation to the extremely nice way they behaved when I went on board the ships, or met them. And all our Fishery Protection vessels lived like kings on fresh cod and so on when they were up in those areas. We got to know quite a number of the personalities involved, who were very much a breed of their own because, by Jove, it's a tough life. I came back after Christmas. I had been working actually in the Barents Sea, opposite the Russian coast and I was shadowed all the time by a Russian warship, which thought we were up to some evil. I got home at the end of January, after about six weeks in as cold a type of weather as you could wish to experience.

Each nation has its own fishery protection vessels: the Danes, the Norwegians and the Icelanders, of course, were the three main nations, and then there was an enormous number of Frenchmen. We were acting really as an escort. We visited the various fishing areas and there we checked on the observance of Regulations; that is to say, we examined fishing vessels and saw that their mesh was not smaller than it should be and that they weren't misbehaving in some way and breaking the fishing laws. It was an international job, combined with the fact that we were an official Minesweeping Squadron in the fleet – from time to time we would be taken out of fishery work and put into exercising with NATO ships and so on. We answered directly to the Admiralty and the Ministry of Agriculture and Fisheries. So we were really outside the normal Naval Fleet set-up, and trying to do what was a quite tricky job – sometimes as a result of enormous anger on both sides, or questions of search and rescue or what have you. Of that time, I think I remember the weather more than anything else because all the deep sea fishing takes place in the wildest bits of weather, off Iceland, off the Orkney Islands and right across to Bear Island. You can't choose a more awful place for gales, with ice and driving snow and so on. So these little ships were wonderful seaboats but you had to be a fairly rugged sailor to take the bashing you got and be able to keep going.

I have very fresh memories still of gales off Iceland, standing at night on the bridge of this little ship watching the wave apparently going to crash down on me, and looking up, straight ahead and seeing the crest of the wave apparently 20 feet above me, then down it came and these little things, like ducks, just rode up over it. They really were very fine seaboats. We received special rations to keep us warm – we got an extra tin of sardines or soup – and we wore so many clothes. We were so wrapped up in the warmest clothing that we simply couldn't move; we wedged ourselves on the bridge and stayed there until the weather eased. It was quite an alarming experience, being in a full Atlantic gale in one of those little ships, or in a trawler for that matter. It was an entirely new aspect of nautical life.

During my time in *Coquette*, I visited Copenhagen and Amsterdam and all along the north French coast. I had a charming little cabin. There was the bridge, and then the Captain's cabin, which was a sort of structure at the front end, with a gun for'ard of that, and then the fo'c'sle and anchor gear. Generally, I had a very comfortable little place, although I had to fix myself in my bunk so that I didn't get thrown out, because these ships bounce around rather; but you got used to it. On the whole, they were also quite comfortable little ships for the Ship's Company. We didn't have a very big crew and I think they liked it, except at that time there was a certain amount of discontent in the Navy to do with the length of service which people had signed on for. Some were disgruntled, and wanted to get out of the Navy and couldn't get out of it until they'd served their specified time. So there were one or two hotheads around, and perhaps they were sent to the Fishery Protection Squadron to sort them out.

I had one or two tiresome sailors to deal with, who were quite good when they were doing the job but inclined to be rather troublesome when they went ashore. They all got drunk, or tended to, so they were setting a bad example. I mean, they were lazy; they weren't well-dressed; they failed to turn up promptly when they should do. They did all sorts of little things to annoy. Although they constantly got punished, it didn't stop them. They hoped, I think, that by making sufficient nuisances of themselves, they would wear us down and get discharged. Well, once you'd let that happen, of course, you'd find the whole Navy wanting to get into it, or start doing it. Captains, however, have very strong powers of discipline and one just had to use those powers and punish these men.

I was away, of course, a good deal of that time. We used to get leave three times a year and for that time we went back either to

Portsmouth, Chatham or Devonport, according to where the ship was based and one didn't see much of one's family at all. It wasn't the sort of job where we could entertain very much. It was a good, hard seaman's slog, but quite fascinating. I took my wife across to Copenhagen. We went over there for three or four days and then I took her on to Oslo, not on board, she travelled independently, but she saw a little bit of me at work, and I also took her down to the Scilly Isles when we were there for a few days.

THE IMPERIAL DEFENCE COLLEGE

In January 1955 I was selected to go to the Imperial Defence College. This was the Senior Staff College to which they sent people of Captain's or Colonel's rank for a year's course in broadening their minds. It consisted of a whole series of studies on many subjects, such as Communism, China, re-supplying Europe from America, and what have you. I mean matters of considerable strategic weight. We studied them and there was a Directing Staff who examined us. Then our papers were all handed back to us with remarks about where we should do further study, if we wanted to improve our knowledge on a subject. In other words, it was just like a Staff Course, a Staff College, but it had very high-class people who came and lectured. During the year, subjects which were going to be examined in some depth were laid out in a programme and experts came and lectured to you. There were foreign people, Government people, MPs, coal miners: all came and lectured on their particular subject and then we discussed it afterwards. So it was an education. It was to polish you up and bring you up to date and improve your education about all matters of defence, of Government and of the wider issues that were being discussed or legislated for around the world.

We also travelled around a bit. A whole aeroplane of us went on a tour of Africa, to practically all the states. At each place we went to, we were addressed and brought up to date in the affairs of that particular country. We went to Kenya and actually went and saw the Mau Mau [who had recently been in revolt]. After that, I saw all the countries in Africa in the course of six weeks. This included a visit to South Africa. We went down to Durban, then Cape Town, flew up to Southern Rhodesia [now Zimbabwe] and then across to West Africa.

The College had a Directing Staff of three Rear Admirals, or equivalent, and one hand from each of the Services and the Foreign Office. Students came from the whole of the Commonwealth when I was there, and later on from non-Commonwealth countries, so of the sixty or so students that were there, there was an amalgam of British Services people, Civil Servants and other people who had been sent on the course, for the benefit of what they would get out of it. On my course we had people from India, Pakistan, Ceylon, Australia, New Zealand, South Africa and the USA, as well as our three Services and the Civil Service.

We all lived at home, but of course we all used to get together, and our wives used to come up once a week and we'd all go to a cinema or restaurant in London. We got to know quite a lot of them and in the course of the year we probably had a meal with everybody and their wives, so, socially, we spread our friendships. Later on we met a number of these people again, in different circumstances. When I was in Ceylon, for example, I found that the Colonel, who had been the Ceylon member, was Chief of the Ceylon Army; the Chief of the Pakistan Army became a great friend of mine while we were doing the course, and likewise in New Zealand and Australia. One knew all the top brass, and that's very useful. We'd all studied together; we'd all pulled each other's legs; we'd all gone out to dinner together.

CAPTAIN OF HMS GAMECOCK – NAVAL AIR STATION

Before I went to the Imperial Defence College, the Naval Secretary sent for me and said, 'You're not to tell anybody at all, but you're going to the IDC in order to be polished up to come in as Director of Plans [at the Admiralty].' This was a top job.

I said, 'Thanks very much,' and off I went.

Well, at the end of the course, the Naval Secretary sent for each Naval member and said, 'Now this is what we're going to do with you. You're going to go here and you're going to go there.' Now he didn't send for me and I thought, well that was quite natural because he'd already told me. However, eventually he sent for me and said, 'Oh, I've got a very good job for you. You're going to go as Deputy Director of Naval Intelligence.' And I looked at him. He wasn't the same Naval Secretary who had been there when I first went to the College.

I said to him, 'Well that's a bit odd, because I understood that I was going to go as Director of Plans.'

'Ah, yes,' he said, 'but the First Sea Lord has selected somebody else.' The First Sea Lord was Mountbatten, and he wanted an aviator and someone he knew. So, having been told that I was going to do it and then not having got it, I was naturally somewhat disappointed.

However, I didn't get to be the Deputy Director of Naval Intelligence either. I wasn't disappointed about that. I thought there was a great deal of lengthy writing in Intelligence, and a good deal of it designed never to commit yourself particularly to one view or the other. I had taken a dislike to anything that was not in the main stream of operations. This was the second time they'd wanted to put me in the Intelligence division. So I managed to avoid it, but of course I then had to try something else. Well, everybody else had clearly been slotted into something, and I knew nothing, or had no personal experience, of the Fleet Air Arm, so I asked if I could get a job in the Fleet Air Arm, and was rewarded, in January 1956, by the command of an air station in the Midlands, HMS *Gamecock*.

I was the Captain in command of *Gamecock*. Although not a front-line Air Station, it had two Squadrons of RNVR aircraft, and it was a very active station right in the middle of England. It was the most convenient station for any of the other air stations to drop off at or to land at on their way somewhere else, and because it was so central, it hosted quite a number of interesting and useful events. I learnt a great deal. As the Captain I was responsible, of course, for the training in general, and I had a Commander, an engineer, to advise me. There was also a Commander in charge of the aviation. My job was to run the station which meant regular inspections of the young men, watching them do their work, and keeping in touch and flying a bit with the volunteer airmen who worked at the weekends. I mean, I did what the Captain of a ship did, just like any other barracks really.

The Air Station had been one of the air stations built in the thirties, when they first started to rearm the RAF, and these were lovely air stations. But, of course, they only had grass airfields, with grass runways. Although I had a jet Squadron there, we had to fly them from a companion air station with concrete runways. These stations were not only well built, they also had very large quarters for the Commanding Officer – we had a very nice house, built by Sir Edwin Lutyens – but they were impossibly expensive to run. It was quite a business, therefore, to keep one's head above water, money-wise, and live in the house. We had to be very sparing with the central heating. My family lived there with me.

One of the interesting parts of life here were the boys who came in as 'Skinheads'. They had their heads shaved and they wore jeans and they looked like the sort of youths that you saw in towns and avoided. But as soon as they put on a uniform, they were quite different people. To begin with, you gave them some kind of status which they'd never had before. They didn't look out of place because everybody wore uniform at the station and they very, very quickly took to the kind of comradeship that comes from working with a group of boys or people who've all been brought together for a common purpose. Within three months, their mothers wouldn't recognise them. Their hair had grown, they looked smart, efficient, and what's more they were. Their intelligence had been aroused.

We had to get hold of whatever VIPs we could to present prizes regularly, about every two or three weeks, and we gave the trainees what you might call the 'full drill'. They were inspected and they marched past, and the band would play and everything, and they were immensely proud of themselves. At that time

Admiral Caspar John was the Admiral commanding the Fleet Air Arm, who was a tremendous character in himself. But we were in direct command of a Rear Admiral who was called Flag Officer Ground Training [Rear Admiral Willoughby], and he used to come up at regular intervals and if we got, you know, the Lord Mayor of Birmingham or the Lord Mayor of Leicester to come and inspect the troops, it was a great boost for them.

During my time there, the Queen agreed to present the First Colour to the Fleet Air Arm. The Navy doesn't have many Colours like the Army does, but they have one for the Home Fleet, and the Mediterranean Fleet and that sort of thing, and this was for the Fleet Air Arm. Admiral Caspar John, who was then the Flag Officer Air, invited me to command this performance which was to cover the whole of the Fleet Air Arm and, therefore, involve the presence of men from all the air stations, of which we had about six at that time. The business of training a Royal Guard on an occasion like that from six different places is quite complicated and involved me in flying round from one place to another, trying to get six different contingents trained up to the right standard of rifle drill and so on, and then taking them down to Lee-on-Solent for a week's final training together before the great ceremony.

Well, we did this. We all were still down at Lee-on-Solent when, for some obscure reason, the Queen decided to present the Colour on a Monday, which was very worrying for me because we didn't want to stop the men going on their weekend, which would have been very unpopular. But there was a danger that some of them might not get back in time for the Monday performance, but there it was. We just had to take a risk that their morale was such that they would turn up, which, in fact, proved to be true, because they, by that time, had gained a considerable *esprit de corps*.

The Royal Guard consists of something like a hundred men with rifles, tuned up to a very high standard. On the weekend before this ceremony, there was the most awful gale and it blew away all the wooden stands which had been specially erected for this occasion. The whole lot were blown away down the runway:

so on Sunday, panic stations. What were we to do about having no stands? We made a general call to Gosport, for every sailor who was available to turn up at the Air Station and man-handle the whole lot back into position. By Monday morning we had the stands back in position, but were very anxious about the weather, because it was still blowing a bit. The weather men said that the wind was going down, and they thought that it would be all right by eleven o'clock when the Queen was going to arrive.

We had a large number of sailors and Wrens fallen in on the runway with a Guard of Honour of one hundred seamen in the centre and a dais and so on for the Queen. In front of the dais, we were going to pile the drums, in the way that is done for a presentation of Colours. Five or six drums are planted on the ground and then another layer above and then the new colour is placed on the top. The Parson stands there to bless it, and so on. All this was arranged and on Monday morning it was still blowing. They said, providing the wind is 35 miles an hour or less, you can do it. Well, it was just about 35 miles an hour, so we went ahead. Here were all these people fallen in, standing up bravely to what was quite a strong wind, particularly on a runway with no kind of shelter. The Queen looked rather cross about the weather because it blew her clothes about; it was all rather disturbing. She mounted the dais though, and went through the ceremony.

The first part was to produce the drums, which was being done by a whole lot of young Air Artificers, and they were looking very smart. Each one marched and put his drum in position with the top drum on the top. At the moment the Colour was produced, the top drum blew off, and bowled away down the runway at ever-increasing speed. Up to then the Queen had looked rather bored. She didn't care for coming on a Monday, and in this very heavy wind was even less entranced. But once this unusual event happened, she took a great deal of interest. The drum eventually ran into the front row of the Wrens, who were fallen in across the runway. With great valour, they stood firm, though one of the girls received this drum in her midriff.

It was brought back and put in position and it stayed there as the flag was put on, and we went ahead with the presentation. Then off they marched with the Colour among them, and did the rest of the ceremony with very great skill in the face of considerable difficulty. The ceremony was completed and Admiral John, who had been horrified at the proceedings, went into lunch with the Queen, who more or less indicated that it was one of the best Colour performances that she had been to. It was such fun because of this drum blowing away. Admiral John then gave a pair of nylons to the Wren who stopped the drum, and next day, there was a cartoon in one of the papers, showing the drum bowling away, and some caustic remarks about the Navy and its Colour performance, all quite good humoured.

CAPTAIN OF HMS CEYLON – 6-INCH CRUISER

My next appointment was to the cruiser HMS *Ceylon*. I took command of her just before Christmas 1957. She had just become the Flagship to Vice Admiral Sir David Luce [Flag Officer (Flotillas) Home] and was in the last few months of a commission normally of Home Service but which had, because of the Suez operation, been entirely spent overseas. The Ship's Company were far from happy at having to spend their last two months abroad again on the spring cruise of the Home Fleet to the West Indies. On top of this problem, I was not at all happy with what I inherited. The ship was dirty, the Ship's Company slovenly and the officers unimpressive. The previous Captain had permitted smoking at work anywhere in the ship; on the bridge, on the upper deck, on the mess-decks and in offices. The result was cigarette ends everywhere, and this slovenliness had communicated itself to the whole conduct of the vessel. I realised that until the ship paid off in three months' time I would have great difficulty in effecting major changes in the face of a none too co-operative Ship's Company, a Commander who thought his way of running the ship was the right one and a Wardroom that was, to put it kindly, running down.

We sailed for the West Indies in company with other ships of the Fleet and made for Jamaica. There were ups and downs. Knowing Admiral Luce personally made that side of my job easier and together we made some delightful visits to Caribbean islands. There was an amusing incident at Montego Bay when the Admiral and I were returning on board by barge in very rough seas and he fell between the barge and the gangway ladder. With some presence of mind, I pushed him under the lowest platform and had the Coxswain go full ahead to clear the ship. Although the Admiral was very wet and perhaps shocked, I reckoned I had saved him from being crushed; but he was not convinced of my altruism and relations between us were less than easy for some days. Happily his wife, hearing from mine that I had pushed him under the ladder, thought it very funny and when, a few days later, she arrived out by air, bought him a new camera to replace his waterlogged one as a souvenir of the day the Flag Captain pushed the Admiral down as he came up for the third time.

During our visit to Barbados we had what was not far from a mutiny. About twelve bloody-minded sailors got extremely drunk on rum and then shacked up in a local brothel and refused to return on board. The Commander and the Master at Arms became very worried and wanted to send a party ashore to capture them and bring them back under arrest. But I could see this would merely worsen the position and possibly lead to more trouble and publicity. So I decided to leave the ratings where they were and await the outcome. For two or three days nothing more was heard or seen. On the fourth day we sailed and, just before weighing anchor, a boat was seen approaching with a number of very untidy, dirty and disconsolate men. No doubt money, rum and women had run out. Our friends were back and spent the next days in the cells waiting for our return to Portsmouth where, on arrival, they had the depressing sight of their shipmates going on leave while they went to the Detention Quarters. The ship then paid off, refitted for a couple of months and re-commissioned with an entirely new company and wardroom. It never looked back. Under the cry of '220', standing for 'Second to none', we completed as happy and successful an eighteen months' foreign commission as one could wish, and a commission with a great deal of fun and variety.

The *Ceylon* worked up in Malta and, after visiting Toulon flying the flag of Rear Admiral Ewing [Flag Officer (Flotillas) Mediterranean], was rushed off to the Persian Gulf to render assistance to a mammoth tanker which had been badly damaged in a collision. HMS *Albion*, which was operating off the Trucial Coast, managed to get a line aboard and to tow her as far as Muscat. Bearing huge steel sheets welded to our bridge structure and miles of steel girders, screws, bolts, rivets and so on, plus a small team of Maltese dockyard men, we hurried through the Suez Canal, refuelled at Aden and pushed on up to Muscat.

We found the great tanker lying at anchor 2 or 3 miles off-shore. You could have driven two double-decker buses through the hole in her side and still have room to spare. Fire had damaged her upper-works and we soon found the ship to be in a dreadful state internally. Her cool and cold rooms were full of rotting provisions, her cabins had been looted by the *Albion*'s fire fighters; she was anchored by a bare minimum of cable; there was no light, no refrigeration, no water, no power. The task of getting her into a condition fit for towing back to some large port where she could be repaired was daunting. Day after day the revolting task of cleaning up was done by *Ceylon*'s sailors in temperatures hot enough to melt the soles of your rubber shoes. But clear it up they did and restored enough machinery to working condition to provide power, refrigeration and ventilation. Meanwhile the Maltese, aided by a few *Ceylon* artificers, patched up the huge hole in the tanker's side and pumped out the hundreds of tons of sea water in the bottom.

Just as this job was coming to an end, with visions of pushing on to Singapore appearing, a signal came from Admiralty ordering the *Ceylon* to embark the heavy equipment of a battalion from Bahrain and take it to Aden, subsequently proceeding up the Red Sea to the port of Eilat in the Gulf of Aqaba to collect the last British battalion in Jordan and take them to Mombasa. So off we set, leaving the tanker, by now patched and reasonably sea-worthy, for some tug to collect. We reached Aqaba prepared to take on board about 900 men with their light arms and equipment. Information indicated that they were the Cameronians, reputed to be the toughest and most ill-disciplined soldiers in the Army, and that among their lot were three or four soldiers under arrest for trying to kill one of their sergeants with a tent pole. I conferred with the Commander and the Master at Arms and we agreed that they would have to sleep on deck for the nine-day passage to Mombasa. Each man had a camp bed and a pack, while the men under arrest were consigned to the cells, which, being right in the bows of the ship, are no place for anyone suffering from sea-sickness. We had no trouble with the culprits on passage! After a farewell parade ashore, King Hussein came on board and walked round the *Ceylon*. Then we were away.

By great good fortune the trip to Mombasa was fairly smooth and we had no rain, so that the soldiers on deck fared comfortably and thrived on Navy meals. We entered Mombasa with the regimental band playing and pipers on the forward turret. It was a great occasion, the troops were in good heart and very soon were ashore and on a train for Nairobi. Next day we sailed at last for Singapore. However, the day after that the Cameronians ran riot and took Nairobi to pieces, causing immense damage and great hostility. Alas, they lacked our Master at Arms.

At Singapore we took over the flag of Rear Admiral Varyl Begg [Flag Officer 2nd in Command, Far East Station] from our sister ship, HMS *Newfoundland*, and settled into the routine of the Far East Fleet. Life on board was far from pleasant for the majority of sailors as the ship was not air-conditioned and conditions between decks on the equator were dreadfully hot and sticky. But a visit to Hong Kong at Christmas made up for a lot and the ship was seldom in one place for long. There were a few particular incidents which stand out in my memory.

The first was the visit of the Duke of Edinburgh in the Royal Yacht *Britannia* to Singapore and Hong Kong. The *Ceylon* was detailed as guardship and her Captain made Officer-in-

Command of the escort force. We made a rendezvous off Penang in great style, accompanied by four destroyers. We raced down on *Britannia*, turned and steamed close aboard and cheered ship before taking up our allotted stations. The entry into Singapore commercial harbour was like a ticker tape reception. Hundreds of small boats came out to meet the Yacht, tugs and ships sirens were blowing and all Singapore was en fête. The Duke stayed for a few days before moving on, escorted by *Ceylon*, to Hong Kong, where the same reception was waiting.

On board the Royal Yacht as a guest of HRH was Admiral of the Fleet Lord Fraser of North Cape, victor of the *Schnarnhorst* sinking and an old friend of mine. Bruce Fraser was a bachelor and a character who didn't care much for official dinners but he had to attend that given by the Governor of Hong Kong. He was provided with a car and Chinese driver, and duly arrived at the dinner in full mess kit, orders, decorations, the lot. Just as soon as he could after dinner, he slipped away, summoned his driver and said, 'Now what's on in Hong Kong. Take me to a good show.' The driver brightened up and decided that the place for the Admiral was the circus. Arriving at the circus the driver instructed Bruce Fraser to stay in the car for a minute or so while he fixed seats, explaining to the manager, with great excitement, that he had 'One great piecey Warlord outside.' The manager took a look and, seeing Bruce Fraser in all his uniformed glory, ushered him to the premier box in the auditorium. The evening was an immense success. The audience was thrilled, Bruce loved every minute and when the show was over he went round the back to visit all the circus actors and animals. His driver was ecstatic. Everyone in Hong Kong knew the great Warlord had been to see them. Bruce Fraser reached his hotel at some hour in the early morning still in full mess dress but satisfied.

The next incident was of a very different nature. The *Ceylon* was sent on a goodwill visit to Colombo. Arriving in that harbour, I went ashore as soon as we had secured to a buoy, to pay my official calls, closely followed, as was customary, by the Wardroom Chief Steward, the most respected Senior Chief Petty Officer of the Hong Kong Chinese Division and wearer of a

BEM. It was his job to arrange appropriate supplies for the Wardroom Mess. As soon as I returned on board I was met by the Commander who explained that there had been some incident ashore involving the Chief Steward who had been taken off by the Customs Officers. Not a very propitious start to the visit, but I did not worry too much, for the Chinese were a pretty crafty lot – but not crafty enough.

Before long a message was brought to me from the Chief of the Ceylon Customs saying that a gold bar had been found on the Chief Steward, apparently in the heel of his shoe, and that the Customs demanded access to search the ship. Now Her Majesty's Ships do not allow Customs or any other people to search unless it is asked for by the Captain. But in this case I did not want any such action, nor did I like the tone of the message. In law, what is on board is entirely a matter for the Captain and if his ship is stuffed with gold that is his affair so long as he does not try to land it without authority. So we could not allow any searching by the Customs, nor was it any business of theirs what we might be carrying. A suitable reply was made and the Governor informed. The situation became tense. The Customs railed, the Governor rather weakly suggested I let them on board and I firmly rejected all such suggestions. Instead, I made an urgent signal to the Admiralty reporting my stance and asking for backing. Meanwhile, I told the Commander to organise a search of the Chinese messes to see what else was around.

I am happy to report that the Admiralty fully confirmed the correctness of my attitude and told the Foreign Office so; but the Commander's reply was less happy. He had found a waistcoat loaded with gold bars in the Chief Steward's locker and fifty gold watches wrapped in one of the Captain's towels in a steward's locker! The rest of the visit was a trifle tense. Each time I landed I expected to be arrested, but was not, and eventually we managed to have the Chief Steward brought to Court where he was fined, lost his gold bar and sent back on board. Meanwhile, in my safe I had accumulated about thirty gold bars and fifty gold watches and it took many weeks and much correspondence to deal with that lot and with the luckless Chief Petty Officer Steward.

Not long before we returned to England the *Ceylon* visited Japan taking Admiral Begg on his first official visit there. I had not been back to that country since 1945 and was not sure how I would care for it. However, with an old friend as Naval Attaché, Captain Denis Chilton, and an Admiral I knew well with me, this was no time to be squeamish. We arrived in Yokohama at the very berth, or so it seemed to me, where I had been rudely hustled ashore as a prisoner. But what a change: a Guard of Honour, the police band, many officials and three pretty little Japanese girls labelled 'Miss Yokohama 1959'. As Captain of the ship, the latter presented me with roses while the Press plied me with questions: had I ever been to Japan before? Yes, I said. What did I think of Japan? It had changed a bit, I said. And so forth, with me trying to give away nothing of my former visit. The Admiral was billed to make all the official calls in Tokyo while I was assigned to make on his behalf all those in Yokohama. At the end of these calls the Admiral was to give an official lunch on board the *Ceylon*.

Off went the Admiral accompanied by the Naval Attaché and then off I went, to call upon the Consul General, the Mayor of Yokohama, the Chief of Police and the Senior US Army Officer. I duly completed my calls and returned on board with a little time to spare before the return of the Admiral and the arrival of his lunch guests. I was sitting in my cabin when my secretary brought in a message to say the Mayor would not be able to lunch as he had a meeting in the afternoon. This got my goat. The Admiral's official lunch had been arranged through the Attaché weeks before, anyone falling out now would upset all the seating plans. Who did this beastly man think he was, to treat a British Admiral's invitation like that? I recalled how the Japanese had treated me when I was their guest and resolved to get a bit of my own back. I telephoned the Mayor's secretary and indicated without any doubt that the fact that the Mayor had a meeting was of no consequence at all. He had been given the honour of an invitation to lunch by the Admiral and it would be a grave matter of disrespect if he did not attend. His meeting could be changed very easily and I, the ship's Captain, expected an immediate notification that the Mayor would attend. If not, I hinted, I should call the British Ambassador and that would lead to a diplomatic incident which I felt sure the Mayor would wish to avoid. Bingo! I felt much better. If necessary I would go and bring him back myself.

I waited for results. They came first from the Consul General, deeply worried and alarmed. Was it true, etc? Yes it was, I said, and I didn't spend three and a half years in Japan being ordered about by them, not to know that it was exactly what they understood. I hoped very much that the Consul General would convey to the Mayor that I would not take NO for an answer and, if necessary, the Mayor had better be told precisely why. He came, all smiles and bearing a gift for the Admiral!

There were two more incidents worth recording in that commission. The first arose at the time of the ship's annual docking and self-maintenance period. This spell of some six weeks was a time when living on board was almost intolerable, and the officers and men lived ashore in the barracks. It was a time too, when the annual overseas leave allowance of fourteen days could most easily be taken. Unfortunately, virtually no sailors and only a very limited number of officers and Chief Petty Officers could afford to take two weeks on holiday away from the ship and Singapore; but all on board needed a change away from the heat and cramped conditions of life on board.

Having seen other ship's companies living ashore in the barracks doing virtually nothing except drinking and womanising for their leave, I decided to organise our own holiday camp and make everyone who could not afford a proper 'away from it all' holiday, take at least one week in the camp. The Gunnery Officer was put in charge of a plan which involved borrowing one of the recently vacated Army jungle camps, where people could live in rattan huts and look after their own housekeeping. We also arranged various outings and entertainments.

We were very fortunate in these latter affairs. The Army offered to provide trained instructors to take teams of sailors into the deep Malayan jungle for two or three nights, a feature which was much enhanced by the report of a tiger being on the loose. Then the local rubber planters offered facilities such as bathing, tennis and bars at their clubs, the Army provided sports grounds and excellent transport for stores and men, the RAF laid on a daily mail and paper drop from an aircraft and other kind helpers produced film shows and talks on the jungle flora and fauna, rubber growing, survival, and so on. To make everything as much of a change as possible, the essential work to run the camp was given to others than those who did it on board. For example, the stokers did the cooking, the seamen did the stoking and the cooks did the guard duties. All in all I was very pleased with what we had cooked up, and announced to the Ship's Company what was intended and why. To avoid any kind of uncertainty over numbers to be catered for, the edict was that everyone must spend one week in the Berthus camp.

To my chagrin the idea was received with much hostility. The sailors grumbled and were convinced that they would have to do rifle or other drill every day; the idea was just another gunnery scheme for Whale Island training. The Chief and Petty Officers were highly suspicious and, in any case, thought it was below their dignity. So much so, in fact, that the four most senior Chief Petty Officers in the ship put in to state a complaint, which was in effect that they did not wish to attend the week's camp. It was a difficult moment, yet I was sure that the idea was a good one and that everybody would benefit from a change which took them away from spending their money in bars and brothels.

I invited all four Chief Petty Officers to my cabin and there I said to them that I was most reluctant to order Chief and Petty Officers to attend and would be very unhappy to have to deal with any direct disobedience. But quite frankly I had put myself on the line over this idea, it was in no way intended to be anything but a 'do-it-yourself' holiday and it was quite clear that without the support of the four most senior ratings in the ship, no Captain could expect to succeed. The scheme absolutely needed loyal and full-hearted support or it was a dead duck. They went away, and not long after came back and said in effect, 'OK Captain, we'll back you.' And back me they certainly did.

There was apprehension as the first lot set out for the camp, way up in the Malayan jungle. But before long reports began to come back that everyone had settled in well, and, while not ready to say so, were enjoying themselves. After five days I decided to visit the camp myself. When I arrived, I was greeted by a huge banner across the path to the camp: 'Stalag Twiss' it read. I knew that all was well. The whole scheme proved to be an enormous success and our principal trouble was dealing with the applications to stay on for a second or third week.

I don't think such a scheme was ever run again. Long after we had left the station, and the bills came in for transport, food, fuel and so forth, the Navy had to pay out a pretty heavy sum. But as the bills were largely one Service charging the other, the Dockyard eventually accepted them and paid up. But they were not likely to be caught for a second lot. What was nice, however, was that when the ship sailed away from Singapore after docking, the four senior Chief Petty Officers came to me to apologise for their original action, and to say how much they admired the way the whole operation had gone and how greatly they had enjoyed the Stalag!

Not many months later our time was up in the Far East and we set sail for home. The ship was in wonderful shape, clean, efficient and all systems go. But it was to be her last commission before the scrap heap, or so we thought until the Admiralty signalled 'Peruvians wish to purchase *Ceylon*. Team of experts will join you at Aden for passage home and to assess suitability of ship.' My heart sank. Instead of a nice quiet passage home we were going to have to endure endless questioning, testing and inspection by the Peruvian experts.

We put into Aden to refuel and three Peruvian civilians, each bearing two huge leather briefcases presented themselves on board. As we had feared, I thought, they have brought endless plans, diagrams, graphs and statistics, which we shall have to explain and justify. How wrong I was. A couple of hours out from Aden one of the Peruvians came to the bridge and said, 'Captain, we would like to give a Pisco party to you and your officers this evening.' How nice, I thought, as I gratefully accepted, but what was Pisco? It was explained. Pisco was a famous Peruvian drink unequalled anywhere in the world. They had brought a good supply with them, enough for us all to have a good time. The briefcases and their bulging contents were not after all the plans and papers we had feared. The party was a great success and the Peruvians soon became friends of everyone on board. They asked no questions about the ship. After all it was steaming along very well and everything seemed to be working, so why bother? Peru eventually bought the *Ceylon*, renamed her the *Coronel Bolognesi* and, so far as I know, she has served faithfully in the Peruvian Navy for over twenty years.

We had a very active Wardroom, that helped to ease things. We had three bachelor Commanders who were very good indeed and who took charge of things and set a very good example, and we had a number of people who were quite talented. We had a very good concert party, where we used to do what was called a concert, a knock-about show, wherever we went. We had an extremely good cricket side, and nearly defeated the Mediterranean Fleet on the way through, and a good hockey side and soccer side, so we had a good games performance. The ship was clean, with very good morale, excellent Chief and Petty Officers, and a very good Ship's Company. So it was a very happy ship, and everybody knew each other and things worked quite easily. I knew the Admiral very well, so that side of the business went all right, and I greatly enjoyed it. I mean, it was a wonderful commission. I was promoted to Rear Admiral in April 1960.

CHAPTER NINE

Flag Officer, 1960–1967

NAVAL SECRETARY TO THE
FIRST LORD OF THE ADMIRALTY

I was appointed to be Naval Secretary to the First Lord of the Admiralty, Lord Carrington, in April 1960. I did just over two years in this post, a fascinating job altogether. The First Lord of the Admiralty at that time was still a member of the Cabinet, and the Admiralty Board was still an independent board. The Naval Secretary had responsibility for helping or advising the First Lord of the Admiralty on matters to do with the Navy and particularly with the personnel.

The First Sea Lord, you see, is the senior active sailor. He commands the whole Navy and is the senior Naval Officer on the Admiralty Board. He is now known as the Chief of Naval Staff and not the First Sea Lord so much, although the title still remains. His equivalent, therefore, is the Chief of Naval Staff in America or France or wherever it may be. The First Lord of the Admiralty is the naval politician. He represented the Admiralty in the Cabinet at that time, and spoke on naval matters in the Houses of Parliament. Lord Carrington, of course, being a peer, did his speaking in the House of Lords, in the same way as he did when he was Foreign Secretary later on. The First Sea Lord is made an Admiral of the Fleet and is the only active Admiral of the Fleet on the list. All the rest are retired. He is born and bred a naval man, and has spent his whole working life in the Navy, whereas the First Lord of the Admiralty may have been the Minister of Agriculture or something else before he becomes First Lord of the Admiralty. He is, therefore, a politician and would look at the politics of the matter as much as the naval aspects.

As Naval Secretary to the First Lord, then, my job involved travelling round visiting the whole of the Navy ashore and afloat, as well as visiting foreign navies and foreign Chiefs of Staff. As well as that, the Naval Secretary handled the processing of the promotion of officers to the rank of Rear Admiral and above. The First Sea Lord had to approve all senior Naval appointments. The Naval Secretary was merely part of the link producing the names. He also looked after the Captains' List of the Navy and was open to being approached by anybody, any Captain or Senior Officer on matters which affected them personally or on which they wanted advice, or to be advised on what they were likely to do next. It therefore led not only to a close working relationship with the First Lord of the Admiralty, but also to getting to know pretty well every officer of Captain's rank and above in the Navy.

At the time I took up the job, the office of the Naval Secretary maintained a large book in which were inscribed the names of all the Captains, and the possible posts they might fill were noted against them. This was the system of advising the First Sea Lord who to consider for promotion, and all Captains going to jobs in ships at sea were known colloquially as Post Captains (which was from the old Nelsonian days). So it started really with the Naval Secretary making proposals as to how the post should be filled, the First Sea Lord considering these and exerting his own personal views, and the result going to the First Lord of the Admiralty who had to agree them, and who, in turn, had the Naval Secretary to advise him on any technical points. It was, I think, a sound personnel system. It seemed, I think, to work well and kept the Naval Secretary not only in touch with all the active officers, but also with a very large number of retired officers, who regarded it as important that from time to time they should call upon the Naval Secretary when they were in London, to have a bit of a chinwag and see how the Navy was getting on.

During my time, Harold Macmillan was the Prime Minister of a Conservative Government and the really big issue was the replacement of the carrier force, and for that reason it was extremely important that we should have at the head of the Navy an aviator. In fact, when I took over as Naval Secretary that wasn't so. We had an Admiral called Sir Charles Lambe, an extremely able officer, who had been a great friend of Earl Mountbatten and who had been First Sea Lord for a relatively short time when I took over. The day I actually moved into the office, the man I was relieving said to me, 'Well, there's one thing you needn't worry about at the moment, that is the process for finding a new First Sea Lord.' He also said 'There's a file here and I advise you to look at it some time, but you needn't bother about it now.' And off he went into another job and I sat down in his chair and took over the post of Naval Secretary. That was about eleven or twelve o'clock in the morning.

Later that day Admiral Lambe invited me to go and have a word with him in his office. He was going to the opera that night, so he said, 'If you come along at six o'clock, we could have about half an hour together and just run over the points that I have in my mind for certain promotions and things, in the future.' So I duly did that at six o'clock and somewhere about quarter to seven I left him, and he went off and changed for the opera, and I went home. He went to the opera and had a heart attack and when I came back next morning, consternation reigned. The First Sea Lord was in hospital with a severe heart attack and this file, which dealt with the question of how you found the next First Sea Lord, was obviously one I should look at fairly quickly.

It was by no means certain whether Admiral Lambe was going to recover sufficiently to carry on with the job, but I went down to see him in hospital and he gave me various instructions and the system went on running with the Vice Chief of Naval Staff taking the load. Sadly, Charles Lambe didn't recover and died only a week or two later. We were left, therefore, without a First Sea Lord at this critical moment when the important matter of the carriers was coming up. Furthermore, various changes were looming in the future over the whole question of Captains and above, due to the fact that the General List was now producing officers with qualifications for a wider range of jobs than had hitherto been the case.

The first question, of course, was who was going to become the First Sea Lord? It was apparent that there were really three runners, and it was in fact a policy of the First Lord to try and keep three possible candidates always in mind in case this sort of thing happened. Of the three candidates, one was in America where he was in a job, but was on leave somewhere in the Far West and was very difficult to reach. One was Admiral Sir Caspar John, who only the week before had been relieved as Vice Chief of the Naval Staff and had gone on holiday prior to becoming the Admiral commanding the Home Fleet. And the third one was the Admiral currently commanding the Home Fleet. And of those the Admiral of the Home Fleet was the only one we could get hold of. So I had the business of trying to get hold of the other two, so that the First Lord could interview them and decide who to put in the place of Charles Lambe. It was in many ways a laughable situation. I managed to find the man who was on holiday in America, but Caspar John, being a very strong character, had made sure that nobody could get in touch with him when he was on his holiday. He didn't want to have his holiday interrupted. He disappeared into Europe in a caravan – and there was nothing we could do. We tried Interpol; we simply couldn't find him. Eventually, of course, he returned. I managed to get hold of him and Lord Carrington was able to interview him.

Now the long and short of all this was that the First Lord decided that Sir Caspar John was the man to become First Sea Lord. Caspar John, however, was extremely unwilling to do it. He'd just done two years and a bit in the Admiralty as Vice Chief of Naval Staff and he wanted a rest from Whitehall, and was going to go to command the Home Fleet. Poor man; he had his arm heavily twisted and eventually was appointed. It was, of course, a very good appointment because here was an aviator taking the top post in the Navy, at the very moment when this critical matter of the replacement of the carrier force was coming to the boil.

The carrier debate was really no business of mine. My job was people, and Senior Officers in the Navy, and so on. At the same time, though, because I was closely in touch with the First Lord and was supposed to be his man to give advice on naval matters as papers on this matter came to me, I couldn't resist commenting. I think it was easily accepted, my giving my own personal views on these papers as they came through. Not that I think I necessarily affected anything at all, but it was a matter on which the Navy was considerably divided. The new carrier was going to be immensely expensive and having one was no good. You needed three or four to make a force at all. So any discussion I might have had with the First Lord of the Admiralty was simply slight interference on my part or, as it were, gossiping.

My actual job really divided itself up into two areas: one, the question of promotions, and two, accompanying and assisting the First Lord of the Admiralty. He was required to go round and get to know the Navy and its ships and their companies, so he travelled quite a lot. He visited various naval bases, training establishments and overseas places. He went to Australia, Canada, and America, always accompanied by the Naval Secretary. Thus the First Lord always had at hand a Naval Officer of experience whom he could either consult, or tell to get on with something that he wanted done, in respect of what he was having to decide. A very close association between the Naval Secretary and the First Lord was needed to do this and I travelled with Lord Carrington a good few times. And I tell you, with enormous enjoyment, because he's an able and amusing and capable man. Extremely charming, and very able, he was highly popular in the Navy, and a man of decision. It was a great loss when he resigned from being Foreign Secretary over the Falklands affair.

We went out to Australia once, which was a fascinating tour because we spent about a week there altogether, and he had only recently been High Commissioner in Australia so was extremely well known there. We flew out by BOAC and we landed at Singapore. Then we went on from Singapore to Darwin in the middle of the night, arriving at Darwin at four o'clock in the morning. And on the way chatting to me Lord Carrington said, 'Have you ever been to Australia, Frank?'

I said, 'No, I've never been. I know a lot of people there because I've been a prisoner of war with a great many Australians, but I've never actually been there.'

'Fine country,' he said, and left it at that. We landed at four o'clock in the morning in Darwin and there was a welcoming party to pay their respects to Lord Carrington. We were the only people that got out of the aeroplane, and went down the steps to shake hands with these people, and we advanced towards the welcoming man who was the District Commissioner for that part of Australia. He shook hands with Lord Carrington and then he looked round and said, 'By golly, Frank! How good to see you!', and he rushed up and shook me by the hand. When the same thing happened at Sydney, Lord Carrington said to me, 'Look here, I thought you hadn't been to Australia, and everywhere we go people rush up to you, not just to me, and shake you by the hand. What's going on?'

'Oh!' I said, 'It's just that they're all ex-prisoners of war.' There were a good many, of course, in Australia.

We travelled quite a bit. We went from Sydney to Canberra and on to Melbourne while we were there. And then later on we went to America, where we visited the Chiefs of Staff, and one or two places, training establishments and shipyards in America and soon got to know the form. (The welcoming form in America is a fairly standard procedure and after you've done it once you begin to know just what you're in for in the way of speeches and protocol.) We went out to the Mediterranean Fleet and to the Persian Gulf. We also went to the Home Fleet and to various ships in and around England, and most of the training establishments. Lord Carrington would be received with whatever ceremony was appropriate, and it wasn't necessarily guards and bugles and things. He would be received, if we went to a naval air station, by the Captain, who would introduce him to his officers and then he would be taken round the air station inspecting all the departments, shaking hands with the people in the hangar and the people in traffic control and so on, making himself known to, and acquainted with, the essential elements of the Navy, including trips to sea in ships and staying with the Commander-in-Chief in Malta. There was only a limited amount of ceremony on these occasions. He was interesting himself and he was deeply interested in the Navy, getting to know people, some of whom might come up for promotion or an appointment somewhere else, and he'd have to put his chop [stamp of approval] on them. I would take him round the ship with the ship's officers and arrange a little tour for him, so that he could meet the Chief and Petty Officers, talk to the Coxswain, have a chat with the Bosun's Mate, or whoever it was, and go all round the ship. So in a way, one was educating this politician into the Service which he represented on the Cabinet. And with a man like Lord Carrington it was an extremely good education, of course.

FLAG OFFICER FLOTILLAS, HOME FLEET

My next job, in September 1962, was as Flag Officer Flotillas, Home Fleet. The Home Fleet had a Commander-in-Chief who lived in an underground shelter, so to speak, in Northwood. He's shore-based and the whole of his Staff and the supporting services are in offices which are deep underground. The sea-going part of the Home Fleet was commanded by a Rear Admiral, who was known as Flag Officer Flotillas Home Fleet. He was the Second-in-Command and he had a Flagship and ran all the exercises and training for the Home Fleet. In a way, he was the man who could be used if a naval force had to be sent of sufficient size to warrant having a Rear Admiral in command (and in the Falklands that was more or less what happened). So I, therefore, was the Second-in-Command of the Home Fleet and I flew my Flag in three or four different ships in the two years that I was in the Home Fleet. It was during that time that the Cuban crisis came up, and, had we got involved in that, it would have been from the Home Fleet that the ships would have been picked to go out and join forces or whatever, with the Americans off Cuba. And I was the Admiral who would have gone with them.

Flag Officer Flotillas, of course, in the Home Fleet is a very busy sea-going job because not only have you a large variety of ships with all their Commanding Officers and their problems, but also the Home Fleet takes part in pretty well all sorts of sea-going NATO exercises. I suppose I did three or four major NATO exercises while I was there, and these are very interesting to take part in, with many foreign ships. We always seemed to choose places which had lots of rough weather: that I'm afraid is a feature of the naval side of life in home waters.

During my time in the Home Fleet, as well as the Cuban crisis, Malta gained her independence. This represented quite a change in naval situations, because that had been a very large base of ours and it was lost. I was present at the Independence ceremony. In fact, I was sent out with a small force to represent the Royal Navy.

COMMANDER-IN-CHIEF, FAR EAST FLEET

Early in 1965 I was appointed as Commander of the Far East Fleet, as a Vice Admiral, at a time when we had just got embroiled with Indonesia, which was in many ways a very big affair. I went out to Singapore knowing the man who had been appointed Commander-in-Chief of all three Services out there, Admiral Sir Varyl Begg; I had been his Flag Captain and knew him very well. So I went out to command the British Fleet when we were getting deeply involved with the attitude of Indonesia, who wanted to re-take North Borneo. North Borneo, which had been British-controlled for years, had just become part of Malaysia. The Indonesians said the island of Borneo was split, partly under the British and partly under the Dutch, and now that they had got the Dutch bit under their control, then they ought to have the British bit as well. They proposed to take it by force and started a whole series of infiltrations in an endeavour to do this. Well, it started to escalate. Allied to this of course, the Americans had just got themselves involved in Vietnam as we were trying to hold the ring in Borneo and Malaya against the Indonesians, who were being assisted by the Russians. The Russians gave the Indonesians a great deal of armament, including a lot of fast patrol boats with missiles, which were a very formidable kind of force if they ever tried to use them, especially in that part of the world that consists of a large number of islands.

We sent a lot of soldiers and airmen and ships out to Singapore to support Malaya against the Indonesians. There was fighting in Borneo, and there were raids coming across from Sumatra and attacking Malaya and causing a certain amount of alarm, by shooting up things and going away again. The business of containing this without actually getting involved in the war took a very large proportion of our naval forces. You see, it's a big area and we had responsibilities for supporting the Army in Borneo, with boats up the rivers and using our helicopters. I ended up with the Malaysian Navy, Australian and New Zealand contingents and British ships, numbering something like eighty ships, helping to keep the peace and

35. *Lord Carrington being greeted on arrival in HM Ship by jackstay transfer,
c. 1963. (Crown Copyright; RNM Collection, neg. 2224)*

36. *Vice Admiral Twiss on board HMS* Hampshire, *Guided Missile Destroyer,
with Captain White, July 1963. (Crown Copyright; RNM Collection, neg. 2225)*

37. NATO ships dressed overall, Grand Harbour, Malta, 1964.
(Crown Copyright; RNM Collection, neg. 2183)

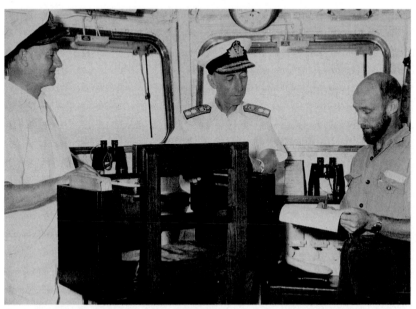

38. On compass platform of Ajax *with her CO and Communication Yeoman.*
(Crown Copyright; RNM Collection, neg. 2192)

*39. Admiral of the Fleet, the Earl Mountbatten of Burma meeting various RN
Officers during Far East Visit, HMS* Terror, *1965.
(Crown Copyright; RNM Collection, neg. 2191)*

*40. Meets 40 Commando and 848 Squadron in Borneo, 1965.
(Crown Copyright; RNM Collection, neg. 2193)*

41. Arrives by helicopter at Royal Marine Establishment, 1965.
(Crown Copyright; RNM Collection, neg. 2254)

42. Scene from Vice Admiral Twiss's inspection of an RN Establishment, 1965.
(Crown Copyright; RNM Collection, neg. 2253)

43. In Amphion's *galley, 1965.*
(Crown Copyright; RNM Collection, neg. 2190)

44. Attending a cookery exhibition in Royal Naval Dockyard Canteen,
Singapore, c. 1965. (RNM Collection, neg. 2188)

*45. With HRH Duke of Edinburgh, Singapore, 1965.
(Crown Copyright; RNM Collection, neg. 2234)*

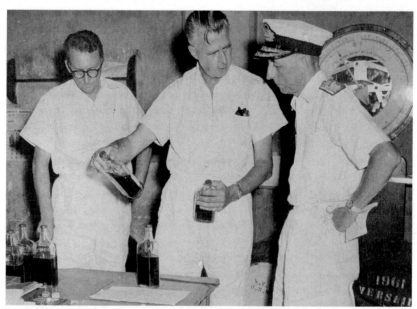

*46. Vice Admiral Twiss visits Victualling Department, Naval Base, Singapore,
1965. (Crown Copyright; RNM Collection, neg. 2257)*

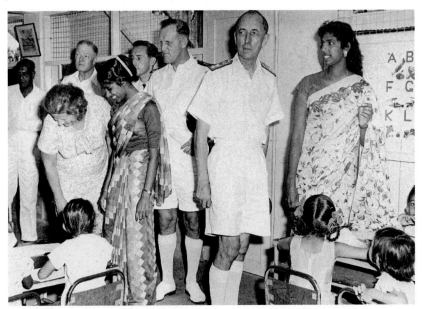

47. Vice Admiral and Lady Twiss visit Singapore Naval Base Asian School, early 1966. (Crown Copyright; RNM Collection, neg. 2204)

48. Greeted by US Vice Admiral Hyland on board USS Oklahama City, 1965. (Crown Copyright; RNM Collection, neg. 2233)*

49. Visiting a carrier, 1966. (RNM Collection, neg. 2198)

50. Addressing ship's company, HMS Hampshire, *early 1966.*
(Crown Copyright; RNM Collection, neg. 2203)

51. Port bow aerial view of HMS Hermes, *1966.*
(Crown Copyright; RNM Collection, neg. 2230)

prevent the Indonesians from escalating the confrontation, because we didn't want to get into a Vietnam situation. As the rest of that part of the world was influenced by what was going on in Vietnam, I had to keep in very close touch with the Americans to make sure that we didn't get into the parts of East Asia in which they were operating.

At home the debate about replacing our aircraft carriers was still under way, with all the implications to the naval budget. When Macmillan went out in October 1963, Sir Alec Douglas-Home was Prime Minister for a short while. In October 1964 the Labour Party came in and their policy was not to replace the aircraft carrier; they reasoned that it was too small a force unless there were four carriers, which we couldn't afford. In other words, we were trying to play a role in the naval concept of world defence which was greater than we could accept. The Labour Party was convinced that we couldn't afford it and that we, as a world power, would have to pull in our horns and come back to defending nearer home.

I was the Commander-in-Chief of the Far East Fleet – which at that time was the biggest Fleet we had – when the decision was made not to replace the carrier. This decision, as you might imagine, caused an immense amount of dissatisfaction in the Fleet Air Arm. Here was their pride and joy being thrown away, and they organised a great deal of opposition. When the decision was announced, I had been a Commander-in-Chief for about a year, and had had sufficient experience in operating, both as the Second-in-Command of the Home Fleet, and then Commander of the Far East Fleet, to form the opinion that we really couldn't go on running carriers. The way we were doing it at that time was really exhausting our naval resources and it wasn't producing the kind of striking power that we claimed it would. In Singapore, for example, we had one carrier there all the time, and it was one hell of a business to keep that carrier operational. Everything had to be devoted to this end, and one couldn't say that the results, even then, were absolutely useful.

Anyway, when the news came through, I gathered everybody in Singapore and addressed them, as Commander-in-Chief, on this matter. I said to them, 'Look, I know this is frightfully contentious, but I want you to know from my experience that it is, in fact, the right decision, and we mustn't therefore get wound up in gloom. There are other things that can be done and we've now really got to buckle to and find out what they are and do them.' But, of course, anybody who said a thing like that would hardly be popular with the Fleet Air Arm, whom I admired tremendously, I mean, they're a wonderful lot.

Denis Healey [the Secretary of State for Defence] came out to Singapore and I actually took him round the Fleet and he went round the Army and the Air Force, addressed us all and made it quite clear that he was not only going to do away with the carrier force but, when all the troubles were over, he wanted to do away with the whole military presence East of Suez including Singapore, which at that time had built up into a very considerable amount: I took him round the Fleet, and that was not without its amusement.

He had devoted a day to going round each of the Services and on the day he was going round the Fleet, I was to take him out in a helicopter and take him on board an aircraft carrier and he was to address all the officers in the carrier and tell them why he was proposing to get rid of the carriers, which of course was an extremely hot number at the time. He arrived at the helicopter pad at Admiralty House and before he got into the helicopter he said to me, 'Now Frank, I'm going to speak quite openly to these people, but just tell me quickly anything I should avoid saying which would really make everyone jump up and down madly.'

And I said, 'Well, it's perfectly all right Minister; you'll be received quite politely, just so long as you don't refer to anything being done which the RAF can do and the Navy can't. If you do that you're in trouble.'

And he said, 'Thank you very much Frank, that's a very useful piece of advice.' And out he went and landed on board HMS *Eagle*, had a look around the ship and eventually we got down to the Wardroom where the Captain had assembled every possible officer and senior Chief Petty Officer. There were more than a hundred people there. He made a very good address indeed, very moving, until at the end he got onto Rhodesia, which at that time was involved in this thing called UDI [Unilateral Declaration of Independence], and he commented, 'Of course, the trouble about Rhodesia is that that's not a job which anybody but the RAF . . . I mean, we could only take any military action there by the RAF flying in.'

Well, the Navy had a feeling at that time that they could have done it perfectly well – Healey was doing just what I'd advised him not to do. And the Wardroom, which had been listening to him very politely, all stood up as one man when he said that and shouted, 'Balls!' and sat down again. I mean it was the most astonishing performance. I could never have organised it, and no one was in any way aware of what was going to happen. It absolutely took Healey by surprise, as you might imagine. But he got himself out of it in a skilful, political way. And I think, on the whole, except for that, he spoke extremely well, although I don't know that he necessarily changed people's minds at the time.

However, the rest of that day at sea with Healey was interesting. The trouble with civilians when they go on board ships is that they have to go through hatches, you know, up and down decks, and they nearly always hit their heads on them, because they're a little bit awkward to go through. Healey hit his head on the hatch in the *Eagle* and bruised it a bit, and I then took him to a guided missile destroyer where the hatch was a little smaller, and after he'd gone round that he hit his head again. Then I took him to a minesweeper, and he went round that and the hatches were smaller still, and he hit his head again. Finally I took him to a submarine which we had to enter through the torpedo loading hatch after landing by helicopter on the sloping deck – it was quite a tricky business to get in. When I finally got him home, for he was staying with the Commander-in-Chief, who was an Air Chief Marshal, Healey was bleeding from his head and looked as if he'd been battered a bit. The Commander-in-Chief came out to welcome him back in the motor car and he saw Healey there with blood streaming down his head, and I said to him jocularly, perhaps rather stupidly, I was sorry to bring him back in this condition, someone must have hit him over the head with a bottle in the *Eagle*, and Healey laughed and thought it was quite a good joke. Then they went in and he washed the blood off. I mean he wasn't seriously injured, but handing him back to the Commander-in-Chief after his day at sea, it rather looked as if the Admiral had been at him with an axe.

My time in the East was a time of transition. In many ways, I witnessed the demise of the British Empire East of Suez. Before I left that job, Healey and the Government had decided that they were going to close Singapore, remove all our dockyard and all the ships and everything else, and the Navy was going to withdraw from keeping forces out in the Far East. In other words, we were going to throw in our lot fully with NATO and the Western Alliance, and that was all we could afford to do. And that meant running down Singapore.

It was a very busy time, then, because the ships were changing over all the time and, of course, I wanted to get to know all the new Captains and so on. We had a very large number of wives and families out there. My own children were in school at home, but they used to get flown out from boarding school. My daughter was with me, or she was with me part of the time. I didn't think it was best for her to stay all the time in Singapore and I sent her to Australia to work, where she went and got a job. But my two other children used to come out from time to time.

Living in Admiralty House, my wife had the business of running the domestic side of it and enabling me, so to speak, to get on with my naval work. And we had, of course, a large number of British dockyard people of all grades who had houses and lived out there with their families, and a certain number of resident people running training establishments, dockyard barracks and things, to enable the complete naval life to be carried through, to accommodate drafts arriving or waiting to be sent back. There was also a military hospital. It was in fact, a whole three-Service base, and therefore it took a lot of unscrambling because we had rented an immense amount of housing and things, not only on Singapore Island, but in the State of Johore as well.

Various people used to come out and visit us, and I remember particularly, a singer who did a lot in the war in one of those famous programmes; anyhow, he came out and there was a man who plays the clarinet very well, Acker Bilk, who played a lovely tune called *Stranger on the Shore*. I invited him to come up to Admiralty House, which he did, and he was giving a concert there, and I told him how much I enjoyed the clarinet and wished I could play it myself. In fact, I had played a trumpet in a dance band, and I said I often wished I could have stayed on. Maybe if I'd stayed on I might have made quite a name for myself in a band or something. He looked at me and he said, 'You don't seem to have done too badly do you, living in Admiralty House,' which was a palatial place. And he went on to give his concert.

A TURNING TIME – 1960–1965

This period in the Navy, 1960–1965, was really very much a turning time. Money for Defence shrank and there were endless Defence reviews. At the beginning, in 1960, we had a number of problems, which had to be addressed. One was recruiting: it wasn't easy to get the number of recruits we wanted or the right quality of recruits. And the next thing was that there were a lot of sailors in the Navy who were very dissatisfied with the terms of service, which up till then, had been to sign on for twelve years from the age of eighteen with a further ten for pension. And there was little opportunity to get out once you'd signed on at eighteen. You were stuck. It was very difficult to get out of the Navy unless you were invalided or had some very pressing family affair that you simply had to go to. And it was quite clear that the wish of people at that time was not to be committed for so long. They were prepared, perhaps, to join the Navy, but they wanted, if it didn't suit them, to get out. Because of this, lots of sailors who were disgruntled were devising ways of getting out of the Navy by making a nuisance of themselves.

Their view was that if they behaved sufficiently badly and at sufficient intervals, they would eventually reach a stage where the Admiralty would say let's get rid of this chap, he's not worth keeping. And in order to do that, which was known as 'working your ticket', you had to commit at least three crimes which got you punished by Detention. By the end of that, the authorities would say this man is useless, he spends all his time in prison, we'll get rid of him. And he was discharged, what was called SNLR, 'services no longer required'. He didn't get a pension or anything. He was just flung out. But there were quite a number of sailors who were prepared to go through this somewhat traumatic experience in order to get out of the Navy, and they were just rotten apples in the barrel. They were tiresome on board. They sometimes persuaded other people to do things that were against discipline, and it was a plague which simply had to be cured.

The only way to cure it, of course, was to alter the terms of service, to get away from tying a man up for the first twelve years of his adult career, and find ways in which he could get out of the Navy with honour, without upsetting the whole balance of the Fleet which depended, of course, on having the right numbers of the right trained class of man available for sending to ships, and available in the right state. That is to say, if he was going to sea, that he hadn't just spent three years at sea and was due for some shore job which was near his family. Today it's an extremely flexible system and sailors get the opportunity to opt out after a very much shorter period. But at that time it was a real sore, and in every ship, if you had two or three of these men, they were a bad influence.

Technology, in the sense that it affected the men's general life, was also going ahead very fast at that time. In 1960 we were still in the age of the hammock. We were still in the age of what was called 'general messing', where somebody went to the galley, collected the food, then took it out and served it to his messmates, in his mess where he lived. We didn't allow men to have plain clothes when they went ashore. They always went ashore in uniform, but there was a great desire to go ashore and not be recognised immediately as a sailor. We had very strict rules about entertaining on board. When a ship went into a foreign port there was usually a well co-ordinated programme which always involved a cocktail party on board, given by the officers to entertain people ashore who were interested in the Navy or helped in the visits and one thing and another. And the Chief and Petty Officers, in particular, felt that they, too, should be able to hold some entertainment on board for people they met ashore. And that hadn't been accepted up until then. Now these were the sort of problems which were pressing down on us, and unless they were solved we weren't going to get out of the so-called old Navy into the new.

Allied with that, the composition of the Fleet was changing completely. At the beginning of the 1960s, we brought into the Fleet the County Class guided missile destroyers, which were an enormous improvement on anything we'd had before. Their living quarters were very good – they had mess halls and cafeteria messing, they had bunks, they had air-conditioning – they had gas turbines and, of course, they had the Sea Slug anti-aircraft missile. So they were a great advance in technology of both living and fighting material. And they were the forerunners of ships which were quite out-distancing anything that had been in the Fleet before. By the time I'd finished being in the Home Fleet, we had not only the guided missile destroyers but also we had the Tribal Class of frigates which were smaller vessels without large missiles but with the same degree of improvement in living conditions on board. At last we were getting to a state where to live on board a small ship, a destroyer compared to the old battleships, was much more pleasant than it had ever been before.

We were also getting into the whole business of servicing replacement. We were moving out of the era where if something broke on board, your artificers could probably manufacture it or you had a spare. That isn't possible any longer with the highly technological gear of today; if a unit is wrong, you take it out and put in another one. These advances in technology meant advances in training and the skills of the men, and their skills became less of the hammer and anvil type and much more of the electronic-analysis type with the use of replacement packets which were so made up and sealed that you couldn't do anything with them other than put them in or take them out. In other words, we were at last becoming technologically quite advanced; before, if it didn't work, you hit it with a hammer.

Training also had to change. In order to get the best out of ships, it had been agreed some little time before, that it was necessary to train the whole ship specifically with a team of experts, in a concentrated period as soon as it re-commissioned. It was no longer possible just to commission a ship, sail it away and leave the Commanding Officer and the Ship's Company and so on, to go through a series of training exercises themselves. And so the training base at Portland had been very highly developed, with a team of experts coming on board; the curriculum, methods and process of working a ship up, until it was worthy to join the Fleet as an action ready ship, had become very sophisticated and, I think, very effective.

Most ships went to Portland where they did six weeks of intensive practising, under the eye of people whose job it had been to study the methods and techniques, and who at the end of the six weeks, carried out a kind of exam on the ship and passed it or didn't pass it, as the case may be, as fit to join the Fleet as a fighting unit. This had entirely transformed efficiency and meant that when a ship joined the Fleet you knew that, not only was she up to the mark, but probably a little better than the rest of her compatriots in the Fleet, who hadn't been to the work-up base, perhaps for a couple of years.

As these technological changes took hold, and as the conditions under which men lived and worked on board moved on, the behaviour, so to speak, of everybody changed. And a number of desires of the past which hadn't been possible, started to become so. These included, of course, a raising in the standards, if not in education, then at least in the understanding of the men who worked. It became necessary for them to be more competent and more intelligent and more up-to-date. And as they did that, their way of life had to be altered. Great studies were going on, under the heading of Work Study, to find ways of running ships, that is to say the routine and the general work which went on on board, which produced the best results with the fewest men. At this time, you see, the number of men on board was becoming critical not only from the point of view of its demand on recruiting, but also from the point of view of the demand on living space. The more sophisticated the machinery became, the more space it seemed to take up inside the ship and the less room there was for the humans to live. So we were having to develop a man-economic and machinery-economic ship to meet all these new trends.

The men's attitudes had also changed. The whole attitude of separation had changed completely since the war, for example. It was no longer possible to take men and send them away for two years to some foreign station where they didn't see their families, and return at the end. You were not going to get men to join the Navy if they were separated from their wives and families for long periods. The length of the period which they could be separated from them was, of course, the minimum that was possible. You can't have people away in ships at sea from their families simply for twenty-four hours and run a Navy on that. There must be longer periods. But what has come to be much recognised is that if it's known in advance when people are going to be separated, if it's realised that the times of separation are either essential or necessary for political or other reasons, and if they're kept to a reasonable minimum, then sailors will accept them and be content. But if they're simply flogging away, away from their families, apparently for no reason, then they get discontented. It's difficult to say today what those standards are, because men move around and ships move around so much, but very few sailors are away from families for more than a matter of a few weeks, except on the occasions when ships, shall we say, go round the world, or go out to Australia or South America, on some particular flag showing or political requirement. Ships may then be away for two or three months. But that's the maximum that people will be away from their families and that will only be on reasonably rare occasions. So I think we have achieved a degree of family stability, with not too much separation, which will be accepted by the ordinary man of today.

Welfare, I think, has moved along with this very same

problem. Whereas before the war men were used to, and accepted, being away from their families for a long time, and their families equally accepted that their menfolk would be away, that hasn't been the case since the end of the war and it would seem as if the wife has not been as self-sufficient post-war as she was pre-war. But then that must be set against the fact that there were a number of things that were highly desired by wives and sailors before the war but which were not feasible because of, for example, the travelling. It was simply not possible for a man's wife to travel out to Singapore within twenty-four hours. The arrival of air travel has greatly cut down the time taken to bring two people together, and has made equally possible a decrease in the time families are separated, the swift transportation of reinforcements, or whatever it may be. There is no question that the improvements in travel and communication, the extraordinary way it has been speeded up by the aeroplane, and the arrival of things like package tours and package holidays, have set standards outside the Services which are extremely difficult to match inside them, but which must be allowed for because they've become part of the modern way of life.

As the mess-decks got better, air-conditioning was provided, the galleys became more effective and separated from the messes, so the ships became more habitable. At the same time, the Chief and Petty Officers began to feel that they were not, perhaps, as fully allowed to act on their own as they might be. And they rather naturally wanted to do some of the things that the officers did. For example, they wanted to be able to entertain, in their own messes, people from shore on a par with what had been possible for the officers in the Wardroom. This was a very reasonable request, but it did mean a change in the attitude towards the whole Ship's Company on arrival in a port. Whereas before it was the officers who did the entertaining and the sailors went ashore and had a good time or got drunk, it was now the Chief and Petty Officers who were taking the lead in activities ashore, which featured both the ship and shore people. We had very few people, for instance, who played golf before the war. Many of the things which officers did were not done by the Chief and Petty Officers, but that was changing. These activities were being done ashore, where a much more classless society played golf, sailed, bicycled, played tennis, went to the opera, whatever it was. They had been carried over the class divisions, and likewise it was expected that the same would happen in ships. Chief and Petty Officers started to want to do exactly what the officers did. This not only fitted in with what was going on ashore but simply had to be provided if we were going to keep a contented Ship's Company.

The desire for the Chief and Petty Officers to have dinners, or mess dinners was accompanied by a desire to wear what the officers wore in the evening, some sort of evening dress with bow tie. It gave the activities some kind of acceptability. To allow this to happen required some considerable changes, not only in the relationships between officers and men, but also in the provisions made in Chief and Petty Officers' messes and elsewhere.

We are now very much more on a level. People talk of a classless society, which frankly, I think, is an impossible idea, but it is true that this has come about much more in a ship than ashore. There is a tendency, in some ways, for the moving spirit in a ship no longer to be the Wardroom Mess but the Chief and Petty Officers' Mess. I don't think it's a very healthy result. I think it's important that the Officers' Mess should be taking the lead in things. But where you get an Officers' Mess which is not quite as good as the equivalent in the Chief and Petty Officers' Mess, it's the latter that will take the lead in the ship. And maybe that will work but it's not meant to be that way.

Along with all that I've been talking about, and for many years before, there had been a great desire in the Navy to equate the highest rate of the non-commissioned ranks, the lower-deck, with those of the other services, and both the Air Force and the Army had a Warrant Officer. Of course, before the war we had a Warrant Officer who was, so to speak, rather a higher class than the Warrant Officer in the Army but not quite regarded the same as a Wardroom Officer. That had been done away with after the war. And there was now a feeling that the Chief Petty Officers should be a higher rate of Chief Petty Officer to equate with the Warrant Officer in the Army and the Royal Air Force.

The difficulty was to insert a higher rate than just the Chief Petty Officer, required you to define just what he was wanted for. What would be his job in comparison with other Chief and Petty Officers? This is not particularly difficult to do, shall we say, in the seaman branch. A higher Chief and Petty Officer can take on regulating duties or higher skills, but it is much more difficult to do for cooks and stewards or sick berth attendants, those two in particular. The seamen, or the engineering branch, can pick out people with higher competence to become a Warrant Officer type in their branch and to keep it in proportion to its total numbers; whereas, that's very difficult to do with cooks. How can you make a Warrant Cook? How can you find enough billets to justify paying a man extra to cook? You might say, well all Commanders-in-Chief should have a Warrant Officer Cook, but there aren't a lot of Chief Cook posts around, and in some cases they are taken on by Chinese, and to have just one is not enough and to have just the same proportion as other branches may be too many.

So the provision of the rank and the fairness of chance to achieve it has been quite a stumbling block. But it was eventually met by the introduction of an up-grading of the top Chief Petty Officer, into what is known as a Fleet Chief Petty Officer and grading him as a Warrant Officer. I don't think they still carry the same kudos as a Warrant Officer in the Army, except in the Navy itself. I think that in a Warrant Officers' Mess in an Army regiment they would be regarded as being only slightly higher in rank possibly than a Chief Petty Officer, but it hasn't been going for very long and no doubt it will grow together.

As for discipline, the main change really has been in punishments, because we have adopted a system of using fines. There was no such thing before. Men either lost leave or they did extra work or rifle drill or whatever it was, or they got dis-rated. Now they can be fined. Not only can the lower-deck be fined, but the officers can too. And this seems to have worked; it's very much in line with what happens ashore. If you're brought up before the Magistrate, you don't just have thirty days' leave stopped or whatever it is, or the equivalent punishment from the other Services but you get fined. You get fined for speeding offences in your motor car, or you may be fined for something which you've done, if not criminal, at least against the rules somewhere. Therefore, fines have been introduced into the Navy and have changed perhaps the degree of disciplinary control, since I think they lend themselves to more variation to meet the actual requirements of the investigation. Detention Quarters were very much disliked by the Labour Government. They were very much against Detention Quarters, I think on two grounds. One was that they thought the routine was too harsh compared with what was being done in civil life, where there's no doubt about it, there has been a softening in the treatment of prisoners over the years. Detention Quarters certainly up until the late sixties were places where the prisoners were treated humanely all right, but very toughly. They had very little time to do anything for themselves or think for themselves. They had some difficult rules. They weren't allowed to talk for the first week. They weren't allowed to write as many letters home or what have you, compared with what happened in a civil prison. The Labour Party interested itself in changing the routines in the Detention Quarters in the direction of rather less toughness, and although a lot of people have objected rather strongly to it, it has had to be so, in order to keep in line with what goes on ashore. And so nowadays, Detention Quarters are not the really hard life. It used to be always the rule that men held in Detention Quarters had a very hard life; it was thought that at the end of that time, although they would be considerably fitter and smarter, offenders would not want to go through it again and this would stop them committing crimes. According to statistics, this is not so, and people come back for more, not because they want to but because they just can't stop it.

I think probably the change that had the most effect on the Fleet at this time was the change in the catering facilities. Improvements in messing had the biggest effect during that particular five years, 1960–1965, together with the effect of other improvements in living conditions, that is to say, bunks rather than hammocks, and air-conditioning. Cabins weren't changed very much, though. They were probably made a little smaller than they used to be, because we got much better at fitting them out, but these things and the changing of the lengths of service to get away from this sore discontent by the people who had joined and didn't want to stay on, were the most striking changes. Later on we were to get to deal with the matter of rum, which had been a running problem for years, and which nobody had managed to solve. Looking back on it, generally, I think it was a period when there was an emergence of an entirely new spirit, which marked the new Navy as quite separate from the old Navy.

CHAPTER TEN

Second Sea Lord, Chief of Naval Personnel, 1967–1970

A bout six months before I was appointed Second Sea Lord in 1967 I started thinking about what I would do next, as one does in the Navy; you look ahead to see what possible jobs you may have when you come to the end of your present one. I had relieved an Admiral called Sir Desmond Dreyer, who had taken the post of Second Sea Lord, therefore his period as Second Sea Lord and my period as the Commander of the Far East Fleet tallied. It was clear that he was due to be relieved soon anyway as he had become involved in a re-organisation of the Ministry of Defence, and was selected to become the Head of all the Personnel of all three Services in the Ministry of Defence.

In due course, I was told that I had been selected for the post. There was a slight hiccup, because Admiral Dreyer was moved to his new appointment before I had been relieved as Commander of the Far East Fleet, so somebody had to take over the job of Second Sea Lord temporarily while I finished off my time in Singapore and came home. I had interested myself in personnel affairs because it was quite clear that if I was going to get any further in the Navy that was what I had to do.

The title of Second Sea Lord is the first part of the whole title, the rest of which is Chief of Naval Personnel. Naval Personnel is a fairly broad subject, involving not only the welfare of officers and men in the Navy, their careers, their training, their education and requirements of entry and recruiting and legal matters, but also, in fact, anything that is non-operational. I attempted to tackle a number of problems which were of concern to us at that time, including the training of officers, the rum issue, certain social conditions, and legal and welfare matters.

A SERVICE UNIVERSITY?

At that particular period in our history, the importance of personnel was becoming much greater because we were having extreme difficulty in recruiting the right numbers of the right quality people that we wanted. We were also having difficulty in holding them in the Service because of the Service conditions which they didn't like. Because of this, there was enormous pressure to reduce the number of sailors in ships and submarines, and to run a more efficient, personnel-wise, Navy. And indeed, unless the right number of naval officers and men were provided at the right time, the Navy certainly couldn't go on achieving what it was aiming at. And so, whereas before the war we had no great difficulty in recruiting people, and, therefore, the primary line of action lay with the operational side of the Navy, this had now swung round, and it was the Second Sea Lord on whose shoulders the problem fell. One was in the position, at Navy Board meetings, to be able to dictate to some extent the future requirements of the Navy, in the terms of what could be provided in the way of manpower in order to meet them.

The Labour Party was then in power, and the Services were headed by two extremely powerful people, Denis Healey, Minister of Defence, and Admiral Lord Louis Mountbatten. Mountbatten was forging ahead with plans to make a unified command of the Navy and appoint what eventually became the Chief of Defence Staff, and a Joint Staff to run all three Services. That was his objective, and he was working hard on it. Healey was very much concerned with qualifications, particularly educational ones. He appeared to have decided that practically all the officers in the Services were illiterate; they hadn't been taught properly, they hadn't got degrees, and anybody who hadn't got a degree was regarded as inferior. Healey had set his mind to alter the whole educational stream and requirements of entry into the Services, and to this end he wished everybody who was capable of it to have a degree.

This was much opposed by the Services, each of whom had its own particular set-up for entering and training officers. The Army didn't go much for higher education, the RAF on the whole had more highly educated people, particularly just before the war because they had a university entry in the shape of a University Air Squadron. The Navy was somewhere between the two. We had very few people with degrees, although we did set the standard of entry at two A-levels, which at the time was sufficient to get you into a university, and we had started working on a scheme for sending a few naval officers of the rank of Sub-Lieutenant to university to do a degree course before rejoining the Fleet.

To turn those three systems upside down in one swoop naturally brought Healey into conflict with the three personnel officers, the Second Sea Lord, the Adjutant General and the Air Force Chief of Personnel, who didn't want to make such sweeping changes. However, Healey was a powerful operator and he was gradually forcing the personnel officers of the three Services to adopt a method of recruiting all Service officers through a university which he was going to set up as the Service University, to be located in the Royal Military College at Shrivenham. He was pressing us very hard to accept this aim, but accepting it meant doing away with, or greatly altering, a number of very well-established methods and places – the Army at Sandhurst, the Navy at Dartmouth and Greenwich, and, of course, the Air Force at Cranwell. It meant, in many cases, doing away with those forms of entry. We struggled with Healey on this matter and fought all the way to try to avoid being pushed into it, and it fell to each Chief of Personnel to meet with Healey and his advisers and to discuss it.

As far as the Navy was concerned, we were not absolutely against adopting a degree form of entry or degree form of training, but what we didn't want to do was to exclude people who didn't get degrees. That is to say, we felt that there was an enormous number of highly qualified people who might join the Services, but who weren't quite up to being able to take a degree at a good university. As far as the Army was concerned, they thought the whole thing was a hideous waste of time. They were prepared to put a few people up to get a degree, but generally speaking their view was that what you wanted was a jolly good chap, so to speak, a man who had had a good education but wasn't absolutely a professor. And as far as the RAF were concerned, they felt they were well on the way to doing it without anybody interfering.

Healey's ideas had got quite a long way down the line when we ran out of money and the British economy hit a difficult time. We had had to devalue the pound and the money just wasn't there to provide this kind of training. Personally, I got on quite well with Healey. But he was a very tough customer, and very accomplished. Like so many politicians, when they've set their mind on something, it takes an awful lot to change it, and to that extent Healey had pulled his team together and they held the ultimate power. I think if we hadn't run out of money we would have finished with this rather odd university at Shrivenham.

The Navy was already moving towards sending a few of its Sub-Lieutenants to universities after they'd finished both Dartmouth and sea time, and in the early 1990s the first of those officers were coming up to be Admirals. We had sent two or three to Oxford. Of course, at that time the Navy had a feeling that if you didn't go to Oxford or Cambridge, you weren't really going to university. It was very difficult to overcome this prejudice even though, not long before, the number of universities and degree training programmes in the country had greatly increased and a report showed that a number of these universities had shown themselves to be extremely competent. But the old Navy people, as I'm sure many other people, regarded only Oxford and Cambridge as true university training and anything less than that was something very odd – 'red brick' universities weren't highly regarded. However, since it was clearly impossible to get all your entry of Naval, Army or Air Force officers to go to Oxford or Cambridge, it did mean looking round for other universities or polytechnics.

Although the idea of university degree entry was continued, the business of Shrivenham was abandoned because of the price. We were now left with having to agree certain projects which moved towards Healey's idea. I was deeply concerned; first of all that we should have as many officers with degrees as possible. I took the line that the right way to do this was to take the candidates after they had finished their sea time as Midshipmen, and instead of returning them to Dartmouth for a short period before going to sea as a Sub-Lieutenant, as we had been doing, we should send them to a university. For years the training of officers had [taken place at] Dartmouth, where the passing out standard was certainly up to university entry, but of course they didn't go to university. They went to sea and then came back and did a short time at Dartmouth before going into the Fleet. The short time at Dartmouth was accompanied by professional training at Portsmouth in gunnery, navigation, torpedoes, and so on. My idea was that we should take this period and make it into a period of training for a degree, and the degree should be tailored to what the Navy required in the way of technological knowledge. I mean, much of what we do in the Navy is much more technical than is done in the Army certainly, and probably the Air Force as well. We live with computers and radar sets in our ships; everything that's done, the way the ship is driven, the way the ship is navigated and so on, is all done in some technical way. Thus, the training of naval officers has a good deal of technology in it. And it was my idea that we should invite a university to, as it were, work with us in producing a degree for young people, young officers, which enabled the brightest ones to get a degree and the ones who couldn't get a degree to get sufficient technological training to take their place as they would have done under the old scheme. To this end, the business was to find a university.

One of the competitors, of course, was Exeter, because Exeter was next to Dartmouth, and the Captain of Dartmouth and all his officers were very keen that Dartmouth should play a part in this scheme. However, I felt that that wasn't a sensible thing. I felt that once a young man had done his early training at Dartmouth it was no good sending him back to school in the same place, and I was also extremely anxious to bring Greenwich into the scheme. The reason for that was that the Labour Party had made a very strong bid to get rid of Greenwich. It's a very expensive place to keep, but then it's a national memorial. I think I'm right in saying that the Government tried to get the London School of Economics to take it over, but they and other places, wisely enough, could see that the expense of maintaining those buildings was too great. And my idea was that Greenwich, which was where all young officers or Sub-Lieutenants used to go for a six months' educational course to bring them up to scratch before doing the technical courses, would make an ideal university campus – it looks a bit like a university and it's got a lovely situation. I felt that what we needed to do was to bring it up to university standard but to do it in conjunction with somebody else.

Eventually, I got an agreement with the City University. Now the City University, which is very much supported by the City of London, had been a polytechnic, and had just been regraded as a university. It had university living accommodation in London, and was quite reasonably close to where the living accommodation for the naval contingent would be in Greenwich. My hope was that we could have a mixture of civilian and naval students taking a degree which was specially tailored to produce a good, technology-trained and, in general, well-educated student.

Greenwich would be the campus of the Navy side and the City University would use their own campus, and the two would amalgamate. This would be very good for the City side, which would get the benefit of naval discipline. Generally speaking, you see, the Sub-Lieutenants would be more disciplined, having been in the Navy for three or four years before going there. This mix would be a good one, would produce a good degree which would be popular and would enable all naval officers to get a degree in a subject which contributed towards their naval professional service. I took this proposal to the Board, but I met constant opposition, opposition which simply failed to see, as I saw it, the great advantages of this scheme. When I finished my time as Second Sea Lord, and handed over to somebody else, he killed the scheme, almost certainly. We did run a programme with the City University for a while, but it was never as intended, and that was a very great disappointment to me.

THE RUM ISSUE

Another area I looked at was the rum issue.[1] For years the Admiralty had been worrying over the rum issue, and the essential problem with it – drunkenness. All through my time in

[1] For an extended discussion of the issue by Admiral Twiss see Captain James Pack OBE, RN, *Nelson's Blood: The Story of Naval Rum*, Stroud, Gloucestershire, Alan Sutton Publishing in association with The Royal Naval Museum, 1995, pp. 101–8.

the Navy, the 1920s, the 1930s, right up to the 1950s and 1960s, there was a problem of how to deal with the issue of rum. It was undoubtedly bearing down upon efficiency. There were many opportunities to use it inadvisedly, that is to say, to bribe people or to get intoxicated, and so on. It was cheap, just under tuppence a tot and it was strong. The sailor was undoubtedly less reliable when he had had his tot of rum, but we couldn't weaken the tot. We couldn't simply say, 'We'll give you less rum', because that would have caused a fearful disturbance. The problems, however, were greatly shielded by the fact that ships were spread about all over the world.

Nobody could think of a way of getting rid of rum which wouldn't be grossly unfair to the sailor. The Treasury was asked whether it could be replaced by beer. But before the war you couldn't replace it by beer because you couldn't carry beer on board. The methods of making and storing beer, tinned beer and so on, didn't exist then. You either had a million bottles or you had barrels of beer, and neither of those could be carried on board a warship. So there was no question of replacing it by beer, and there was no question of the Treasury paying for it, because while a tot of rum cost tuppence, beer cost more

We couldn't say we were going to stop the rum issue but we'd give the men the money it cost instead, because that would only be tuppence. Well, you can hardly win the men over for tuppence can you? So, if we were going to replace the rum, we had to provide something that was, if possible, equivalent to it, something which carried as much use or enjoyment, was a lot of fun and games, but did not produce drunken sailors, who were not in the best condition to deal with the growing complexity of our equipment. It was simply unreasonable to expect a sailor who had had a tot, and possibly a bottle or a can of beer as well, to go into a modern jet-propelled aircraft which relied on its radar to find its way around, and check it and put right something that was wrong, carrying with him a small instrument and a few screwdrivers or whatever it was. He was in just the same position as a chap who drives a car when he won't pass the breath test. You can't run a Navy on that basis. If you do, you run it at considerable risk to life and limb.

The problem had to be dealt with, but nobody could think how to do it. How were you to replace tuppence and rum with something which the sailor would accept? Nobody came up with much of an idea. Various things were suggested. People said, let's just phase it out bit by bit, as from a certain day every sailor who joins the Navy won't be entitled to rum. Well, that would take twenty-five years to finish. It would be a hopeless situation. So we couldn't simply phase it out. The other way was to say that we would phase it out ashore, because they used to get it at sea and not ashore. Well, it was at sea, in many ways, that it was most tiresome, and one wanted to get rid of it. What were we to do? How were we to produce an alternative which enabled us to stop issuing rum which would be accepted by the Navy and regarded as a reasonable replacement? The problem was a very great one and had baffled everybody.

While I was Commander-in-Chief of the Far East Fleet, the Commander-in-Chief of the Mediterranean Fleet was a man called Admiral Sir John Hamilton, who was the same term as me at Dartmouth, and the Commander-in-Chief of the Home Fleet was Admiral Sir John Frewen, who also was about the same time as me. We all wrestled with this problem. We put up suggestions and we said to the Board of Admiralty that we really had to tackle this. It must be grasped to see if we can find a solution. Well, nothing happened of course. I came back and found myself Second Sea Lord, and by that time I had evolved in my mind a way of dealing with it. I might say that by that time, I'm now talking of 1967, I had been an Admiral in command of ships at sea since 1963, and, of course, before that I had been Captain of a ship for four years. I had visited practically every sea-going ship in the Home, Mediterranean and Far East Fleets. As a result of this experience, I had had the opportunity to address a very large number of sailors and talk to them about matters to do with the Navy and things that fell within my particular responsibility.

I had made a point, always, when I spoke to people, particularly to the Chief and Petty Officers, to discuss rum. 'The question of rum in the Navy was really not only a very difficult one,' I said, ' but one that was really quite out of line with the day's standards.' I explained to them the difficulties and they understood that, but they were, of course, strongly wedded to the rum issue. In the course of talking to all these men, I had formed a conclusion that I was not talking to a body of men who would die at the last ditch to save the rum ration, if somebody came along with a reasonable solution. In fact, I was amazed at the number of sailors who accepted that rum was an anomaly, but didn't want to give it up because they enjoyed it. There were, of course, a number of sailors who loathed rum, and a lot of them drank it because they were too frightened not to. It was considered not manly, you know, not to take your tot. I arrived as Second Sea Lord, therefore, with the feeling that I was not simply fighting against all the personnel of the Navy, that underneath I had a very responsible and responsive body of people, and that if we could work out some sort of scheme, I was prepared to try it.

When I arrived to take over as Second Sea Lord, Admiral Sir Peter Hill-Norton had been doing the job temporarily for me while I was getting home. He had been my Second-in-Command in the Far East for some time, and had therefore discussed and talked about rum, and knew my views on it and had, indeed, started a paper on getting rid of the rum ration. He had made quite a bit of progress on it, and so when I arrived I took up this docket but I didn't agree with the proposition he was putting forward. So, I put forward my own.

My own proposition was, first of all, that Chief and Petty Officers should be given the privilege of having their own bars in exactly the same way as the officers. Now up to that time they had their own bars, but only to drink beer. There were no spirits. I said, 'Well, they're all highly responsible men. We have high-class Chief and Petty Officers in the Navy and I think one of the things we should give in return for doing away with the rum ration, is that they should be able to buy spirits in their own bars, and that the amount of spirits that they could buy should be regulated in exactly the same way as it is for officers.' Officers have a wine bill and are not allowed to exceed it. If they do, they are brought before the Captain who admonishes them or may even punish them. And in the case of the sailors, since we couldn't provide a liquid replacement then they should be provided with some form of monetary fund which they could use to replace the rum issue and which they could spend on anything they liked. We couldn't really provide bars for all the sailors – it's not possible to provide a bar for two hundred sailors in a frigate, for example.

In other words, sailors who lost their tot in the future, who entered the Navy but didn't get a tot, would be able, together with those who were already there, to dispose of funds for buying the things they wanted, like ski boots, or sailing dinghies, or golf clubs. It could be anything but it would be run by a committee and it would be a fund known as the 'Rum Fund'. And that fund could, if it was big enough, provide a wonderful range of benefits for the sailor. In the case of the Chief and Petty Officers, their position socially, so to speak, and in the ship would be greatly enhanced by having exactly the same booze opportunities as the officers. So this was the scheme; the sailors would have the benefit of the Rum Fund and the Chief and Petty Officers would have the benefit of the Rum Fund, but could buy their drink, pay for their drink in a bar, in their own mess. Meanwhile, the sailors of course could go on getting what they were getting at the time, which was a can of beer at the dinner hour, but which they paid for.

Now clearly there was a connection between giving up rum at tuppence a tot for the whole Navy and providing this large sum of money to finance the sailors' Tot Fund, or Rum Fund, or Sailors' Fund, or whatever you like to call it. I put forward this scheme to the Board of Admiralty, and eventually I got approval to go forward with it and find out what the Treasury would do. I proposed that I should go to the Treasury and say, look, rum costs you, the Treasury, or the Navy finances, so many million pounds a year. The cost of it is the actual liquor itself, and the storing and issuing of the liquor, because it all has to be recorded. It was a very detailed system. A sailor, before he drank his tot, had to have it issued to him, measured out, mixed with water; if he didn't take it, it had to be recorded so that he could get two or threepence instead. A small staff in an aircraft carrier were solely concerned with keeping the rum issue going. But by the time they'd got it on board, stored it down below, drawn it every day, issued it out to each mess, measured it out with water, given the CPOs and POs their own and so on, it required two or three men doing nothing else. So I took into account their wages; I took into account the cost of the rum, the cost of its distribution, the number of people who worked on barrels, because you see in the Victualling Department, the barrels and barrels of rum were looked after by people who are experts in barrels, coopers. We had a large number of coopers in the Navy, really well-paid men.

I took these sums of money and I added it all up and it came to something like £3m a year. That is to say, at that time, there were 175,000 men in the Navy and at that time a tot was tuppence, so it was about £3m a year. And, I thought to myself, well, if I can get £3m invested we shall have a jolly good fund, and they really will be able to buy things, won't they. So with the then Permanent Secretary of the Naval Department, Sir Michael Carey, who was a very accomplished man, I went personally to the Treasury and had a meeting with two of the top Treasury men, and we laid this out before them, and we said, 'Look, if you will give us this money to amortise the rum issue over ten years, we will do away with rum, and after ten years you won't have to pay for any rum, the sailors will not be taking rum, but they'll have three million pounds.' So that must have been the cost over ten years, mustn't it? It must have been £300,000 a year. I didn't for one moment think the Treasury would wear this. I mean, from what I knew of the Treasury I'd be lucky if I got £100,000. But I had the assistance of the Permanent Secretary, who, as I say, was a much more able man at handling this than me. We had, I suppose, a twenty-minute discussion with these men, and they said, 'Okay, we think you're exaggerating a bit with three million. We wouldn't expect you not to ask for a little bit too much. We think you're exaggerating though; so you can have two million, seven hundred and fifty thousand.' In other words they knocked off £¼m from my £3m, and gave me £2¾m, or that's what they said they'd do. Well, I nearly fell off my chair. I could hardly contain myself long enough to get out of the room. We went back and eventually reported to the Board of Admiralty that I could get this large sum of money, if we did this scheme. And the Navy Board then agreed to it.

By that time, Admiral Sir Varyl Begg had retired from the post of First Sea Lord and was now Governor of Gibraltar, and it therefore fell to the First Sea Lord, Admiral Sir Michael Le Fanu, to put this proposition forward, and it was a hideously difficult thing to do, of course. I mean it was a really big moment. First of all it was a large sum of money invested in shares, and, allowing for the rate of inflation at that time, it was going to produce a lot of money for sailors to buy things with. But, at the same time, it was the kind of thing which might lead to a mutiny in the Navy. This had to be judged by the First Sea Lord and, of course, by my recommendation on it, too. Was the risk worth taking? Well, to Michael Le Fanu's great credit he took it on, and he went to Healey and he said that this was what we wanted to do. And Healey said, 'Okay, good idea.' And he wrote to the Second Sea Lord, me, and said, 'This scheme of yours, is there going to be a mutiny?' Well, I don't suppose I've ever been asked a more difficult question. How could I tell? It was no good replying, 'Well, I don't know.' So I replied to Healey, 'In my opinion, there will not be a mutiny. There will be an enormous amount of, what the sailors call "chi-acking". They'll make a tremendous song and dance, but there'll be a great deal of humour in it. Because by and large, they all know that the rum ought to go.'

And, of course, I was right. They had had enormous fun on the day that the rum was taken away. They buried it in coffins, and they did this, that and the other. And you might have thought that we were looking after Tutankhamun's tomb or something, and so it went through. The day it was approved, Michael Le Fanu called the press and gave them all a tot of rum, and I might say they were amazed how woozy they were when they left the press conference. So it went down, and, indeed, the Fleet did not mutiny; it accepted it in the most balanced way, and it really was a tremendous feather in their cap. And the Sailors' Fund was set up, £2¾m. The Chief Petty Officers got their bar, and the rum ration has now faded. Practically all the old sweats who had rum have by now left the Navy, and you know, it's a bit of history.

The Sailors' Fund, though, is now doing extremely well. It is run entirely by sailors. It has one officer, whose job it is to see that the minutes and things are properly kept, and the decisions are in accordance with the foundations of the fund and so on, and that there's no jiggery pokery going on. That's quite interesting; it's the only, so to speak, committee in the Service entirely run by the lower-deck without a smattering of officers. Anyhow, that's the story of the rum issue and it was a very fundamental moment in the history of the Navy when it was done away with.

OTHER STEPS FORWARD

The abolition of rum was entirely in keeping with the ways things were going, with the way that more liberty was being given, with the way that living conditions had improved. Since the war, catering in the Navy has improved beyond belief. That was another tremendous step forward. In the old Navy, the messing and cooking and the preparation and things, was largely left in the hands of the people who ate it. And although we have a Cookery branch, they were not much sought after as chefs at the Savoy. But with the introduction of cafeteria messing, and the equipment that went with it in galleys, and the issuing of the food in the dining hall, an enormous improvement took place in the standard of feeding in the Navy. And what's more it began to attract much better men into the Cookery branch.

The chefs became much more interested. They became much more accomplished, and as is reflected in the way that today quite a number of television programmes deal entirely with eating, this became an important issue in the Navy. The branch that looked after it was the Supply Officer's branch, and they put their minds very much to helping and designed a really good cafeteria system, with the result that not only did the catering greatly improve, but the whole standard of the messing on the lower-deck, and at Chief and Petty Officer level as well, improved. We began to find that people who served in the Navy and became Chief Petty Officer Cooks were sought after for jobs in hotels and restaurants when they left the Navy. So this was all good for recruiting.

It was also part and parcel of improving living conditions further, with which I was concerned as Second Sea Lord. With the improvements in catering came, as I mentioned earlier[2], the abolition of the hammock and the introduction of bunks. Living conditions slowly became better and better. The design of the bunks, the fitting, the messes, the lockers that went with them, then the air-conditioning as well, meant that people were now sleeping and spending their leisure hours in places which were a great deal better they had been only five or six years before. So, by the end of the 1960s, we had a Navy which had good food, good messing, good accommodation, good sleeping accommodation, good air-conditioning and considerable changes for the better in its uniform.

However, recruiting had been a problem for a long time. And recruiting became involved in an entirely new pay scheme, which was revolutionary, and whether it's actually improved the Navy or not, I think would be difficult to say. What happened was that pay in all the Services was in a category of its own. It was always said that allowance was made for your pension, and your salary therefore was not necessarily equal to that of somebody who you thought was doing the same sort of job in civilian life. But recruiting became very difficult because people said that they were so badly paid in the Services, that they weren't really worth going into. To some extent, that was quite right. The naval pay was low, and although naval pensions were available to all, they were not very handsome; a comparison with civil pay, when done scientifically, showed that the Navy, the Army and the Air Force were all behind-hand. And this all came to a head in a proposition which was known as the 'military

---

[2] See earlier, pp. 182–6.

salary'. Now the military salary was a scheme whereby naval pay was based on the pay of somebody of equivalent capability, training, age and so on, in civil life. Large comparative assessments were made of what people got ashore and what people got in the Services, and the new standard of pay was introduced but, of course, in order for it to compare favourably with civilian life, we had to alter a lot of our allowances.

Now these allowances, which were part and parcel of naval pay, were many and varied; they included, for example, a messing allowance. Sailors got so much a day for their messing, and they could buy a limited amount of a variety of food at very low rates, which was provided by the naval Victualling Department. They also got free accommodation in barracks, as they did in ships, and when they were not at sea and were in some shore job, if they weren't in their own house or a married quarter, they were accommodated and given free lodging in a naval barracks or building of some sort. All these things had to be reviewed, if they were to be compared with people in civilian life. Part of the military salary involved charging for accommodation ashore in barracks. If you were going to live in barracks, you paid for it. You didn't get a victualling allowance; your pay was supposed to include that. Therefore, in naval messes, gunnery schools, signal schools, aviation, airfields and so on, all the accommodation became chargeable, and the allowances, the free living and the cheap living all went by the board. In return you were supposed to get a salary which was equivalent to what your civilian opposite number would be drawing, who would be paying for his own food, paying his rent and so on.

This system was accepted, but it was promised that it would include a thing called the X factor – a multiplying factor to increase the military salary to allow for the disturbed life of the Service man. It would compensate for the fact that he might be plucked out and sent away at short notice, that he might be separated from his wife and family. Allowances also had to be made for people in ships; sailors were blowed if they were going to pay a rent for being in ships. They said they should be paid extra for being in ships, so we devised a sea-going allowance. All these kinds of adjustments took time to work out and be applied, of course.

The result of these changes has been that few people now live in barracks at all. If they are ashore, they find their own accommodation, and they pay for it. In many cases, young officers clubbed together and shared a flat, and that's what still goes on. They find their own accommodation and to that extent they are not under the same degree of naval leadership and discipline as when they were in a barracks, where they could be called on to take part in Mess Dinners and so on, and indeed, where they lived a more club-like life than living ashore individually. It has had a strong effect on the *esprit de corps* of the whole Navy.

I don't think the military salary has necessarily improved the general morale of the Services, but there it is, we've got it. The result is that Service people now get paid very much more than I did, I mean, in my generation. We regard their pay today as enormous, but, of course, we don't understand the costs of living because we don't face them in the way that they do. You will find, for instance, the pension of people leaving the Service is much bigger. It's quite interesting. I left the Navy in 1970, having joined it in 1924 at Dartmouth, so I've done quite a long time. I had the maximum pension that an Admiral could draw; that is to say, I had done enough years as Admiral to get to the top rate, and my pension was £4,000 a year. I don't know what it is today, but it's much nearer £40,000. And that is something people of my generation can't really grasp.

THE LEGAL SIDE

Another of my responsibilities as the Second Sea Lord was to look at all the Courts Martial. Courts Martial are reported, and some of them, of course, get involved in further litigation. There was an appeal system in the Courts Martial, but all Courts Martial were reported to the Admiralty and they came in the form of a docket. Before they reached the Second Sea Lord, all the records of the trial were examined by a Naval Judge Advocate,

52. *Vice Admiral Sir Frank Twiss,*
   c. *1966.*
   (RNM Collection, neg. 78)

53. Visiting troops in the jungle, 1966. (RNM Collection, neg. 2200)

54. *With Denis Healey, Secretary of State for Defence, Singapore, 1967.*
(RNM Collection, neg. 2215)

55. *Children's party, Admiralty*
House, Singapore, 1967.
(RNM Collection, neg. 105)

56. *Lady Twiss presents gift to*
Singapore child, Admiralty House,
Singapore, 1967.
(RNM Collection, neg. 2212)

57. Presenting CPO Urry with the British Empire Medal, August 1968.
(Crown Copyright; IWM, HU 69912)

*58. Signing his autograph for a young admirer at the 1968 London Boat Show.
(Crown Copyright; IWM, HU 69910)*

59. *Talking to Chief Petty Officers of Clyde Submarine Base, 24 June 1969.*
(Crown Copyright; IWM, HU 69911)

60. *Last rum issue, HMS* Forth, *31 July 1970.*
(Crown Copyright; RNM Collection, neg. 4083)

61. Second Sea Lord, 1968. (Courtesy Godfrey Argent; RNM Collection, neg. 98).

62. Gentleman Usher of the Black Rod, c. 1971.
(Courtesy of the Daily Telegraph*)*

63. With grandson, Miles, and his second wife, Rosemary, after their wedding, 19 August 1977. (Courtesy of the Bristol Evening Post)

64. Commodore Michael A. Johnson receiving Admiral Sir Frank Twiss's stars and medals from Lady Twiss (l), Sir Frank's son, Hugh, and daughter, Gill, at the Naval Base Museum, Devonport, 13 June 1995. (Crown Copyright, 1995)

who was either a Judge or a senior Recorder. He was a well-trained legal man and he looked at all these things to see if the conduct of the trial had been carried out entirely as it should be and if he had remarks on it, he would write those remarks and before the Second Sea Lord actually put his chop on it, the Judge Advocate would seek his opinion first. He could hardly go against that opinion without at least getting hold of the Second Sea Lord and discussing the thing, and agreeing whether the Second Sea Lord should approve it or whether it should be altered in some way. So the Second Sea Lord had responsibility for the legal side.

The legal side was strangely divided, because there was a Legal branch. Naval Law was one of the naval branches and the Head of Naval Law was a long-serving legal civilian, who commented on all legal matters, including Courts Martial, which came to the Second Sea Lord before he had to make decisions on them. So we had Naval Law, which worked closely with the Judges Advocate and advised the Second Sea Lord, but Naval Law was a little world of its own and, like a lot of those people, was somewhat entrenched, and if the Second Sea Lord didn't agree with those opinions, it was quite a business to get it altered, you know. When you are wrestling with senior Civil Servants, you can get involved in the most hideous discussions on quite small details. So there was Naval Law, the Judge Advocate and Second Sea Lord trying to make certain that the Naval Discipline Act was enforced and the legal side of it conducted in the proper way.

There was one aspect of the legal side with which I was very dissatisfied, and that was the inquiry side. There is a thing in the Navy which was simply an inquiry into a problem, in which evidence was taken before a board, and it was called a Board of Inquiry. If you had a problem as a Commander-in-Chief, or that you wished to have investigated further, you set up a Board of Inquiry. You appointed some senior officer to be President of the Board of Inquiry and you collected together some members, and they then investigated the evidence and wrote a report, and that report could involve some sort of action, disciplinary or otherwise. It was a very good system for assisting a Commander-in-Chief in getting to the bottom of things. Indeed, it's the sort of thing that's used in Government, isn't it? Whenever something happens now, people jump up and say there should be an inquiry. It had some legal status and was conducted rather like a Court Martial, but evidence was not taken on oath, and there was no cross-examination. It was just a question of witnesses, and asking, and papers, and a report, and so on.

Now the final opinion of the board at the end of a Board of Inquiry could be that there was some gross failing by Mr X to Able Seaman Y. A recommendation was then sent to the Commander-in-Chief who would decide whether further disciplinary action was required. Now further disciplinary action could take the place of a Court Martial, conducted with all its pomp and ceremony, or what was called an Administrative Step. That is to say, the defendant's record could be marked, for example, that he was behaving in an unseemly way on board HMS so-and-so, and that would go on his record or various forms of official punishment be arrived at without a Court Martial.

Now in many cases those recommendations were quite satisfactory, but there was no form of appeal. If you were the chap who got into trouble over it, it was no good you saying you wanted to appeal, you couldn't do it. If the Commander-in-Chief said no, that's that and sit, that's all you could do. I thought this was very bad. I thought that when there were occasions when somebody had been found guilty, or was suspected of being guilty of something, at an Administrative Board, and was going to be put on Court Martial, then either they should be given the opportunity to appeal or the evidence of the case should be subject to cross-examination. I didn't feel that the evidence given at these boards was as impeccable as it should be. I got nowhere.

THE WELFARE SIDE

Welfare was another of those difficult subjects which fell to the Second Sea Lord, and it was handled very personally by the Second Sea Lord. Each barracks had a welfare organisation, with a Welfare Officer and a staff who did their best to look after the welfare of sailors and their wives, both afloat and ashore, and, in my opinion, were doing a very good job. They were not, perhaps, as instructive as welfare in the Social Services of the country and they were also largely reinforced by a thing called the Second Sea Lord's Liaison Unit, which consisted of a senior Chief Petty Officer and one or two other ratings who spent their entire life going round the Navy, visiting ships and establishments and talking to the men. They would arrive on board a ship, the Captain would give them all the facilities they wanted and they could go freely and talk to the men about any subject to do with welfare. They would then write a report, and therefore provide a very easy way of getting information direct from the point of issue. A ship might raise some problem and make considerable criticisms which they couldn't readily do in any other way, to the Second Sea Lord's representative. By virtue of his position and the authority that had been given to him, he, as a sailor himself, could record and make recommendations on matters which could well escape Admirals and even Captains of ships. The Liaison Units went round and made these reports and very valuable they were too, because they could be viewed against the whole concept of welfare. The results of the reports were available to welfare organisations in the barracks and, of course, the welfare organisation in the Second Sea Lord's office.

In my opinion, at the time I went to Second Sea Lord, I think it was a very good system. But the Navy Minister at that time, Dr David Owen, was a Labour man, and therefore deeply taken up with social problems. He was also the member for Plymouth or one of the constituencies of Plymouth, and he took the line that he understood welfare much better than the Second Sea Lord, which aggravated me enormously; although he may have known a lot about welfare, and he may have had all sorts of ideas which Socialists would like but others wouldn't, I certainly resented his interference in the Navy. He regarded himself as a great expert on social matters and he dived into the whole welfare system of the Navy and greatly, he would say, improved it. I don't know whether he improved it or not.

The period of service was one area of concern, as I've

mentioned before. The period of service which men had to do when they entered the Navy, was quite long. Before the war, they could sign on for a period of twelve years from the age of eighteen, followed by a further ten. And, in the course of their first twelve years, they went around saying, 'Roll on my twelve', hoping that they'd get out of the Navy after twelve years, but probably ending up by signing up for the further ten. And they took their pension at the age of forty-two, which was quite young. A limited number of people could sign on for short services afterwards. That period of service, twelve years from eighteen, which was acceptable before the war, was unacceptable after the war. People were not prepared to sign on for such a long period. They were not prepared to perhaps because they didn't willingly accept the naval Service and its discipline. They took it on when they were young, full of bright ideas, and after they'd been in the Navy a few years, they began to get bored with it, but realised they had to go on until they'd done twelve years.

A proportion of them would settle down and say, 'I might as well make the best use of it I can, and if I can become a Petty Officer, I shall perhaps have quite a jolly time for my last ten years.' But a lot of them were disgruntled about it. Since they were in the Navy and couldn't get out, they became rotten apples in the barrel, as I've mentioned before. They made trouble, they were discontented, they didn't like the Navy, they were 'anti' and that's not a good sailor. You don't want people like that in the Navy and in ships; you want satisfied, able people. It was a great problem. It was also a great problem to reduce the time for which they served, and keep an even flow of recruits into the Service, and provide a proper career to Petty Officer, Chief Petty Officer and, of course, from the lower-deck to the Officer status.

But we really couldn't find a way of cutting down the length of service far enough to satisfy these people, and so what grew up was a thing called 'working your ticket' which I talked about earlier.[3] If men were so determined to get out of the Navy, the

[3] See earlier, p. 178.

way they did it was to make such a bloody nuisance of themselves that eventually they got flung out. And, although it was a rough deal it did result in them ending back in Civvy Street, but with no recommendations at all. I mean from a point of view of going to an employer and saying, look what a good sailor I was, well, they couldn't because they were discharged what was called SNLR, services no longer required, which every employer knew meant that they were a nuisance really. However, a great many men took to this, and 'working your ticket' meant committing offences which each time led to a further punishment, until they were discharged SNLR. Then after what might have taken three or four years to work through, he was a free man.

'MY TIME CAME TO AN END'

Heath's Government came in during 1970. It was a time of a great deal of energy, a great deal of debate and it all ended up in a very sad and disastrous way, with the six-hour day, and the coal miners going on strike, and the Government coming down. I was actively in the post of Second Sea Lord and a member of what, at that time, was called the Navy Board, and was involved in a number, as I've described, of really quite crucial problems, finding solutions to which was absolutely essential for the future. To recap, they involved the education and entry of officers, particularly who should go to universities, by what means, and to which universities, how the social gap between the officers and the Chief and Petty Officers should be handled, and the great problem, which I have outlined before – the whole matter of rum. I was in the middle of these matters and had made a great deal of progress in all those fields, when my time came to an end; I was reaching the age of sixty, which, for a Naval Officer, was considered fairly old. In the normal course of things I might have, and probably would have, gone on to be Commander-in-Chief Home at Portsmouth for my last tour in the Navy.

There were a number of candidates for the top post though, and I had reached sixty; it was regarded as time for me to get out and not to go on filling another post, so the First Sea Lord decided it was better that I should retire and someone else should take my place. So I became acquainted with the fact that the end of my naval career was going to fall on 1 April or thereabouts, 1970. Quite an interesting date – apart from being 'All Fools Day', I think it was the date I was made a Lieutenant. Anyway, round about April 1970 I was told that I would be placed on the Retired List. I was not offered Commander-in-Chief Home, largely because of my age and because filling those top posts fell out rather more easily if there was one candidate less. That is to say, if I retired, it would be easier to use the people who were left to fill the post. I retired from the Navy, then, in April 1970, and was relieved by Vice Admiral Andrew Lewis, who was a very great friend of the then First Sea Lord, Admiral Le Fanu, and off I went. Like any other Admiral retiring, having been placed on the Retired List, put on a pension, the question of whether I was going to take any further jobs or just retire and grow my roses was left entirely to me.

CHAPTER ELEVEN

Gentleman Usher of the Black Rod, 1970–1978

When you start looking for a job as a retired Admiral, there are endless people who are very happy to offer you work, provided you don't want to be paid. They're frightfully keen on voluntary work: would I go and do this bit of voluntary work, or that bit of voluntary work, or both. I said, 'Well, I don't wish to take on any work for at least three months, so I can take a look around.' And so I retired into my corner to have a look around, warding off various well-wishers who kept saying, 'Our charity badly needs someone to take over, and you're just the chap to do it.' One offer that came up said, 'You're just the chap to run the "All England Croquet" business.' I knew nothing about croquet I must say, but I did know that the All England croquet matches were extremely competitive. And when I found that the wages for this job were something like £400 a year, I had no difficulty in saying that I didn't think I wanted that one.

In the middle of all this, I was suddenly summoned by Lord Healey who said, 'Now I want to set up a Committee to look into the civilianization of certain parts of the Services, and I would like you to become the Chairman of it. It's a job that will last for about four or five months and while you're in the job you will have the same pay as you had as Second Sea Lord, with the use of a motor car and so on. Are you prepared to take that on?' Well, that was rather a baffler, because it was only a temporary job for three or four months. Very nice while it was going on and, actually, I had been concerned with certain of the items that they were going to investigate, so I did know something about it. Before I did it, though, I thought I would go and see my own boss, the First Sea Lord, to find out whether he thought there would be any disadvantage in my taking on this post, rather than a General or an Air Marshal. Well, the long and short of that was that neither the First Sea Lord nor the Chief of Defence Personnel nor any of the other Chiefs of Staff, I think, were frightfully keen to have an Admiral as chairman of this committee, and in the end I wasn't too sorry not to take it on, so I turned it down.

At the same time, I was asked whether I would be interested in having my name considered to be the Gentleman Usher of the

Black Rod. This seemed a very good thing to have a look at as I knew nothing about it. I didn't know what he did, or what the responsibilities were, or what the remuneration was, but it seemed an interesting job and would get me out of the difficulty of telling the Minister of Defence I didn't want to take up his offer as chairman of this particular committee. And so I said I would be very pleased to have my name put forward.

In due course, I received the approval of the Queen and found myself nominated to become Gentleman Usher of the Black Rod in July 1970. I then had to discuss, with the Chairman of Committees [the Deputy Speaker] in the House of Lords, my terms of service. That might sound odd because the job had been going for a good many hundred years, but in fact, the House of Lords had been having difficulty filling the posts of the two top administrative people in the House of Lords. One was the Serjeant-at-Arms in the House of Lords, who was Serjeant-at-Arms to the Lord Chancellor, the equivalent of the Speaker in the House of Lords. He was the exact opposite number to the Serjeant-at-Arms in the House of Commons, who answers to the Speaker. On top of that, there was the Gentleman Usher of the Black Rod, who did some of the work of the Serjeant-at-Arms in the House of Lords. The Serjeant-at-Arms did the housekeeping and the Gentleman Usher of the Black Rod did the ceremonial work, and he had to be present when the House was sitting. He had to run the State Opening of Parliament, assisting the Lord Great Chamberlain. He only came into work when the House sat and as soon as the House rose, he fell out, leaving the Serjeant-at-Arms behind. This led to a great deal of duplication and they got themselves into an extraordinary muddle. The Serjeant-at-Arms, for example, was responsible for cleaning the Chamber of the House of Lords as far as the Woolsack, from one end, and the Gentleman Usher of the Black Rod was responsible for what happened at the other end, and all sorts of strange anomalies like that.

The man who was the Serjeant-at-Arms at the time was a retired Captain in the Navy. He said that really he had too much work to do, and that he must have an assistant as he couldn't go on as he was. The committee in the House of Lords which dealt with this was very reluctant to add another post, and said to him, 'Very well, this new Black Rod we're appointing, before he takes over, is to come and study this matter and write a report to us suggesting how the posts of Gentleman Usher of the Black Rod, Serjeant-at-Arms and Secretary to the Lord Great Chamberlain, which are all wrapped up, three posts in two people, should be tidied up for the future, and he will lay that before us and we will make a decision then, how we wish to proceed and, therefore, what your job will be and what your salary will be.'

So, I went into the House of Lords and spent a few weeks as Gentleman Usher of the Black Rod doing nothing except writing out my proposals for running the administrative side of the House of Lords. Happily, this was accepted by the House and they put forward a new organisation whereby the Gentleman Usher of the Black Rod and the Serjeant-at-Arms should be the same person, both those jobs should be vested in one person and the post therefore of Serjeant-at-Arms would be, as it were, below that of the Gentleman Usher, although vested in the same person, and, moreover, he would do the work which was due to the Lord Great Chamberlain. I then took over all three of those posts, which, though it may sound a lot, was no more than what was done before, and indeed was done more simply.

So in 1971, we ended up with me as Black Rod and Serjeant-at-Arms, my assistant, the Yeoman, a Staff Superintendent to help with all the staff that came directly under me, two ladies in the office and that was it. Quite a small team to run all the ceremonial and security tasks; particularly at that time, because the [IRA] bombs were starting to go off, and we had to take extra special precautions. We also had to look after the Queen's premises in the House of Lords, because HM still retains the Robing Room and the Royal Gallery and they're looked after by the Lord Great Chamberlain. So whatever the Lord Great Chamberlain did, he had the Usher of the Black Rod to help him, and it was a compact little organisation which worked very well during the time I was there.

Black Rod did all the ceremonial. When the House of Lords sits in the afternoon, the Mace is carried in by the Serjeant-at-

Arms, the Lord Chancellor walks in behind the Mace and Black Rod brings up the rear. In the House of Commons, the Mace is carried by the Serjeant-at-Arms. Well, as Black Rod and Serjeant-at-Arms in the Lords were now one and the same person, he couldn't be at both the front of the procession and the back, so we arranged that the Yeoman Usher carried the Mace in the front, and Black Rod marched at the back. The House goes in every day at half-past two for prayers – the procession comes from the Lord Chancellor's office, through the Prince's Chamber, down the lobbies and then enters at the end of the House. The Mace is put on the table in front of the Woolsack. Then, the Speaker of the House of Lords, who is the Lord Chancellor or somebody who is nominated in his place for some of the time, because he can't sit there all the time, sits on the Woolsack. The Mace represents his authority and is placed in front of the Woolsack when the House is in session.

The Mace is historically the ceremonial representation of a weapon – your powers are supposed to be represented by the Mace as a fearsome looking weapon with which you can defend your job. In both the House of Commons and in the House of Lords they have a Mace, but in the Order of the Garter they have a rod, as do the other Orders of Chivalry. Each of the Orders of Chivalry have an Usher who carries, in place of a Mace, a rod, and the top rod is the Black Rod and he is the Usher of the Order of the Garter, which is the highest of the various Orders which the Queen has in her gift.

I remember my first State ceremonial quite well because Black Rod wears a rather unusual uniform, the same, in fact, as is worn by Judges and people at the ceremonial. The uniform comprises silk stockings and black patent shoes with a black-fitting on the top; a pair of breeches; a cut-away coat with a waistcoat underneath; and a sword, a ceremonial sword, which sits on the left side and hangs from the cut-away coat. A white cravat, black gloves and, of course, medals and Orders such as Black Rod possesses are also worn on ceremonial occasions. So, at the State Opening of Parliament Black Rod is there in all his finery with his medals and his black rod, and he walks in front of the royal personages, that is to say the Queen and the Duke of Edinburgh. The Queen puts on the Crown, she comes out of the Robing Room, is received by trumpets and goes down the Royal Gallery, preceded by the Lord Great Chamberlain and the Earl Marshal of England, walking backwards, and both dressed in their appropriate ceremonial uniforms. They actually make up the centre of the ceremonial body that comes out of the Robing Room, goes down through the Royal Gallery and comes up behind the throne in the Chamber of the House of Lords. There the Queen takes her position, which consists of these two, the Lord Great Chamberlain and the Earl Marshal, and in front of those two go Garter King-at-Arms and Black Rod. They lead the Queen's procession right into the House of Lords where the Queen takes her place on the throne. Black Rod then dashes down one of the division lobbies to reappear at the other end of the House of Lords, ready to be commanded by Her Majesty to go to the House of Commons.

You don't see that bit, because he breaks off quietly when he gets into the Prince's Chamber and the whole business of the Queen and the train bearers and arranging the Queen's train on the dais and the appropriate people, members of the Royal Family and so on taking their places, takes a little time and gives the Black Rod a chance to move down from one end of the Chamber to the other, outside the Chamber, and reappear at the other end. There he stands waiting for the order to go and bring in the Commons, which is done by the Queen asking the Lord Great Chamberlain to summon the House of Commons. The Lord Great Chamberlain, with great dexterity, raises his white wand of office in the air, which Black Rod can see, and that's his order to turn about and march through the Palace of Westminster to the House of Commons and do the act of banging on the door.

It's quite a long way from the House of Lords to the House of Commons, and it's all polished stone floors, so you come out of the House of Lords and you walk 50 yards, and you then arrive at the entrance to the Chamber of the House of Commons. All the way down, there are door-keepers and policemen and one thing and another, lining the route. When you get to the House of Commons, the Serjeant-at-Arms of the House of Commons calls out to the Speaker, 'Black Rod' and slams the door in your face, and this is the tradition to indicate that the House of Commons cannot be pushed around by the Queen. She can send someone to summon them, but they can't just walk in, and as it were, take charge, and, therefore, she can't turn up with a few soldiers behind and rush the place.

If the Queen has a message to deliver and she's delivering it by the Black Rod, then they'll only let him in to deliver the message and, to some extent, consider whether they will obey it or not, and then follow him back. This is re-enacted every time the House is summoned. Black Rod is told by the Queen, 'Please summon the Commons.' He then walks down to the House of Commons, has the door shut in his face, and knocks on the door with his rod, three times. The Serjeant-at-Arms then opens the door, announces again to the Speaker and the House of Commons that Black Rod is at the door. Black Rod advances to the Mace, bows and delivers the message from the Queen, 'Her Majesty desires this Honourable House to attend her immediately in the House of Peers.' A fairly simple, straightforward order. On receiving this message, the Speaker gets up, and comes forward and joins Black Rod with the Serjeant-at-Arms, who picks up the Mace, and the three of them then walk back to the House of Lords, up to the bar end. When they get to the bar end, they halt, bow to the Queen and she delivers the speech. And at the end of the speech they bow again, and go back. And that is the ceremonial part of the State Opening of Parliament.

The greatest respect you can pay someone, of course, is to walk backwards in front of them. If you walk facing forwards, of course, you can belt off and leave them standing and, indeed, it is a moment of considerable anxiety at the State Opening of Parliament for the Earl Marshal, the Lord Great Chamberlain, Black Rod and the Garter King-at-Arms, who are the four people just in front of the Queen as she comes down the Royal Gallery. The reason for this is, that with two people going forwards and two people going backwards, it's only too easy to step on each other's shoes and the sort of shoes worn on those occasions are ones which come off very easily; they're not laced-up boots or anything. Thus it's perfectly possible for Black Rod or Garter King-at-Arms to finish up entering the Prince's Chamber, which is just behind where the throne is placed, with one or more shoes missing. I always used to take the precaution of having a spare pair of shoes tucked away in the corner there, so that when I broke off from that procession and made my way down to the bar end of the Chamber of the House of Lords, if I was minus a shoe, I could put on another one and have two shoes to make the passage from the House of Commons to the House of Lords and back again.

My life as Black Rod continued until I retired in 1978. My day was really divided fairly comfortably into two parts. In the morning, that is to say from about nine o'clock onwards, I ran the business, the offices and the correspondence of the administrative side of the House of Lords. The administrative side consisted of seeing that the proper door-keepers were on duty in the proper places at the proper times, and really everything that concerned the daily running of the House of Lords. Any matters which affected the running of the House, whether it was special parking for, shall we say, a specific visit by a Judge to the Lord Chancellor, some exercise in protection against bombs, practice evacuations or that kind of thing, a problem with ordinary parking facilities, complaints by people, requests by Peers for special facilities, and so on, I handled in my office. There was quite a lot of correspondence. A lot of Peers would write to Black Rod when the Opening of Parliament season was coming on, that is to say, from about September onwards. There were endless special requests for seats and a whole series of performances leading up to the final draw for the seats, both in the Chambers and then in the Galleries. That, together with things like the broadcasting of the State Opening or any other broadcasting that might go on, the visit of any foreign Statesmen who might come to address one or both Houses in the Royal Gallery, everything really which maintained the running of the House of Lords and its work, which wasn't particularly dealt with by the Lord Chancellor in his judicial capacity, everything which came under the broad heading of administration, fell to Black Rod. That included cleaning the House once a year, repainting, refurnishing, repairs, alterations to rooms to make extra space, or where we thought space could be obtained. You name it, if it was of a practical nature like that and not anything to do with politics, the Black Rod had a hand in it. And that took you really up to the lunch hour.

At lunch hour, I changed into my Black Rod uniform (I wore plain clothes in the morning), and appeared on duty at about quarter past two, ready to escort the Lord Chancellor and the Yeoman Usher of the Black Rod, carrying the Mace, into the Chamber, because the House sat from half past two onwards. Before that sitting started, there was the procession of the Lord Chancellor and the Mace, the reading of prayers by the duty Bishop, and then the admission of strangers to the Galleries before the first start of the session's work. Once the House, therefore, had gone into session, Black Rod was expected to be in or near Black Rod's box, just outside the main seating of the House of Lords, to deal with any matter that arose. It might be some particular arrangement to do with the King of Saudi Arabia coming to listen to a debate. It might be the ceremony admitting new Peers. Every new Peer goes through a ceremony and takes the oath when he joins the House, and that is done immediately after prayers and before the beginning of business. All that would start up at the beginning of the sitting, and then the debate or series of debates would start.

If, in the course of the sitting of the House, it came to a Division, the conduct of that Division was overseen by Black Rod, who has in his box a push button for ringing the Division bells and who sees the doors are open and closed at appropriate times, so as to let in the people who are voting and let out those who have voted. In other words, to see the thing was conducted in the proper fashion. Other minor things went on the whole time. There could be trouble in one of the galleries. There were occasions when someone in the Stranger's Gallery would try and create a kerfuffle, and would have to be taken out. I remember on one occasion an enormous amount of water suddenly poured down through the roof on top of the Strangers' Gallery, when an old water tank, installed during the war to provide water for fire fighting, rusted through and burst open. Gallons of water came pouring down, not only onto the Strangers' Gallery but right through onto the people sitting in the Chamber.

People who misbehaved themselves would be taken away by the door-keepers, and would be taken to the Police Headquarters in the Palace and their fate would be decided upon by Black Rod. Usually you detained them there for an inconvenient time and then let them go. If they were drunk or violent or something else, they might have to be carted off elsewhere. In other words, all the possible odd things that could go on in a place like the Palace of Westminster, if they were in any way likely to interfere with the business of the House, would have to be dealt with by Black Rod. He was, so to speak, in command of the militia.

Black Rod takes no part at all in the political debate, the Bills, that side of things. He is never asked his views and he never expresses his views, except at special committee meetings. For example, he attends the Offices Committee, which runs the housekeeping of the House and deals with what rooms can be allocated, what special things can be undertaken, who shall be hired and fired, like, perhaps, finding a new principal door-keeper. This committee runs the business of the House.

My reflections on my experiences as Black Rod don't, perhaps, fit together very well. The first thing that comes to mind, is that it is very nice to be involved in what's going on at the top. When I say to be involved, I mean to be sufficiently involved to be able to follow it and take some sort of active part in it. There's nothing like being in the main office. The second thing is that it's never dull. Things happen with astonishing speed and, then again, what you think is going to happen tomorrow doesn't happen. You are mixing with a very large number of extraordinary, able men and women. Not all able in the same way necessarily, but skilful, powerful, ambitious politicians, whose names appear in the news and the papers regularly. So you've got to be on your toes, whatever you're doing. It is all done in the Palace of Westminster, which is a huge and extraordinarily complex club. All those people there with any number of axes to grind, all working to fairly well-conducted methods of operation. Whether I'm talking about the way the Commons does its work, or the way the Lords does its work, it is a very fascinating profession to be in. To that extent, working in it keeps you on your toes and keeps you up with the news.

*****

Looking back, then, my career has meant everything to me. From the time I actually joined the Navy as a cadet at Dartmouth I was deeply involved. I was enthusiastic. I was keen. I was able to hold my own and I was working with people, many of whom I had known for a very long time. I was serving, certainly when I started, in the finest Navy in the world, the largest Navy in the world and to that extent far and away the most influential, probably, in world politics. It was a very exciting job. Though there were a lot of very boring things about it, I could never say there was not a great deal of variety. It was full of variety. It enabled me to travel all round the world and see places and do things which there was no hope of doing at home in other professions or occupations. I not only loved the Navy, I was also extraordinarily proud of it and the sailors who served in it. Generally, I regard myself as having had the most wonderfully lucky time and having been fortunate to progress up the naval ladder, in many ways without even being aware of it.

EPILOGUE

A TOTALLY DIFFERENT NAVY

The years immediately after the Second World War, then, were pretty turbulent and busy, mainly with politics, demobilisation and sorting out the threads of a large Navy built up during the war. The Socialist Government had an immediate effect upon the personnel of the Navy. The Warrant Officers' Mess was abolished, followed by that of the Gunroom in company with the change, first to the Sixteen Entry (which was a flop) and later to the Eighteen Entry, the short service and the University entries, all of which with their accompanying educational standards were originated by Socialist governments. The outcome has been to dismantle the old officer class recruited from the upper-middle (public school) class.

So it seems to me that the five years after the war were a period of immense struggle, in which the major powers were not only looking to settle the old war but also had simultaneously to build up a new political and technological world. The chaos in Europe and the Korean War, together with the impact of new technology on weaponry, made change quicker all round, and the world moved into the age of mass-destruction, satellites, fast travel, instant communications and all those new possibilities which have been developing since the 1950s.

The changes which have come upon us since the middle of the century, and which have been thought necessary to keep up with the race, are so great and so numerous that it is hardly surprising that there is so much turmoil in the world today. The change in the country's social climate, for example, after two world wars and the politics of Socialism, have led to complete change in the class, ability and selection of officers. Up to 1939, officers were mainly recruited from private schools and from the upper classes, principally in the southern counties. Only a few officers came from the lower deck, in the main due to lack of education.

The turning point came with the abolition of the Thirteen Entry at Dartmouth after the Second World War. Whether this was in every way a success can be argued, but as it was done for political and class reasons, it does look as if the resulting selection of new officers has been strongly slanted towards state-educated applicants in the past three decades. Because of this and other changes, it is clear that Wardrooms today contain a very different mix of officers. This trend has been set against the quality of the Chief Petty Officers, whose professional skills, selection and salaries had given them a chance to take over the lead which the Wardroom previously gave to the ship. The abolition of the old WOs' [Warrant Officers'] mess, the introduction of the short-service entry, the demise of the tot and its replacement by mess bars *à la* Wardroom-style have all contributed to the speed of change.

During the 1960s, the world and society altered very rapidly. The budget for defence shrank under almost endless reviews, our Empire disappeared and the impact of technology, not just in hardware but also in methods and performance, started to make the whole way the Navy was run seem very out of date. In the technical field, chips, computers, calculators and wholly new materials took hold. It was clear that working practices would need changing to fit the new world. In the technological field there were nuclear-power, gas turbines, Polaris missiles and greatly improved communications. To meet these we had to raise educational standards, improve training and quality controls. Manpower, which had become the largest slice of the budget, had to be used much more effectively. This has called for work study, revision of daily routines and maintenance schedules, replacement rather than on-board repair and improved dockyard support and fleet maintenance.

Then family welfare, sea/shore ratios, living conditions, social and salary changes all had to be up-dated. To list but some of these: official entertainment had to include serials to meet the needs of Chief and Petty Officers, uniform changes were introduced to make dress less formal and less expensive, and evening wear for Chief Petty Officers (bow ties) to enhance their status all came forward. The long-discussed Master Rate produced the Fleet Chief and the Warrant Officer (Army style). Along with all this came a complete revision of pay and allowances, with parallel matters like living-in charges, married quarters' rent charges and comparability with civilian salaries in what became known as the military salary. Husbands and wives are away from each other for much less time. Most wives work to meet a budget, which, while no more demanding than forty years ago, has to be met without the harsh denials that were part of the sailors' lot. Centralised drafting, discipline, fines, defaulters, types of engagement and the removal of 'working one's ticket', which did away with many bad apples, all had an impact. Finally, there were certain outstanding changes which had considerable further impact – the abolition of rum and the enormous improvement in messing, for example.

Today, we have a totally different Navy to the one in which I and my contemporaries were brought up. The hours of work are longer, and the Navy has fewer ships, although the commitments do not seem much smaller. It is said the Navy is leaner and fitter. It may be, but it certainly is not so much fun.

SELECT BIBLIOGRAPHY

The following sources were consulted, although this is not an exhaustive list:

PRIMARY SOURCE MATERIAL
OF ADMIRAL SIR FRANK TWISS

Twiss, Cdr. F.R. DSC, RN and Lieutenant (S) N.J. Power RNVR. *HMS* Exeter: *March 1941–August 1945*. Unpublished Manuscript. (Royal Naval Museum Collections [RNM], 214/90)

Midshipman's Journals, 1927–1929 (RNM, 294/78)

Midshipman's Journals, 1929–1930 (RNM, 295/78)

Diary, 1946 and 1953–1954 (RNM, 293/78)

Photographic Albums F59–F75 inclusive (RNM, 289/78)

Visitors' Books (RNM, 292/78)

Newspaper cuttings (RNM, 296–298/78).

Oral History Interview Tapes (RNM, 407/91, 1–23)

Private Letters to Chris Howard Bailey, 14 September 1992–27 July 1993

Letter to his family from Yokohama, 10 September 1945

Letter to Admiral Sir Desmond Dreyer, 16 October 1977

Correspondence in Ministry of Agriculture and Fisheries (MAF) files, 1953–1954 (Public Record Office, MAF 209/1627)

SECONDARY SOURCES

The following sources provide a relevant context; the place of publication is London, unless otherwise stated:

Defence Council Instructions (Navy)

Naval Review

Navy Lists

Royal Navy Broadsheets

The Army and Navy Gazette

The Mariner's Mirror

Barnett, Correlli. *Engage the Enemy More Closely: The Royal Navy in the Second World War*, Hodder and Stoughton, 1991

Bartimeus. *The Long Trick*, Cassell, 1917

——. *A Make and Mend*, Richard Cowan, 1934

——. *The Navy Eternal*, Richard Cowan, n.d.

Benstead, C.R. *HMS* Rodney *at Sea*, Methuen, 1932

SELECT BIBLIOGRAPHY

Bush, Captain E.W. *How to become a Naval Officer*, Allen and Unwin, 1963

Carew, Anthony. *The Lower Deck of the Royal Navy, 1900–1939*, Manchester, University Press, 1981

Carrington, Lord Peter. *Reflect on Things Past: The Memoirs of Lord Carrington*, Collins, 1988

Chatfield, Admiral of the Fleet, Lord. *The Navy and Defence*, Heinemann, 1942

Coles, Alan. *Invergordon Scapegoat: The Betrayal of Admiral Tomkinson*, Stroud, Alan Sutton Publishing, 1993

Dewar, Vice Admiral, KCB. *The Navy from Within*, Gollancz, 1939

Grove, Eric. *From Vanguard to Trident: British Naval Policy Since World War II*, Annapolis, Maryland, US Naval Institute Press, 1987

Hackforth-Jones, Gilbert. *Life in the Navy Today*, Cassell, 1957

Hampshire, A. Cecil. *The Royal Navy Since 1945: Its Transition to a Nuclear Age*, Parnell Book Services, 1975

Healey, Denis. *The Time of My Life*, Penguin Books, 1989

Hogg, Anthony. *Just a Hogg's Life: A Royal Navy Saga of the Thirties*, Solo Mio Books, 1993

Hughes, E.A. *The Royal Naval College, Dartmouth*, Winchester Publications, 1950

Jackson, Bill and Dwin Bramall. *The Chiefs: The Story of the UK Chiefs of Staff*, Brassey's, 1992

James, Admiral Sir William. *Portsmouth Letters*, Macmillan, 1946

Johns, Chief Ordnance Artificer William E. *No Surrender*, George Harrop and Co. Ltd, 1969; rpt. W.J. Allen and Co., 1989

Kemp, Peter K. *The British Sailor – A Social History of the Lower Deck*, Dent, 1970

Lodwick, John. *The Cradle of Neptune*, Heinemann, 1951

Marder, Arthur J., Jacobsen, Mark, and Horsfield, John. *Old Friends New Enemies: The Royal Navy and the Imperial Japanese Navy, The Pacific War, 1942–1945*, Oxford, Clarendon Press, 1990

Owen, Charles. *No More Heroes: The Royal Navy in the Twentieth Century*, Allen and Unwin, 1975

Pack, Captain James. *Nelson's Blood: The Story of Naval Rum*, Emsworth, Kenneth Mason, 1982; rpt. Stroud, Alan Sutton Publishing in association with the RNM, 1995

Poolman, Kenneth. *The British Sailor*, Arms and Armour, 1989

Rodger, N.A.M. *The Admiralty*, Dalton, 1979

Roskill, Captain S.W. *The Navy at War, 1939–1945*, Collins, 1960

——. *Naval Policy between the Wars*, Vols 1 & 2, Collins, 1968

Troup, Captain J.A.G., RN, *On the Bridge*, London, Rich and Coward, 1932

Wells, Captain John G. *Whaley*, HMSO, 1980

——. *The Royal Navy: An Illustrated Social History 1870–1982*, Stroud, Alan Sutton Publishing in association with RNM, 1994

Wettern, Desmond. *Decline of British Sea Power*, Janes, 1982

Winton, John. *We Joined the Navy*, Michael Joseph, 1959

Ziegler, Philip. *Mountbatten: The Official Biography*, Collins, 1985

INDEX

Foreword, Introduction, Prologue and Epilogue have been indexed. Headings are arranged alphabetically, but subheadings of persons and ships are arranged in chronological order. Figures in italic refer to illustrations.